GENDER
AND
INTERNATIONAL RELATIONS

GENDER
AND
INTERNATIONAL RELATIONS

ISSUES, DEBATES AND
FUTURE DIRECTIONS

SECOND EDITION

JILL STEANS

polity

First published in 2006 by Polity Press
Reprinted 2008, 2009

Polity Press
65 Bridge Street
Cambridge CB2 1UR, UK

Polity Press
350 Main Street
Malden, MA 02148, USA

ISBN-10: 0-7456-3581-4
ISBN-13: 978-07456-3581-1
ISBN-10: 0-7456-3582-2 (pb)
ISBN-13: 978-07456-3582-8 (pb)

A catalogue record for this book is available from the British Library.

Typeset in 10 on 12 pt Sabon
by SNP Best-set Typesetter Ltd, Hong Kong
Printed and bound in Great Britain by MPG Books Ltd, Bodmin, Cornwall

For further information on Polity, visit our website: www.polity.co.uk

CONTENTS

Acknowledgements

My thanks to all colleagues who helped in the preparation of the first edition, especially Andrew Linklater, Roger Tooze and Margaret (Sara) Law and members of the British International Studies Association's (BISA) Gender and International Relations Working Group. Chapter 9 of this book is based on a paper on 'Constructing Collective Identities, Negotiating Differences, Forging Solidarities', presented at the BISA Working Group on Solidarity in International Relations at the University of Aberdeen in Spring 2004. I am grateful to Martin Weber who provided helpful feedback on the first draft. Part of chapter 8 is based on a paper entitled 'Debating Women's Human Rights as a "Universal" Feminist Project: Defending Women's Human Rights as a Political Tool', the first draft of which was presented at a BISA Gender and IR Working Group at the University of Surrey in July, 2004. My thanks to all participants at the Workshop and especially to Roberta Guerrina, who subsequently provided written feedback on the first draft of this paper. Part of chapter 10 has previously been published as 'Engaging from the Margins: Feminist Encounters with the "Mainstream" of International Relations' (*British Journal of Politics and International Relations*). Marysia Zalewski was kind enough to read the first draft of that article. My thanks are also extended to two anonymous reviewers who read the manuscript for the second edition and who supplied thorough and thoughtful comments. Louise Knight, Ellen McKinlay and Gail Ferguson at Polity provided me with helpful assistance throughout the process of preparing the manuscript. Finally, as ever, thank you to my children Luke and Ria for their continuing love and their full support in all that I do.

Jill Steans
University of Birmingham

Introduction

International Relations (IR) has been described as a 'crudely patriarchal' discourse.[1] Historically, the discipline of IR failed to notice the relevance of gender in international relations/politics and had not, until quite recently, engaged with feminist theory. In 1988 a special issue of the journal *Millennium* on the theme of 'Women and International Relations'[2] began to change this state of affairs, sparking a debate on the marginalization of gender in IR and the invisibility of women in international politics. In the United States, Cynthia Enloe's engaging book *Bananas, Beaches and Bases* first published in 1989[3] was also an important landmark in the effort to 'make feminist sense of international politics', introducing students to the study of IR through stories and illustrations that put the lives of usually invisible women – military wives and workers in export production zones for example – at the centre of our understanding of the world.

During the 1990s, the need for specialist gender/feminist IR texts was recognized and a literature was quickly produced.[4] In 1988 the point of departure for the group of scholars who convened at the London School of Economics and who later produced the *Millennium* special issue was the question 'where are the women in international relations?' Where once 'the elevation of ways of being and knowing associated with men and the masculine over those associated with women and the feminine'[5] in IR and the virtually all-male sphere of international politics was not questioned, there is now a literature that focuses on men and masculinities in IR.[6] This change is largely due to the efforts of feminist International Relations scholars who have pointed out that, while frequently ignored, gender issues are deeply embedded in what is conventionally taken to be the 'mainstream' concerns of the discipline. Through various means and forums during this decade, the visibility of feminist work in IR was much heightened.[7]

Today, the discipline is certainly more open than previously to the questions and issues raised by feminism. Feminists working in the field of IR have produced a body of work on: IR theory; the state; political identity, the construction of the boundaries of political community; international feminist ethics; war, peace and security;

international institutions; political economy and development; and (women's) human rights.[8] Foregrounding issues of gender and employing feminist tools of analysis has encouraged some of the key concerns of IR to be rethought in radically different ways and as such feminism has contributed to a broader critical debate within IR theory that has challenged 'mainstream' approaches like neorealism and neoliberal institutionalism.

By 2001, Cynthia Enloe could point to 'the success of the feminist project to "gender IR"' measured by 'how much is going on with feminist informed scholarship in lots of different parts of the world'[9] and 'department by department' in which more scholars were 'embracing gender analysis' and rethinking 'what one needs to study, to teach and to make sense of politics'.[10] And yet, in some quarters the relevance of gender in IR and the legitimacy of feminist work continue to be disputed.[11] In the early 1990s, there was some discussion among feminist scholars, initiated by V. Spike Peterson, on whether feminism had the capacity to 'transform' the discipline or whether, as with other critical approaches, like poststructuralism or Critical Theory, it was destined merely to 'expand the margins'.[12] Frustrated by attempts to confine feminism within the limits of a 'mainstream' IR research agenda, feminists were apt to portray encounters with mainstream scholars as akin to 'David and Goliath'-type struggles[13] or to see feminist IR as 'on the outside looking in'.[14] Feminists sought to challenge the dominant conception of what was central and what was marginal in the discipline and, in so doing, refused to be 'disciplined' in the sense of addressing only the so-called 'big issues' as defined by the 'orthodoxy'.

BOOK THEMES

This book provides a comprehensive overview of feminist work in IR,[15] focusing on key areas generally regarded as central to international politics, including: IR theory; war; peace; security; international political economy; development; international institutions, human rights and transnational politics. The text reflects the development of feminist IR since the late 1990s when the first edition of this book was published. Accordingly, more space is afforded to postcolonial feminism and the book also includes new chapters on human rights, transnational feminist politics and the key debates that have taken place between feminist and 'mainstream' IR scholars during the past two decades. The discussion in individual chapters is organized around a number of core themes.

Epistemological, ontological and methodological issues

More so than any other branch of the social sciences perhaps, debates within IR have centred on 'first order' type questions concerning epistemological (what constitutes knowledge) and ontological (what can be said to exist/the nature of 'reality') issues and/or appropriate methodological approaches (how do we go about the task of studying international relations). Feminists in the field have contributed to the wider debate on the epistemological, ontological and methodological challenges posed to 'mainstream' (positivist) IR. These issues arise throughout the text but are addressed explicitly in chapters 1, 2 and 10, where feminist work is located within the context of broader theoretical debates in the discipline.

Practices of inclusion and exclusion

A second theme is the practices of inclusion and exclusion in the construction of boundaries between the international (outside) and domestic (inside) and between the private and the public realms in IR (practices that remove gender relations from the field of inquiry). What might be termed the 'first wave' of feminist scholarship in IR went beyond locating women in international relations, opening up questions about how the theoretical framing and the empirical research agenda of 'mainstream' IR worked to marginalize women as social, economic and political subjects and how discourses on IR were profoundly gendered.[16] Feminist critiques of the (realist/neorealist) 'orthodoxy' particularly raised important issues about the processes of inclusion and exclusion in the construction of theory.

The construction and reproduction of (gendered) identities

In mainstream IR, the nation-state has served as the primary locus for political identity and political solidarity. This reflects the dominance of nationalism (from the eighteenth century onwards) as a discourse on political identity. Nationalism provides a narrative that allows citizens and nationals to 'imagine' themselves to be a community[17] and thus share meanings through which collective identities are constructed and boundaries drawn through practices of 'Othering'. Focusing on processes of inclusion and exclusion in both the theory and practice of IR highlights the way in which state-centric analytical frameworks reduce questions of identity to identification with the state and nation. Chapters 3 and 4 focus on how the boundaries of the state have been carved out and reproduced, notably in war, and how certain constructions of political identity have, consequently, been produced and reproduced in both IR theory and in the actual practice of international relations. In part, chapter 5 is also concerned with how the fusion of 'secure individual identity' and 'secure state identity' has shaped mainstream thinking about security.

The domain of international politics is a site in which gendered identities are produced and reproduced. Feminist work illustrates the complex ways in which gender is central to understanding how political spaces are carved out, how the boundaries of community are demarcated and how identities are constructed in practices of 'state-making', a theme addressed explicitly in chapter 3. Gender is central to the construction of the 'inclusive' and 'exclusive' categories that establish rights of citizenship, while the linkage between the state, political loyalty and combat means that traditional conceptions of loyalty have been highly gendered.[18] When the state is re-visioned as a dynamic entity, made through practices that construct and police political and territorial borders, it is possible to see that the actual business of international politics is profoundly masculinized. Chapter 4 explores the ways in which particular constructions of masculinity and femininity are embedded in and reproduced within the military. Just as war and combat have been conventionally viewed as 'masculine' activities, peace has been associated with the 'feminine'. Therefore, this chapter also includes a discussion of the historical connections between peace and female-identified roles and values, which have been particularly prevalent in the international peace movement.

Questioning identities, contesting boundaries

A related theme is the construction of identities and the demarcation of boundaries as sites of political contestation and struggle. Expressions of collective identity and solidarity can be viewed at the level of inter-personal relationships, the nation-state, or in terms of transnational/international social forces. Indeed, much of the critical International Relations literature challenges received ideas on the boundaries drawn between the international and domestic and the public and private, along with received notions of political community, loyalty and identity.[19] While questions of solidarity have not often figured centrally and explicitly in such works, both historical examples of transnational solidarities and the emergence of new forms of politics at spatial scales above the nation-state suggest that the study of solidarity should not be confined to the nation-state and citizenship. It is possible to stand in solidarity with a group or people otherwise divided by geographical location, nationality, class, and/or ethnicity, on the basis of empathy with their cause, or ground solidarity in perceived shared characteristics, or shared social principles.

Feminism is not merely an academic discourse, but also a social and political movement. Women are not, and have never been, the passive 'victims' of global political and economic processes. Non-governmental organizations (NGOs) and feminist groups have sought to influence policy debates and law-making processes and in the process forged support networks and transnational alliances. NGOs and feminist groups have lobbied in international forums, notably the United Nations (UN) conferences, on behalf of and in the name of 'women'. In chapter 8, the growth and expansion of a discourse on women's human rights, along with the rise of the application of international human rights law in diverse societies, is used to illustrate challenges to what has been conventionally thought of as the international and domestic, public and private. Moreover, women's human rights have been a site of struggle around the tensions between the principle of individual rights and expressions of communal identity. Chapter 9 focuses explicitly on the way in which the construction of feminist identities challenges the nation-state as the dominant form of political identity and allegiance. As Rupp has argued, 'women's internationalism points the way to one form of global identity, to add to the more parochial views we have of ourselves.'[20]

Social relations of gender inequality

A fifth theme is the production and reproduction of (gendered) social relations of inequality. The world order of the early twenty-first century, while radically changed in some respects, remains a world of stark gender inequalities. While there are differences between countries across the world, there are also many commonalities; and while the pattern of gender inequality varies between regions, it is nevertheless a global phenomenon. Feminist scholars have focused on how global political and economic processes and development projects produce and reproduce inequalities. This is the subject of chapter 6.[21] Problematizing the state as the primary form of political community, while foregrounding issues of inequality in international relations, also opens up challenges to how we think about and work towards achieving a more secure world. Feminist (re)visions of security that incorporate the need to address profound inequalities between both countries and specific social groups are addressed in chapter 5.

The politics of feminist transnational relations

A sixth theme is the politics of feminist international/transnational relations.[22] During the past two decades, one of the most important developments in feminist IR has been the increasing contribution of postcolonial feminism.[23] Postcolonial feminism focuses on the intersections of class, race, ethnicity and gender. While not exclusively concerned with the politics of feminism, this is an important theme in postcolonial feminist work. The politics of feminism is addressed at various points in the book, but especially in regard to nationalisms in chapter 3 and the influence of the feminist movement at the United Nations in chapters 7 and 8. A key theme of chapter 9 is the challenge involved in constructing collective identities, negotiating differences and forging solidarities among feminist activists in diverse settings and locations around the world.

The gendered politics of International Relations

The contribution of feminism to IR has been welcomed by many male scholars, some of whom have engaged with the feminist literature in a serious and reflective way, or have drawn upon feminist theories and concepts in their own work.[24] That said, as noted above, one still encounters resistance to the idea that gender is relevant to the study of IR and finds that the credentials of feminist theory are questioned on the grounds that feminist analysis is 'unscientific'. Feminist IR scholars continue to face criticism from some quarters that they produce 'knowledge' about IR and, in the process, make certain claims about the gendered nature of international politics that are, at best, suspect and 'subjective'.

Feminist critiques of the mainstream have proceeded from the position that there is a politic at work in the construction of knowledge claims. Drawing upon the notion of 'discourse' as a socially bounded field of knowledge, feminists have contended that what counts as 'knowledge' cannot be determined merely by reference to an 'objective' assessment of the intellectual merit or academic worth of a work alone. Ideas about what constitutes 'knowledge' arise from consensual understandings and judgements made by those already working in the field. Practices of 'gatekeeping' continue to work to define and police the discipline's subject matter and boundaries. Thus, positivists have demanded that feminist IR address a mainstream agenda in IR. This move has been interpreted as 'highly political' in so far as it is an attempt to 'discipline feminists as "goodies" and "baddies" in accordance with their perceived ontological, epistemological and methodological preferences.'[25] The final chapter in this book is concerned with the gender(ed) politics of IR, covering the key debates between feminist and mainstream IR scholars particularly. This chapter also locates feminist IR within the growing field of critical IR theory.

AN ECLECTIC APPROACH

As with the first edition of *Gender and International Relations*, the approach taken in this book is in sympathy with the view that, whilst partial in themselves, feminist theories collectively produce insights that not only contribute to our understanding of many of the concerns of IR as conventionally defined, but also encourage the rethinking or re-visioning of key concepts and central areas of concern. Therefore, the search for a definitive meaning of 'feminist IR' or singular approach has been abandoned in favour of setting out the diversity of feminist work in a number of discrete areas usually regarded as being within the ambit of 'IR'. Before turning to the substance of feminist scholarship in IR, it is helpful to first introduce the main concepts in feminist theory and to highlight key differences in feminist approaches in IR. This is the subject of chapter 1.

Gender, Feminism and International Relations

Introduction

The aims of this chapter are: first, to unpack the key concept of gender and explain how gender has informed analysis and shaped research projects within the social sciences broadly conceived; second, to provide an introduction to feminist theory in a way that reflects the diversity of feminist thought; and third, to set out a number of feminist approaches in IR.

What is gender?

In everyday usage, the terms 'gender' and 'sex' are frequently used interchangeably. Indeed, one might say the belief that gender differences are rooted in 'natural' and/or essential differences between men and women is so prevalent that the proposition is often simply accepted as uncontested and uncontroversial. In other words the relationship between sex and gender and the 'reality' of essential gender difference is simply imbued as 'common sense'. That this is so can be demonstrated by pointing to how beliefs about gender often give rise to certain prejudices and consequently how pejorative terms are often attached to people and types of behaviour that do not fit into this 'common-sense' view of what the relationship between natural sex and gender should be. Thus 'masculine' women might be derided for acting 'butch', empathetic men might be labelled 'soft', homosexuals characterized as 'queer' and so on. Within feminist discourse, and in much of the social science literatures more generally, this view of gender is now held to be at best unsophisticated and at worst ideological and harmful, serving to justify and legitimize forms of social discrimination by making appeals to 'nature' and/or by constructing those who do not conform to widely held gender stereotypes as in some way odd or deviant.

Gender refers not to what men and women are biologically, but to the ideological (or discursive) and material relations that exist between groups of people called 'men' and people called 'women'. The terms 'masculine' and 'feminine' do not describe natural characteristics, but are gender terms. In all societies and in all cultures there are certain emotional and psychological characteristics that are held to be essentially 'male' or 'female'. Similarly, while sex and gender do not coincide naturally, individuals who are born as biological males or females are usually expected to develop 'masculine' or 'feminine' character traits and behave in ways appropriate to their gender. So, for example, certain social groups come to be labelled as 'queer' not because homosexuality is 'unnatural', but because it is behaviour that deviates from the dominant social norm of heterosexuality.

This view of the social rather than natural relationship between sex and gender challenges biological essentialism or determinist ideas that hold that the constitution of the social world is a reflection of natural differences between different types or groups of people (and indeed animals). Instead, the view of gender as social not natural points to the importance of discursive constructions or inter-subjective understandings of gender; that is, the social meaning and significance attributed to perceived sex differences. Gender is material in the sense that even while one's gender is not necessarily rooted in the materiality of one's sexed body, it is nevertheless embedded in social institutions and practices that reproduce gender identities, gender roles and gender relations. In any given society, one's gender will influence one's entitlement to concrete resources and will be a crucial factor in deciding not only 'who gets what', but also 'who can do what' or what one is permitted to 'be' in any given society.

However, along with these material factors, gender must be understood in terms of ideas or the ideational realm or social life. Ideologies or discourses on gender play a key role in reproducing certain forms of power relationships. That said, 'dominant' (common-sense) constructions of gender are also challenged and contested in various ways, so thinking about gender invites deeper reflections on certain forms of power relations that exist within society and how the social meanings that sustain such relations are constructed, reproduced and are also challenged, contested and renegotiated. Historically, feminism has been concerned with the unequal status of women and so has tended to view gender in terms of unequal social relations that exist between men and women. Feminist groups have struggled to challenge dominant definitions of 'woman' and woman's nature and purpose in order to make arguments in favour of extending economic opportunities and civil and political freedoms to women. Or, taking the example of sexuality, gay liberation groups have reclaimed terms like 'queer' and used them politically to infuse homosexuality with positive connotations in ways that challenge the negative construction of gays as social deviants.

Gender in the social sciences

In the development of the early social sciences, sex differences were largely taken for granted, reflecting perhaps the degree to which gender differences were uncontested (or perhaps unnoticed) among male-dominated scholarly communities in emerging disciplines like Sociology. In the 1920s and 1930s, social scientists regarded gender as a personal attribute and the study of gender was largely confined to the study of character traits and 'sex roles'.[1] This notion of sex roles was developed as a way of describing the social functions fulfilled by and seemingly appropriate to men and women. Generally speaking, social scientists supported the 'common-sense' view that men and women had particular characteristics that made them well suited to the performance of particular social roles. Thus, while social scientists did not see sex and gender as synonymous, they believed that they were closely connected.

Connell has argued that in the 1920s the 'new' social sciences, including Sociology and Psychology, became interested in the social and perceived psychological differences between men and women. By the 1930s the use of personality tests to measure 'masculinity' and 'femininity' was widespread in the social sciences. Approaches that concentrated on personality traits were then synthesized with an analysis of the prevailing sexual division of labour and conventional sex roles. Early social scientists concluded from their studies that the prevailing sexual division of labour reflected the close correspondence between gender traits and sex roles.[2] Gender was thus held to be, if not immutable and natural, then at least relatively stable and fixed and, moreover, socially useful. So much so that it was possible to speak about deviancy in relation to those people who were held to be insufficiently 'masculine' or 'feminine' and who could not be accommodated within this schema.

In the 1960s feminist analysis was brought to bear on questions of gender in ways that began to challenge this view. Feminists argued that sex roles were assigned by society. Furthermore, they argued that male-identified roles were frequently seen to be more important and deserving of greater social rewards than female-identified roles. For example, those performing the role of 'breadwinner', that was strongly male-identified, were usually accorded higher social status than 'housewives'. The status accorded to men and women within societies was not, therefore, equal. Historically, the idea that women possessed certain gender traits, for example that they were more passive, emotional and sensitive than men, and that men, by contrast, were aggressive, rational and logical, had been used to justify gender inequality and often female subordination to male authority. Feminists pointed out that rather than reflecting the personality traits of men and women, ideas about gender were used to justify unequal treatment and thus provided an important ideological justification for a specific form of social inequality. In this way feminists began to challenge the dominant view of society as a natural or 'organic' entity beneficial to the individual by pointing to the harmful and perverse effects of gender inequalities (on women particularly). Feminists condemned the subordinate status assigned to women. They also argued that theories that explained women's particular status in terms of either their 'natural' or 'essential' characteristics were ideological, serving to legitimize an unjust social order that valued men and the 'masculine' more highly than women and the 'feminine'. Connell has argued that at its most basic this 'power analysis' of gender 'pictured women and men as social blocs linked by direct power relations' and this, in turn, led to the notion that women as a group shared a common interest in challenging the prevailing gender order.[3]

Feminists also initially accepted that the subordinate social position of women was rooted in socially assigned sex roles. On the basis of this analysis, in the 1960s, feminists argued that the route to sexual equality and women's liberation lay in challenging conventional sex roles. By the 1970s, feminists had become aware that this was no easy task. Sex roles were deeply entrenched. The ascription of gender involved a highly complex system of stereotyping that was, in turn, supported by a whole range of social institutions and practices. 'Women' and 'men' were not only created by society but conformity to the characteristics held to be specifically 'masculine' and 'feminine' was rigidly enforced through social institutions of various kinds.[4]

By this stage, feminist analysis had become increasingly directed towards understanding gender in social and political terms, as a relationship that had meaning within social practices that, in turn, structured and supported social institutions. This view of gender shifted feminist thinking away from a preoccupation with sex roles to a concern with how gender was constituted by the structure of various social institutions and practices that tied gender into intricate patterns of domination. Radical feminists directed their attention to the social dynamics that underpinned the creation and maintenance of 'sex–gender systems' that institutionalized male control over women. Radical feminists saw men's overall social supremacy as being embedded not only in face-to-face settings such as the family, but also generated in the functioning of the economy and through social institutions such as the church and the media. Indeed, the state itself had to be seen as a patriarchal power.[5] (The implications of viewing the state as a patriarchal power in IR are discussed at greater length in chapters 3 and 4).

Contemporary approaches to gender

In recent years, there has been a move towards understanding gender as both an aspect of personal identity and an integral part of social institutions and practices. In contemporary social science, gender is frequently seen in terms of the interweaving of personal life and social structures. Such an approach avoids the pitfalls of voluntarism (the idea that people exercise free choice over their actions) and determinism (the idea that human behaviour is wholly conditioned by social constraints and structures or predetermined by biology). Such an approach also allows gender to be seen in historical context, rather than as a trans-historical structure that arises out of the sexual dichotomy of male and female bodies.[6]

Since the 1980s poststructuralism has been an important influence in feminist theory. Poststructuralist feminists agree that gender cannot be understood as 'natural', or 'universal' and, therefore, outside of history. However, in this view gender is seen as a process in which the 'body' becomes objectified in discourse that takes for granted the reality of sexual difference and inequality.[7] Michel Foucault provided poststructuralist feminism with the insight that 'masculinity' and 'femininity' were variously constructed and located in specific social practices and discourses. This allowed sexuality to be seen in political terms. Also gender inequalities could be understood and/or analysed without positing a single cause, because the 'body' might be worked upon by gender construction and other functions such as race, class and ethnicity that cut across gender historically.[8] As Judith Butler argued, 'because gender is not always constituted coherently or consistently in different historical contexts and because gender intersects with racial, class, ethnic, sexual and regional modalities of discursively constructed identities . . . it becomes impossible to separate out "gender" from the political and cultural intersections in which it is invariably produced and maintained.'[9] This notion of gender as historical, constructed and difficult to separate from, or even speak about, outside of class, culture and ethnicity, rendered problematic the notion of gender as a stable 'category' of analysis within the social sciences.

Masculinities

Much of the literature within the social sciences on gender and gender relations has tended to come from feminist scholars and has largely focused on the way in which constructions of 'women' and the 'feminine' have been used to legitimize unequal social relations. However, there is now a literature on the construction of masculinity, or more properly masculinities, that focuses on men as men. This literature seeks to 'make masculinity visible'.[10] Much of this work has been in sympathy with feminism in so far as it has been acknowledged that women's issues cannot be addressed in isolation from their relationship to men and that men must also be the targets of attempts to redress gender inequalities. As such, work on masculinities also addresses the feminist concern with how practices of power are bound up with the construction of masculine identities. As such it has provided a deeper understanding of how the meaning of masculinity is constructed not only as a superiority of men (and the masculine) over women (and the feminine), but also involves the exaltation of hegemonic masculinity over specific groups of men.[11]

Connell's work, which was alluded to above, has been important in the study of masculinities within the social sciences. Connell has argued that gender should be seen in terms of social and cultural practices that construct gender relations by 'weaving a structure of symbols and interpretation around them and often vastly exaggerating or distorting them'.[12] In this view, 'to sustain patriarchal power on the large scale requires the construction of a hyper-masculine ideal of toughness, and dominance' and 'images of physical beauty in women'.[13] Thus the male or female body does not confer masculinity or femininity on the individual; it takes on meaning through social practices. Connell has argued that 'meanings in the bodily sense of masculinity concern, above all else, the superiority of men to women, and the exaltation of hegemonic masculinity over specific groups of men, processes that are essential to the domination of women'.[14] Just as contemporary feminist thinking tends to stress the multiple identities of women and the specificity of gender in certain localized, cultural contexts, Pease and Pringle stress the need to understand the multiple meanings of masculinity and how men's practices 'vary across a wide range of socio-cultural settings', while recognizing that men and masculinities must be studied within the 'context of a clear gender relational framework'.[15]

The above represents a brief overview of how gender has been understood historically within the social sciences. There have been, and continue to be, differences in perspective and emphasis, notably between those who argue that gender should be understood in terms of structural or material inequalities and those who argue that analysis should focus on how discursive practices produce gender and reproduce gender identities. What is clear from this discussion, however, is that gender is not synonymous with sex and is social rather than natural. Moreover, despite differences of emphasis and approach, feminists of all persuasions have largely agreed that gender is best understood in terms of power relations (in specific societies).

FEMINIST APPROACHES IN IR

Before embarking on a discussion of feminism or feminist theory, it has become almost perfunctory to note that there is no one feminist approach or single feminist theory. The term 'feminist' covers a wide variety of perspectives and practices. For example, the goal of achieving equal rights for women defines liberal-feminism, but difference, rather than equality, has been a key preoccupation in other strands of feminist thought. There is a common commitment among feminists to uncover and elucidate the nature and functions of gender, but some feminists hold that it is difficult in practice to separate gender from other facets of identity such as ethnicity or to understand practices of gender subordination separately from social inequalities rooted in class or justified by racist ideologies. Just as there is no one feminist theory, there is no single feminist theory of international relations or one feminist approach within IR. Below, four distinctive strands of feminism in IR are set out. In chapter 10, the relationship between feminism and social constructivism – an increasingly influential approach in IR – is also considered.

Liberal feminism

The first approach is liberal feminism. Liberal feminists ask the question 'where are the women in IR?' and in so doing highlight the shortcomings of IR in terms of the dearth of research on the position of women across the world and also the under-representation of women in positions of power and influence within international relations/politics.[16] Liberal feminism can be presented as an empirical project to make visible the under-representation, or marginalization of women, and demonstrate how this is in itself a major obstacle to putting women's interests and concerns onto the agenda of international politics. At the same time, the under-representation of women in the academy is a problem because it is likely to mean that there will be little empirical research on the position of women. In a sense, the first feminist 'intervention' in IR might be said to have been a liberal one, in so far as scholars such as Cynthia Enloe began the project of 'making feminist sense' of international politics by locating women in international relations/International Relations,[17] although it should be noted that most feminist scholars in IR do not self-identify with a liberal position, including Enloe.

In concentrating on women specifically, liberal feminism has been criticized for neglecting the study of gender in IR. Liberal feminism has been dismissed as an 'add women and stir' approach, because liberals assume that the issue of male bias can be addressed by including more women in the academy and by generating more 'woman-centred' research in the field. Moreover, this strand of feminism is rationalist (see chapter 9) and, as such, does not fundamentally challenge the basic epistemological foundations of positivism. Positivism will be unpacked at greater length in the following chapter, but put simply positivists insist that there are certain 'facts' about the world that may be ascertained and understood through empirical research and through the rigorous testing of theories. In this way the 'facts' can be established and our knowledge advanced. The role played by the theorist in interpreting the 'facts' and the possibility of bias or distortion of the 'facts' is either not seriously addressed or it is assumed that, if rigorous scholarly procedures are adopted, bias will be minimized or eliminated.

In defence of liberal feminism, Sandra Harding has pointed out that more feminist research with an empirical focus can work to uncover false beliefs and prejudices that distort the findings of research and thereby achieve an enlarged perspective. This is because 'bringing in' more women as researchers will result in a less biased, partial and distorted view of the world. In this way, feminist empiricism begins to undermine the 'male subject as human' bias, opening up a space for an analysis of the ways in which a culture's best beliefs (knowledge) are socially situated.[18] Furthermore, it would be a mistake to dismiss the value of liberal feminist work outright, because arguments for more research on women in international relations, combined with calls for more resources for women, can serve to push women's concerns higher up the (foreign) policy agendas of states, while in the academy (in this case in IR), it can work against the usual tendency to view women and their lives as insignificant or irrelevant.

Standpoint feminism

A second approach within feminist IR is standpoint feminism. Standpoint feminists are committed to articulating the experiences and perspectives of women. Like liberals, standpoint feminists seek to expand the research agenda of IR by locating women in international relations and/or mapping the status of women across the world. However, rather than take the 'reality' of the world as given, standpoint feminists attempt to move women 'from the margin to the centre' as the subjects of knowledge in IR. As such, standpoint feminism is a postpositivist approach to theorizing in IR (see chapter 2).

The point of departure for standpoint feminist IR is to critique mainstream approaches to IR, especially realism and neorealism. Standpoint feminism draws upon a number of insights from psychoanalytical feminism.[19] Unlike liberals who stressed women's equality with men, psychoanalytical feminism argued that processes of socialization and gender-specific experiences like childbirth and mothering meant that women were different from – though not inferior to – men. According to Freudian psychoanalytic theory, single-sex parenting ultimately explained the different personality structures in boys and girls. Feminist scholars such as Nancy Chodorow, for example, drew upon these insights to argue that the formation of gender identity was necessarily a different process for boys and girls. Since mothers usually assumed primary responsibility for care during a child's formative years, girls related to a caretaker of the same sex throughout their formative years, while boys related to a caretaker of a different sex. Boy children, therefore, developed a sense of 'self' – of identity – through a process of radical differentiation from the mother and by identification with a frequently absent father figure. According to this theory, to be a boy involved escaping the world of women and the home and entering the public realm of men. In contrast, the formation of gender identity in girls involved closely relating to the mother figure, developing an orientation towards the domestic realm and adopting passive and submissive behaviour patterns. This pattern of gender identification formed the basis of a basically unequal social division between the public (male) world and private or domestic (female) realm.[20] Moreover, these different developmental processes created a psychology of dominance in boy children and submissiveness in girls.

Feminist theorists in the academy, who are influenced by standpoint ideas, argue that women's material life activity has important epistemological implications.[21] Socialization processes are held to result in girls experiencing a more complex relational world that is then further reinforced through processes of socialization. For boys, however, a central concern with autonomy arises from the male infant's struggle to establish a sense of separate identity. The move towards separation and autonomy and the development of a sense of self can lead to over-rigid ego boundaries where other people are perceived as threats to be controlled or dominated. The notion of different life-worlds gives rise to a critique of universal theories, since these are necessarily gender biased. Standpoint feminists have argued that representations of the 'human' or universal are those devised by men and are about the male world as seen by men. Moreover, social scientists frequently simply reflect the 'male as norm' standpoint. The lack of men's awareness of this particular bias is in turn a reflection of their privileged social position. The major insight of standpoint is then that knowledge about the world is always constructed from a particular point of view.

In her book on *Gender in International Relations*, J. Ann Tickner drew upon standpoint feminism to both critique mainstream IR and to suggest how the field might be (re-)visioned, particularly with respect to security.[22] Tickner critiqued realism and neorealism on the grounds that the sovereign state, personified as a 'rational subject' (implicit in conceptions of the 'state as actor' or 'national/state interests'), could not represent women epistemologically or politically.[23] Tickner argued that adopting a standpoint feminist position allowed for both the development of a powerful critique of dominant approaches in IR and could also form the basis of a radical reconstruction of IR. For example, core concepts central to the study of International Relations, such as autonomy, power, conflict and security could be rethought and re-visioned from a standpoint perspective. Just how some of these ideas have found specific application in feminist thinking and writing about war and conflict, peace and security is set out in later chapters.

However, clearly attempts to theorize from the position of 'women's lived experiences' are problematic. One of the main objections to standpoint is that there is no 'authentic' woman's experience that can serve as a basis for knowledge claims. Even if one was to accept the idea that gender difference was rooted in socialization processes, and not in biology or 'nature', 'women's experiences' might still differ according to social class and/or cultural context. It has been argued that standpoint feminist reformulations offer alternatives that are themselves based on the idea of an ahistorical 'Other', thus taking for granted the idea that there are distinct realities to which 'male' and 'female' refer. It is important to distinguish between the category 'women-as-Other' – the experience that is generally ignored or marginalized when asserting universal claims – that can be usefully employed in the process of deconstruction or critique and the experiences of real women who are material subjects of their own history.[24] Once the historical and cultural specificity of gender is acknowledged, the subject of knowledge must be seen as multiple and, perhaps, contradictory. 'Masculinity' and 'femininity' are not universal categories, but always categories within race, class and culture so there can only be, at best, feminist standpoints. Some standpoint feminist thinkers have acknowledged that there can be no one standpoint. However, while standpoint feminism produces partial truths, partial understandings of the world, these are nevertheless valid knowledge claims.[25]

Critical feminism

A third approach can be characterized as 'critical' feminism. To some extent, critical feminism shares affinities with earlier schools of Marxist-feminism in so far as critical feminists focus on gender as a social relationship of inequality.[26] Marxist feminists understood gender to be a form of social inequality that was rooted in the 'privatization' of women's productive and reproductive labour power, the control of women's sexuality and the subordination of women to male authority through a range of patriarchal institutions. Thus, gender inequality was understood in terms of the intersection of two sets of social forces, capitalism and patriarchy.[27]

However, critical feminists have departed from Marxist-feminism in so far as they place more emphasis on the power of ideas and ideologies in reproducing gender relations. In focusing on how social relations of inequality are structured and reproduced, critical feminists have pointed to both material structures and the role played by dominant (hegemonic even) ideas about the social significance of gender. Moreover, while recognizing that we all live within one capitalist world order and so are all involved in a system that reproduces certain forms of social inequality, critical feminists have paid closer attention to the specificity of gender relations within different countries and societies across the world.[28] Critical feminists are also inclined to afford a greater role to culture in sustaining and reproducing gender inequality in specific societies than Marxist feminists had previously done.

While attempting to categorize or pigeonhole particular scholars can be problematic, since they often utilize rather eclectic theoretical and analytical frameworks, Sandra Whitworth's work is informed by 'critical feminism'.[29] Whitworth has contributed to the development of a feminist international political economy and, in this context, her work will be revisited in chapter 6.[30] However, in her first book on feminist theory in IR, she focused on the role of international institutions in formulating policies that had an impact on everything from labour laws to population policies and reproductive rights. Whitworth argued that social forces and material conditions combined to reproduce social practices, institutions and international organizations. Institutions, social practices and ideas combined to sustain gender relations of inequality. Thus, one had to always question the meaning given to the 'reality' that constituted gender and ask how ideas about gender were expressed in and through social and political institutions. Whitworth insisted that while gender relations had to be seen in the context of social class and/or ethnicity or race, a feminist analysis must, nevertheless, be able to demonstrate how institutions and practices embody forms of power relations that are patriarchal, allowing men (even the most disadvantaged) to exercise power over women. Whitworth argued that the focus should be on gender relations rather than women per se, because this forced us to think about how gender relations operated in different contexts and were affected by both international and internal factors.[31] At the same time, feminist analysis had to account for how relations between women and men could be transformed in specific social and historical contexts.[32]

Critical feminists also share some affinities with Critical Theorists in so far as they embraced the historical commitment of feminism to an emancipatory project (see chapter 9). The central insight of Critical Theory is, perhaps, that the activity of 'theorizing' is intimately connected with social practices. Critical Theorists see part of the critical project of theory as being to understand the activity of the knowing subject and moments of reflection and self-understanding. Critical feminists similarly view knowledge as a 'moment' of emancipation. Feminist theorizing involves constructing 'knowledge' about the world, not in the interests of social and political control, but in the service of an emancipatory politics. Critical feminists are committed to the project of women's emancipation while also recognizing the historical and cultural specificity of gender. From this perspective, then, feminist theorizing is not an abstract activity, but infused with a political purpose: to elucidate the role played by ideologies and social structures in constructing, reconstructing and reproducing gender identities and gendered relationships and to suggest ways in which these might be changed in the interests of securing greater gender equality and more autonomy for women.

Poststructuralist feminism

Perhaps the most radical challenges to mainstream IR have come from poststructuralist feminist interventions in the field, since these have ultimately called into question the very possibility of 'IR'. From a poststructuralist perspective, 'truth' and meaning are always in doubt and forms of identity in question, so sovereign claims to shape human identities, construct linear histories and impose social and political boundaries are necessarily problematic. Therefore, even while in agreement that of all institutionalized forms of contemporary social and political analysis IR has most neglected gender, poststructuralist thinkers have resisted 'reconstructive projects' (such as Tickner's attempt to re-vision security from a 'woman's perspective' for example)[33] because attempts to develop a single perspective or coherent feminist paradigm in IR inevitably marginalize and displace a range of other feminist perspectives and agendas.

Poststructuralist feminists understand categories like 'man', 'woman' and 'gender' (and even sex) to be discursively constructed. From this perspective, there is no essence to 'woman'. Moreover, there is no simple relationship between being a woman and perceiving oneself to have specific interests that arise from one's gender. This calls into question the idea that women necessarily share similar interests or a common perspective on the world. Moreover, the idea that feminist theory can and should serve the project of women's emancipation is viewed as at best problematic and at worst potentially dangerous, since the whole process of theorizing is viewed as a form of domination whereby the theorist comprehends and appropriates the object of knowledge.

The point of departure for many poststructuralist thinkers is to note a paradox. While Enlightenment discourses (including feminism) have championed the values of progress and human freedom, historically, the Enlightenment period has been accompanied by the widespread oppression of many peoples across the world in the name of the 'advance of civilization', of 'progress' and 'freedom'. Discourses on freedom and emancipation have, therefore, merely served to consign to the realm of the 'inhumane', 'uncivilized' and 'backward' whole societies and peoples who do not share the cultural characteristics of (western) 'Enlightenment Man'.[34]

Poststructuralist thinkers argue that, by their very nature, schemes that try to provide universal 'truths' necessarily centre some experiences and, in the process, decentre or marginalize others. The 'truth' only serves to produce and reproduce a series of 'Others' that must be set aside or made invisible to maintain the coherence of the doctrine. The political project must, therefore, be to resist such appropriations. Thus all-encompassing visions of human freedom and emancipation and theories grounded in 'universal' truths are resisted. Here the (feminized) 'Other' is evoked as the experience that confounds that which is held to be 'universal', the voice that is marginalized or silenced when the 'truth' is asserted. Poststructuralists concentrate on exposing the hidden presuppositions and assumptions that underlie all attempts to theorize or tell 'One True Story' about the human condition. Instead, through critique and deconstruction, poststructuralists seek to expose the assumptions, presuppositions and biases that underpin universal theories.[35]

For poststructuralist feminists it is problematic to confer ontological (see the following chapter) status on 'woman', because employing 'woman' as a concept or category of analysis presupposes that all people of the same gender across classes and cultures are somehow socially constituted as a homogeneous group identifiable prior to the process of analysis. In this way the discursive consensual homogeneity of 'women' is mistaken for the specific material reality of real ('concrete') women.[36] Poststructuralist feminists simultaneously resist the notion of uniquely female experiences, because this involves making essentialist or universal knowledge claims on the basis of experiences that are historically and culturally specific. Rather than seek to uncover universal truths, poststructuralist thinkers embrace and celebrate 'Otherness' as a way of being, thinking and speaking that allows for an openness, plurality, diversity and difference.[37] Poststructuralist feminist thinkers have, therefore, celebrated feminist discourses because they are the discourses of 'outsiders', born out of, and attuned to, issues of exclusion and invisibility. As Goetz argued, women have occupied inferior positions in all spheres of life, across most societies and this experience has provided the historical identity upon which feminist scholarship and politics have been based.[38]

Feminist scholars sympathetic to poststructuralism, such as Christine Sylvester, Marysia Zalewski and V. Spike Peterson, for example, reject the possibility of a neutral or objective stance (à la positivism), but also steer clear of epistemological claims made in the name of 'women' (as in standpoint feminism).[39] This questioning of 'woman' or gender as a stable, coherent category leads to a much greater sensitivity towards cultural and historical specificity in poststructuralist feminist analysis. The insight that gender is the cultural means by which 'natural sex' is produced and established as pre-discursive or prior to culture and a product or effect of historically specific power relations[40] gives feminism a useful analytical framework to explain how women's experience is impoverished and controlled within certain culturally determined images of female sexuality and how access to resources might be shut off (or, indeed, opened up) within specific definitions of femininity. Poststructuralist feminist work, therefore, tends to have an empirical focus and stresses the specificity of gender relations in particular societies and their specific effects. That said, poststructuralist feminists are open to the possibility of forging cross-cultural understanding.

Postcolonial feminism

There are similarities between poststructuralist feminism and postcolonial feminism[41] in that both strands of thought emphasize differences among women and not just between men and women. Postcolonial feminism also develops a critique of Enlightenment discourse and draws attention to practices of 'Othering' embedded in Enlightenment projects. Postcolonial feminism speaks to the experiences of women in societies that have been subjected to forms of imperialist and colonial domination and is alert to the new forms of colonialism (neo-colonialism) that pervade the contemporary world.

Historically western feminist theory has been concerned to expose practices that exploit and oppress women. However, oppression takes many forms. Like poststructuralists, postcolonial feminists argue that women are many, not one, and that the experiences of women are profoundly shaped by experiences of racial, ethnic, class and sexual oppression. Feminist theory must, therefore, be able to theorize the way in which class, ethnicity, race and sexuality cut across gender differences. Moreover, in so far as racist assumptions have been embedded in both the theory and practice of western feminism, feminist theory must also be alert to the problem of power and the reproduction of unequal power relations between specific groups of women.

A good example of the problem of power and the reproduction of unequal power relations can be found in the history of colonialism. Both western men and western women often assumed that colonialized people were 'backward', or 'barbaric', and that women particularly suffered the consequences of cultural beliefs and practices rooted in traditions or founded on religion. Western women, who were denied basic rights in their own societies during that same period, nevertheless frequently assumed an inherently superior attitude to women in non-western societies. Colonialism and imperialism were justified by discourses that cast western societies as 'modern' and 'progressive'. Through western political leadership and moral guidance, colonized peoples might be led out of barbarism, freed from ignorance and become 'modern', 'progressive', 'enlightened' societies. In practice, however, colonialist policies and practices actually worked to disempower women.

Postcolonial feminists have been the fiercest critics of contemporary discourses on 'modernization' and development policies that have been imposed on peoples in so-called 'Third World' countries. For example, the Women in Development (WID) movement (see chapter 7) was based on liberal-feminist assumptions that implicitly assumed that western women were more advanced and liberated than their 'sisters' in developing countries. However well intentioned, in practice WID only served to reinforce racial and cultural stereotypes and reproduced unequal power relations between western (colonizing) and non-western (colonialized) women.

Contemporary postcolonial feminists, such as Chandra Mohanty, Gayatri Spivak and Kumari Jayawardena,[42] do not refute or deny the existence of gender inequalities in specific societies. Indeed, the struggle against gender oppression in specific societies is very much at the heart of postcolonial feminism. However, this struggle necessarily involves understanding the complexities of gender and gender inequality within particular societies. It is neither possible nor wise to assume that the experiences of white, western women are relevant to women in non-western societies. Moreover, feminist strategies and practices that have emerged within a particular social, political, economic and cultural context are not necessarily helpful to women's struggles in other places and at other times. Indeed, as the above discussion suggests, the imposition of western feminism on other (and 'Othered') women can be dangerous and damaging. Furthermore, the politics of feminism in non-western societies is shaped by the wider social and cultural context. Activists struggling to challenge forms of oppression justified in the name of gender differences might and often do find that they are charged with collusion with the West, while feminism is apt to be cast by elite men as a 'foreign' discourse and practice that has no relevance in non-western societies. This is often the case in discourses on nationalism (see chapter 3). For this reason, too, postcolonial feminists must negotiate the complexities of class, race and ethnicity in challenging dominant discourses and devising strategies to empower women.

Postcolonial feminists do not discount the possibilities or value of forging alliances between feminist activists across boundaries of race, ethnicity, class or sexuality. However, such alliances must be based on recognition of and respect for the 'Other'. Inderpal Grewal and Caren Kaplan[43] argue that transnational alliances can be forged among reflexive theorists and activists who recognize the links between patriarchies, colonialisms, racisms and other forms of domination and who are similarly alert to power asymmetries and inequalities among both women and men and among different groups of women.

CONCLUSION

This chapter has provided an introduction to the key concept in feminist theory, gender, and provided an overview of the main feminist approaches to IR. Later chapters concentrate on the substantive contribution of feminist scholarship to IR. First, however, it is appropriate to locate feminist IR within the context of the broader theoretical debates within the field. This is the subject of chapter 2.

┌─────────┐
│ **2** │
└─────────┘

GENDER, FEMINISM AND THE FOURTH DEBATE IN INTERNATIONAL RELATIONS

INTRODUCTION

As is evident from the discussion in the introduction to this book, 'feminist IR' has its own specific origins and has been driven by a set of distinctive interests and concerns. However, the emergence of a feminist literature in IR coincided with the 'fourth debate' in IR theory, a debate that opened up intellectual space for a range of 'critical theories' in the field.[1] The fourth debate was concerned, in part, with the politics of knowledge claims and the practices of inclusion and exclusion inherent in all attempts to construct socially bounded fields of knowledge. While there are important differences between feminist approaches to IR, with the exception of liberal feminism, all have shared the common objective of breaking down the positivist 'orthodoxy'. As such, feminist IR should be viewed in the context of 'anti-positivistic, philosophical and sociological trends in the social sciences more generally'.[2] Many of the issues raised by feminism resonate with critical theorists, in a broad sense of the term, in so far as they concern the politics of knowledge claims; the relationship between theory and social practice; and how categories for 'understanding' and 'explaining' international relations have been constructed in ways that delimit the scope of 'legitimate' study in the field.

A CONTESTED FIELD

For much of the post-Second World War period, realism and later neorealism constituted the dominant approaches to IR, so much so that by the 1980s neorealism had come to be labelled the 'orthodoxy' in IR.[3] The dominant position of realism/neorealism explains why it was the target of criticism from critical theorists generally and why it was subjected to feminist critiques specifically. The critique of realism is covered in greater detail in the following chapter.

The first debate

The dominance of realism/neorealism notwithstanding, since IR was established as a distinctive academic discipline,[4] it has been characterized by a series of debates about what constitutes its subject matter and central concerns. In the first wave of scholarship produced just after the First World War, the purpose of the study of international relations was defined in terms of the need to promote respect for the norms of international society and devise institutions that would strengthen and uphold international law. Early IR scholars believed that the purpose of the discipline was to understand the causes of war and suggest ways in which relations between states could be organized according to principles that would sustain an enduring peace.

This first phase of 'political idealism' was displaced after the collapse of the League of Nations and the outbreak of the Second World War. These events brought about a reaction to the idealism of the age – idealism reflected in much early IR scholarship. This reaction possibly reached its intellectual peak in Britain with the publication of E. H. Carr's *The Twenty Years' Crisis* in 1939[5] although it was perhaps Hans Morgenthau's *Politics Among Nations*, published in the United States in 1948, that established realism as the dominant paradigm in IR. [6] Thereafter the study of IR came to be seen as concerned with developing a better understanding of the problems and dilemmas that states faced in achieving security and realizing their strategic and instrumental interests in an 'anarchic' international order.

The second debate

The first debate in IR between the idealists and the realists was settled in favour of realism. This brought about a marked shift away from a normative concern with justice to the problems of power politics. In the late 1950s, during the 'second debate', realism faced a so-called 'behaviouralist revolt'. Both Carr and Morgenthau had argued that the study of international politics should be 'scientific' rather than being driven by normative values and concerns. Behaviouralists took this appeal to science further by attempting to institute scientific research methodologies and positivist epistemological assumptions within the discipline.

The third debate

In the 1970s, both liberal-pluralism and Marxism emerged as competing worldviews in IR, but the existence of competing approaches did not lead to the displacement of realism as a privileged position within IR.[7] It did, however, generate a discussion about the implications of these competing 'worldviews' or 'paradigms'.[8] The existence of multiple approaches and competing paradigms evidenced the degree to which IR lacked an established core. The profusion of approaches and literatures in IR demonstrated that much activity in international relations might be construed as 'political' and that ontological choices are affirmed by categories of inclusion and exclusion and judgements about what is significant.[9] The existence of competing perspectives on the nature of the world raised the question of how competing theories or perspectives could be evaluated. The existence of competing paradigms in IR pointed to how the pursuit of knowledge about the world 'out there' was not a matter of developing better theories through rigorous empirical research and testing, because what was 'out there' was clearly contested within the field. Paradigms did not describe reality but rather constructed 'reality' differently. Furthermore, the construction of theory could not be seen as an activity designed to uncover 'truths' about the world.

Drawing upon the work of Thomas Kuhn, John Vasquez argued that a paradigm should be understood as a shared understanding and way of approaching problems that was accepted by a community of scholars and used to inculcate students with fundamental ways of 'knowing the world'.[10] According to Vasquez, once established, scholarship in the field of IR was characterized by the extensive articulation of the paradigm and that this guided theory construction and empirical research. In a Kuhnian sense it was Morgenthau's *Politics Among Nations* that provided the particular picture of the world, or paradigm, that permitted the IR community to develop a common research agenda. It quickly became the 'exemplar' for the study of IR and was, perhaps, the single most important vehicle for establishing the dominance of realism in the field. Since the publication of *Politics Among Nations*, the IR literature had been fairly systematic and somewhat cumulative in articulating the realist paradigm.[11]

The Fourth Debate

The inter-paradigm debate (or third debate) was quickly overshadowed by the emergence of a fourth debate in IR in the 1980s that was explicitly concerned with the problems and pitfalls of positivism. Everybody engages in the process of trying to 'make sense' of the world and so, in this sense, everybody is a 'theorist'. What then, if anything, makes knowledge within the academy different from 'common-sense' views that circulate in the wider world? The answer to this question lies in understanding the epistemological and ontological claims of social scientific knowledge and methodological issues that relate to how we conduct our research; how we go about discovering what the world is like.

Ontology refers to the nature of the world, how we map the world conceptually and what can be said to exist. So, ontological questions are concerned with, for example, whether we can speak of 'reality' in a material sense or whether we should focus instead on the ideational – that is on 'reality' as an idea or intellectual construct. Epistemology concerns the basis on which we claim to 'know' things about the world (of, say, international politics) and whether the claims that we make about the world are 'factual' and/or 'true' or rather based on belief systems or ideologies. Methodology is concerned with how we go about discovering what the world is like, what methods we employ in our study. Methodology is underpinned, in turn, by 'a theory of how research does or should proceed'.[12] This, in turn, includes 'accounts of how the general structure of theory finds its application in particular scientific disciplines'.[13]

Ontological, epistemological and methodological questions have been extensively debated within the philosophy of science and have been reproduced in key debates in IR. There is a central and important divide between those groups of scholars (often characterized as the 'mainstream' in IR or positivists, including both neorealists and neoliberal institutionalists) who believe that, through adopting rigorous research methods that closely approximate to the methods employed by the natural sciences, it is possible to construct 'objective' knowledge about international relations or world politics. In contrast, postpositivists are apt to view knowledge building as an inter-subjective activity. Both empirical research and theoretical debate within the academic community are driven by a desire to establish a degree of consensus about what the world is like. If, however, knowledge about the world is ideological or inter-subjectively constructed, then knowledge claims cannot be understood apart from the social and cultural context in which they are constructed and propagated.

While classical realism cannot be accurately characterized as a 'positivist' approach (since it is essentially interpretive – more on this in the following chapter), with the emergence of neorealism in the 1980s, positivist assumptions increasingly began to inform the research agendas and methodology adopted by IR scholars. The third debate had gone some way towards challenging the claim that it was possible to understand the world 'out there' objectively. The insight that there is no one unprob-lematic social reality waiting to be explained raised the question of why it was that some theories, or worldviews, had come to be accepted as constituting knowledge of the 'real' world, while others continued to be dismissed as idealistic, wishful thinking, ideological and 'unscientific'.

While the 1980s saw the emergence of a distinctive neoliberal institutionalist approach in IR (which was equally positivist), it was neorealism that became a par-ticular target of criticism, largely because (at that time) neorealism enjoyed a hegem-onic or privileged position within the field of IR.[14] Moreover, the 'widespread sense of crisis' associated with the end of the Cold War also provoked the multi-pronged assault on neorealism.[15] The collapse of the 'old world order' increased dissatisfaction with the neorealist 'orthodoxy' and gave impetus to the search for new conceptual and theoretical tools of analysis in IR. The critique of neorealism was wide-ranging, but largely focused on the following issues and problems.

Philosophical and epistemological issues

The rather more reflective approach of scholars like E. H. Carr was abandoned in 'scientific' realist approaches based on positivist assumptions. Neorealists claimed to have a detached and disinterested view of the central feature of international order (anarchy), the main actors (states) and processes (the struggle for power and pursuit of strategic interests) in IR. Critics of neorealism questioned the 'embedded standards, criteria, norms and principles' in this approach.[16] Whereas positivists tended to 'see the world as something external to our theories', postpositivists argued that 'our theories actually help construct the world'.[17] In making claims about the existence of 'objective facts', neorealism worked to preclude, discourage or marginalize the consid-eration of philosophical or epistemological questions in the discipline. In realism/neorealism what was actually a scholarly convention came to be conceived of as a 'truth' and pre-existing historical phenomenon and explanations about the world were then validated in relation to a posited 'reality' that was actually both the source of and the test of claims about that 'reality'.[18]

When applied to the study of the social world, neorealism denied the role of social practices in making and transforming social orders because positivism perpetuated a belief in the natural rather than historical character of real social and political relations. Positivism objectified and separated the 'knower' from the object of study, so that human beings became the objects of study. The separation of facts and values assumed that it was possible to explain social phenomena without reference to the meanings that people ascribed to social situations. However, there was no one social reality, but different ones that were negotiated and managed by members of any given society.[19]

Problems of reductionism and reification of international order

Neorealism not only privileged positivist knowledge claims but also reified what were historically contingent structures of the social and political world.[20] Thus the notion of structural anarchy was presented as an enduring feature of IR, generating a propensity on the part of states to pursue power and strategic and/or instrumental interests. However, 'structural anarchy' was, at best, a historically contingent phenomenon and not an objective 'fact' or 'enduring condition' of international relations. Neorealism constructed social practice and representations of social practice and, in the process, presupposed that the social world was self-evident.[21] In perpetuating a belief in the natural rather than historical character of real social and political arrangements, neorealism was ideological and, moreover, could potentially be put to the service of conservative political ends.[22] Both realism and neorealism reduced complex international phenomena to relations between reified sovereign states. This not only disguised the degree to which international processes could have an impact on specific social groups (for better or worse) but also marginalized or rendered invisible unequal social relations and many contemporary problems that had an international dimension.[23]

What emerged from the fourth debate was a more reflexive environment in which debate and criticism were encouraged and spaces opened up for scholars to rethink and rewrite IR.[24] Critical theorists of all persuasions acknowledged the socially mutable and historically contingent nature of knowledge claims and defended, and to some degree embraced, methodological pluralism in IR. A growing group of, in many ways diverse, critical theorists began to ask questions concerning the nature of knowledge claims and how meaning and 'truth' were constructed. One of the central themes of the fourth debate was that the production of knowledge must be studied in relation to the dominant social forces and practices of the age.[25] To some extent, the common aim of the various critics of neorealism was to undermine its hegemonic position in IR and open up a space for those voices marginalized or excluded from the mainstream in IR.[26]

Feminism in the fourth debate

The inter-paradigm debate (the 'third debate') provided an early opportunity for feminists to raise issues of exclusionary practices in the construction of knowledge in IR.[27] However, feminist scholars contributed more extensively to the fourth debate in IR. Differences between feminisms notwithstanding, most feminist IR scholars locate themselves within a postpositivist tradition.[28] All criticized the idea that the theorist is simply an impartial observer whose role is to observe and explain an unproblematic reality 'out there' since there is an intimate connection between power, knowledge and interests. Starting from the position that there can be no objective social and political reality, feminists, along with other 'critical' theorists or constructivists working in IR, also pointed to how 'reality' was constituted by inter-subjective meanings about the nature of what was a highly complex social and political world.

However, feminists developed a distinctive critique of mainstream or orthodox IR theory that exposed the gender bias in key concepts and highlighted the profoundly gendered imagery and symbolism employed in realist (and neorealist) texts particularly.[29] In challenging the realist/neorealist orthodoxy, feminist IR aimed to push back the limits of this universe of possible explanation, to give voice to that which could not be articulated or expressed because of the constraints of existing discourse and to open up space for voices and issues previously silenced through the constraints of existing discourse. In this way, foregrounding issues of gender in IR served to both de-reify male reason and objectivity by demonstrating its material and ideological exclusivity and to put 'political subjectivity back into the picture'.[30]

Much of the following is concerned with epistemological issues which centre on the production of knowledge in IR. However, at this juncture it is worth pointing out that one of the problems with state centrism in IR is that it results in the rigid demarcation of boundaries between the international (outside) and domestic (inside) and between private and public realms. Morgenthau insisted that 'politics' had to be seen as a relatively autonomous sphere of action because without this separation it would be impossible to distinguish between political and non-political acts and thus impossible to delimit the field of study of 'international politics'.[31] These choices of 'inclusion' and 'exclusion', made prior to the process of theorizing relations between states, rely upon an existing distinction between 'private' and 'public' realms. Once this gendered distinction is drawn, gender relations (in the private sphere) are rendered invisible.

One of the major aims of feminist critique has been to expose the masculinist bias in neorealist/realist concepts and categories and to show how, consequently, 'claims to know' in IR have been partial and particular. In the following chapter, the feminist critique of realism is set out in some detail. At this juncture, it is appropriate to focus on how dominant ideas in IR construct the core subject matter of IR and also determine what counts as 'knowledge'. The idea that the study of gender is not part of IR because the subject is about the study of the state and its power is premised on certain ideas that privilege a realist/neorealist understanding of what the world is really like, what is enduring and what is ephemeral, what is central and what is marginal.

The major source of gender bias in international relations theory generally is, ultimately, rooted in concepts derived from political theory.[32] Indeed, as Rebecca Grant has argued, 'the whole theoretical approach to IR rests on a foundation of political concepts which it would be difficult to hold together coherently were it not for the trick of eliminating women from the prevailing definitions of [man as] the political actor'.[33] These political concepts are drawn from a wide range of theorists, but owe a great deal to Thomas Hobbes and Niccolò Machiavelli particularly. These key thinkers will be revisited in the following chapter. At this point it is enough to note that the 'problem' with realism is that it is constructed around a series of concepts that privilege masculine identified traits and experiences. As Christine Di Stefano claimed, Hobbes's (a major intellectual influence in realism) thought was shaped by a distinctly masculinist outlook, characterized by dualistic thinking, a need for a singular identity, a denial of relatedness and a radical individualism. In Hobbes's seminal text *Leviathan* (from which realists draw the analogy of IR as a 'state of nature'), one was presented with a picture of atomized individuals who related to each other in entirely impersonal ways and where self/other distinctions were strongly enforced.[34] Hobbes's take on nature was a world in which the solitary subject (state) confronted a dangerous and threatening environment (anarchy).

As noted in the previous chapter, realism should not necessarily be viewed as a positivist approach, since much realist scholarship is not based on positivist methodological assumptions. However, the critique of Hobbes is relevant because neorealism (a positivist approach) in essence grafted a scientific methodology onto a traditional realist approach and in so doing left intact most of the key assumptions and concepts embedded in realism: the state as a sovereign, autonomous and purposive actor; the centrality of power and national interest and so on. As Benhabib argued, one must see in Hobbes's thought the reflection of an early bourgeois world characterized by a division between 'reason' and 'sentiment' and in which reason was male-identified and associated with 'knowledge'.[35] This knowledge was gendered knowledge since it was constructed on the basis of binary oppositions between 'dependence' and 'autonomy' and 'man' over 'nature' (identified metaphorically with the feminine) and as such privileged a distinctly masculinist worldview.

This is not to say that Hobbes (or subsequently realists) made claims about what or how all men thought, but that these categories and concepts reflected historically and culturally conditioned ideas about 'masculinity' and 'femininity' and ways of 'knowing' the world that were identified with a masculine experience. Hobbes viewed the human qualities of autonomy, agency and knowledge as standing in marked opposition to, and threatened by, the forces of nature. In Hobbes's thought, one saw the freeing of the male ego from all bonds of dependence and the male/female dichotomies reified as essential to the constitution of the self. The denial of being born of a woman (mothers, sisters and daughters were simply absent in Hobbes's account of the state of nature – see the following chapter) freed the male ego from the most basic bond of dependence. This was then reflected in epistemologies that embodied a white, male perspective that put the omnipotent subject at the centre of the conceptual universe and constructed a series of marginal 'Others' seen as sets of negative qualities.[36]

Feminists have pointed out that positivism is identified with a distinctly masculinist way of 'knowing the world'. The problem of gender bias is not, then, 'simply the absence of women' but the persistent association of the 'masculine' with the 'objective' and 'scientific'. The construction of 'scientific' knowledge is a process that involves the domination of nature, nature being ubiquitously female. Peterson has argued that, having divided the world into 'knower' mind/subject and 'knowable' nature/object, scientific ideology further specified the relation between knower and known as one of distance and separation. The so-called objectivity of science, then, presupposed a scientific mind and mode of knowing that set the 'knower' apart from what was to be 'known' – nature – and the 'masculine' by association came to connote autonomy, separation and distance.[37]

Nancy Hirschmann has argued that men have historically dominated women and so have exercised control over how they have constructed both themselves and women. This has not only resulted in institutions that socially and politically privileged men over women, but it has also affected the very structure of meaning and reality by pervading our categories of knowledge. Thus, Hirschmann has argued that modern epistemologies affect the kinds of questions asked and the particular modes of inquiry that are considered legitimate. The perspective of a socially constructed 'masculine' experience has been epistemologically validated and imposed on women, preserving male privilege and the social practices and structures that enabled men to consider their own experiences the human experience.[38] In this way, 'by explicitly ignoring gender while implicitly exploiting a distinctly masculine means of knowledge seeking, modern epistemologies have been able to mask their own bias'.[39]

THE SITES OF FEMINIST IR

Having outlined the broad contours of the fourth debate, it is appropriate at this juncture to revisit the various strands of feminism introduced in the previous chapter and revisit the main themes of feminist IR, set out in the introduction to this book. This is not only useful for understanding how feminist scholarship has informed (if not transformed) IR, but is also necessary to understand what has been at stake in engagements between feminism and IR theory generally, engagements that are covered at greater length in chapter 10.

To simplify somewhat, what might be described as the 'first wave' of feminist scholarship in IR could be said to have identified a number of core tasks: first, to point to the exclusions and biases of mainstream IR, both in terms of the limitations of state-centric analyses and of positivism; second, to make women visible as social, economic and political subjects in international politics; third, to analyse how gender inequalities were embedded in the day-to-day practices of international relations; and fourth, and more controversially in terms of my implied consensus, to empower women as subjects of knowledge by building theoretical understanding of international relations from the position of women and their lived, embodied experiences. Feminist scholarship within the field has expanded since the 'first wave' or 'first generation'[40] of feminist scholars endeavoured to 'gender' the discipline of IR. One might add two further 'core tasks' to the contemporary feminist IR agenda. Fifth, to elucidate the ways that 'masculinities' and 'femininities' are forged, shaped and reproduced in relation to global forces and processes. Finally, to highlight specific sites and manifestations of gender relations outside of the western context and address the racialized and colonialized dimensions of international relations.[41]

The exclusions and biases of 'mainstream' IR

Until recently, mainstream/positivist International Relations scholars had not included gender as a category of analysis or as an approach. The few scholars within the mainstream of IR who have engaged with gender and feminist work have proceeded from the assumption that gender is something that is 'out there' in the world, the effects of which can be measured in various ways. In effect, gender is a variable that might be helpful in understanding certain phenomena like war, for example. Indeed 'feminist IR' was initially read by 'mainstream' IR scholars (see chapter 10) as a project devoted to the construction of a single feminist approach or paradigm in IR. In contrast, most feminists are postpositivists of one kind or another and, as such, they argue that we engage with the world and construct our 'reality' as gendered subjects and tend to view the world through the 'lenses of gender',[42] so gender cannot be reduced to a mere 'variable'.

Moreover, from this perspective mainstream IR is a deeply gendered discourse, as evidenced from the discussion above. Part of the project to 'gender IR' has been to engage in the process of critiquing the mainstream to expose the profound gender bias that underpins positivist approaches to theorizing (in IR) and generate a debate about the powerful processes of inclusion and exclusion at work in the construction of theories, worldviews and research agendas in IR. Indeed, many feminist IR scholars have questioned the practices of exclusion inherent in the construction of academic disciplines like IR and in so doing pointed to the politics of knowledge claims.

Making women visible

As noted in the previous chapter, one approach to 'feminist IR' has been to focus on the position of women as subjects in international relations, or women's and/or feminist groups as 'actors' in international politics. For example, some feminist work has investigated why there are so few women in the 'high politics' of foreign policy-making[43] or diplomacy[44] and ask whether this is a consequence of discriminatory practices based on the belief that women are not 'up to the job' perhaps, that continue to hinder the progress of women in these domains. Some of the early contributions to feminist IR sought to locate women as actors in various ways.[45] Asking these questions generates further ruminations about the possible consequences of the under-representation of women in international politics.[46] Some feminist scholars have directed their attention to the task of uncovering and highlighting the economic, social and political status of women throughout the world, pointing to the difference gender evidently makes in deciding who gets an education, access to health care or control of financial resources, issues that are increasingly being constructed as within the domain of women's human rights (see chapter 8).[47]

The first wave of feminist literature in IR included contributions from liberal feminist scholars who worked on (or sometimes in) the transnational women's movement and who were interested in transnational 'legitimized' relationships. Thus, Kathleen Newland described the interactions of women's groups as part of a dense web of transnational relationships that emerged out of the 'Women in Development' movement in the 1970s and 1980s and, as such, provide a prime example of transnational movements in action.[48] Women's human rights advocate Georgina Ashworth similarly highlighted the solidarities forged between women around a range of global gender issues that cut across national boundaries.[49]

The production and reproduction of gendered inequalities

Alternatively, 'feminist IR' has focused on the gendered nature and differential impact of global economic and social processes on men and women respectively, in so far as contemporary globalization, for example, seemingly generates different employment opportunities for men and women, while the impact of global indebtedness is often felt more keenly by women than men, particularly in very poor countries.[50] In so far as ideas and ideologies about gender affect policy-making at both national and international levels, feminists in IR have also sought to understand how institutions play a role in reproducing gender inequalities (see chapter 6).[51]

In distinctive ways, Sandra Whitworth and Sarah Brown have both focused on gender as a socially constructed relationship that has served to legitimize a specific form of social inequality.[52] In her contribution to the special issue of the journal *Millennium*, Sarah Brown argued that gender was not natural but constructed and that when 'gender was viewed as essentially an inequality constructed as a socially relevant difference in order to keep that inequality in place, then gender could be seen as an outcome of social processes of subordination and the issue of gender in International Relations could be treated as a question of systemic dominance'.[53] From this perspective, relations of gender inequality were structured and reproduced at various levels (local, national, international) and through complex ways and means. Clearly some attention has to be paid to dominant forms of political economy in understanding how gender relations of social inequality are produced and reproduced (see chapter 6).

Empowering women as subjects of knowledge

As will be evident from the discussion above, historically feminism has sought to empower or emancipate women. Part of this task involves challenging the construction of knowledge that contains gender bias. Standpoint feminism starts out from the conditions of women's lives and attempts to construct knowledge from women's lived, embodied experiences. Some feminists are sceptical of standpoint claims, believing them to rest ultimately on some form of essentialism. However, the notion of 'feminist lenses' or 'gender lenses' that allow us to 'see' and 'know' the world differently has been widely embraced within feminist IR. Peterson and Runyan, for example, argue that 'the knowledge claims we make, the jobs we work at and the power we have are all profoundly shaped by gender expectations.'[54] Gender lenses or feminist lenses can be used to challenge dominant assumptions about what is significant or insignificant, or what are central or marginal concerns in International Relations. Through 'a gender sensitive lens not only the "what" of world politics but also the "how" we think about it looks different'.[55] However, feminist lenses or gender lenses do not rely upon the premise that men and women are essentially different. As Runyan and Peterson are careful to point out, feminist IR is not exclusively about women, nor need it be only by women. The possibility of gender lenses is not premised on the existence of an unproblematic 'women's perspective'. It is possible for masculine perspectives to be held by women and feminist perspectives to be held by men, 'because those perspectives are politically not biologically grounded'.[56]

To look at the world through gender/feminist lenses is to focus on gender as a particular kind of power relation, and/or to trace out the ways in which gender is central to understanding international processes and practices in international relations. Gender/feminist lenses also focus on the everyday experiences of women as women and highlight the consequences of their unequal social position. The term 'lenses' is, however, preferred to 'lens', because it is recognized that gender relations are complex and it is necessary, therefore, to draw upon a variety of feminist perspectives to get a better understanding of a complex whole. Looking at the world through gender lenses brings into focus the many dimensions of gender inequality, from aspects of 'personal' relations to institutionalized forms of discrimination. Gender lenses or feminist lenses bring into focus the formal barriers to equality of opportunity, or the under-representation of women in decision-making structures, and allow us to see that gender inequality is an integral part of the structural inequalities generated by the operation of the global economy.

The production and reproduction of masculinities and femininities in IR

The feminist project to 'gender IR' goes beyond locating women in IR.[57] That said, much, if not most, feminist scholarship in IR has tended to focus on the position of women in international relations and/or how certain ideas or discourses on gender and the construction of certain notions of 'femininity' contribute to the marginalization of women and perpetuate gender inequalities. This bias towards a preoccupation with women and the feminine is understandable to the degree that 'feminist approaches that remain loyal to an emancipatory feminism based on the subject of women, stress the importance of keeping men out of the centre of feminist analysis and insist on the insertion of women as subjects and objects.'[58] However, both feminists, and indeed their critics,[59] have recognized that since gender is relational, then some attention needs to be given to the production and reproduction of men and 'masculinities' in IR.

Of course, the study of men and masculinities has always been a part of feminist IR. For example, challenging the accepted naturalness of the abundance of men in the theory and practice of IR was one of the first tasks of feminist critique. Men and masculinities have figured in feminist empirical investigations too. Cynthia Enloe has long argued that to understand both the position of women and how gender relations worked, one had to look at 'when and where masculinity was politically wielded'.[60] In turn, the ways in which masculinity worked to sustain inequalities in power could only be fully understood 'if we took women's lives seriously'.[61] Thus, we learned a great deal about 'state anxieties about masculinity from paying attention to military wives'.[62] Part of Enloe's work has focused on 'multiple masculinities' and how they 'got manipulated, the manipulators' motives and the consequences for international politics'.[63] The insights of Enloe have been further developed by scholars such as Marysia Zalewski, Jane Parpart, Charlotte Hooper and, more recently, Bob Pease and Keith Pringle, who have all produced work that is explicitly about the construction of masculinities in IR.

This body of literature seeks to problematize – rather than take for granted – masculinities, the hegemony of men and the subject of men within the theories and practices of IR and as such shifts attention 'from focusing on the categories of women and feminism to accepting that their presence is implicit in any perusal of the gendered category of masculinity'.[64] Just as 'femininities' are seen to be multiple and varied, the study of masculinity in IR endeavours to capture the 'fluid construction of masculine identities' rather than present men and masculinities as 'a fixed set of traits'.[65] Thus the emphasis is on the 'cultural production and interpretations of masculine identities as a political process that informs other, more conventionally defined political and international struggles' and the focus is on international relations as a 'primary site for the cultural and social production of masculinities'.[66]

Making visible the racialized and colonial dimensions of international relations

Contemporary feminist IR is interested in how the politics of gender and the politics of feminism shape the domain of international relations. Feminist politics take place in varied settings. For example, feminists have deconstructed nationalist discourses and practices to show how the discourse of nationalism can be used to appropriate women's voices or 'speak for' women (and other specific social groups) in articulating claims in the name of the 'nation'. Feminist politics also take the form of contesting dominant discourses on development and/or in opposing the activities of multinational corporations in export production zones in many parts of the developing world.

Feminist activists have also played a central role in promoting and defending human rights in varied contexts and settings. The feminist movement emerged in the West and subsequently grew into a transnational network of groups united behind a largely liberal feminist rights agenda. Women of colour participated in early struggles to gain rights for women. Sojourner Truth,[67] for example, was an important figure in early campaigns for suffrage. In her powerful writings she drew attention to the pernicious impact of discrimination rooted in both racial and gender subordination. People of colour were at the forefront of the US civil rights movement in the 1960s, a movement that gained its inspiration from the bravery of a black woman, Rosa Parks, who refused to give up her seat on a bus to a white man in the racially segregated South. Since 1945 the transnational women's movement has campaigned for the recognition of women's rights as human rights. Indeed, equal rights served as the central focus of the women's movement in the West and the mainstay of transnational solidarity among women until the 1960s.

However, it is easy to overstate the degree of unity in the early women's movement. Fissures and splits occurred on substantive issues other than suffrage. The emergence of postcolonial feminism in the 1980s expanded the debate about race, ethnicity and gender considerably, and in so doing both forced western feminists to face up to their own exclusionary practices and exposed the pretence of a homogeneous 'women's experience'. What one might loosely describe as the 'transnational feminist movement' today is comprised of a heterogeneous collection of groups. While diversity and difference does not entirely preclude possibilities for unity among such groups, there are many examples of moments when the 'movement' has been characterized by fragmentation and divisions that have seemingly defied solidarist projects. Liberal feminism particularly has tended to ignore or gloss other major forms of oppression rooted in race, for example, or social class that also structured women's life experiences and potentially militated against achieving solidarity among women.[68] Differences among women have become a much more prominent theme in academic feminist discourse in recent years (from the 1980s onwards particularly) and, moreover, have become much more salient issues in the politics of the transnational women's movement as will become evident in later chapters.

CONCLUSION

This chapter has placed feminist IR in the context of the fourth debate. Many scholars hoped that the legacy of the fourth debate would be the transformation of the study of IR.[69] However, the field could not be 'transformed' unless critical theories – in a broad sense of the term – could demonstrate the capacity to move beyond critiques of the mainstream and forge alternative research agendas. A good place to start this project might be to rethink and re-vision what has perhaps been the key concept in International Relations – the state. This is the subject of the next chapter.

GENDER IN THE THEORY AND PRACTICE OF 'STATE-MAKING'

INTRODUCTION

In the first part of this chapter, realism serves as the point of departure in understanding the place of gender in the theorization of the state in IR. To a great extent, the invisibility or marginalization of gender in the study of IR is a consequence of the methodological individualism in realism. Ann Tickner argues that an 'ontology based on unitary states operating in the asocial, anarchical world has provided few entry points for feminist theories, since these were grounded in an epistemology that took social relations as its central category of analysis.'[1] Realism has been a particular target of feminist critique because it has been an influential – indeed for a long time dominant – approach within IR and has provided a 'common-sense' view of the world for practitioners as well as theorists in IR. As Ann Tickner argued in her critique of realist discourse, 'the most dangerous threat to both a man and a state is to be like a woman because women are weak, fearful, indecisive, and dependent – stereotypes that still surface when assessing women's suitability for the military and the conduct of foreign policy today.'[2]

Feminist work has contributed to a reconceptualization of the state as a dynamic entity that is made and remade through discourses and practices that embed and reproduce both gendered understandings of the world and particular kinds of gender relations in the world of international politics. Accordingly, the second part of the chapter moves beyond critique to set out the various ways that gender is at work in the practice of 'state-making', specifically in the construction of identities and in the boundaries of political community. The third section of this chapter focuses on gendered conceptions of citizenship.

THE REALIST STATE

Sovereign states/sovereign men

Perhaps the defining characteristic of the state is sovereignty. Sovereignty has both an internal and external dimension. Internal sovereignty signifies the holding of authority within a given territory and over a given people, while in the external realm sovereignty involves recognition by other states that governments have the right to represent internationally those people under their sovereign jurisdiction; to make alliances, declare wars and so on. While realists are not alone in highlighting sovereignty as the defining characteristic of the state, what is interesting about realism is that sovereignty is conceptualized as an ontologically secure and stable characteristic of the state, rather than a 'norm' that is established through state practice and so apt to change over time, as social agents produce and reproduce the constitutive principles and structures by which they operate.[3] It is because sovereignty has been taken as given, rather than conceived of in dynamic terms in IR, that realists have been able to speak of the state as a purposive actor.

The 'state as actor' approach works to reify the state by casting the state as a 'thing', an entity that has a concrete materiality or existence. For the purpose of theorizing, realism invests the state with purpose. The state is conceived as a 'purposive individual' with particular characteristics. Sovereign man is a rational choice-making individual able to legitimize violence. The idea of sovereign man is placed firmly at the centre of the conceptual universe in realism and the subject of knowledge. IR is understood as the study of relations between the state (as actor and knowing subject) and a series of marginalized and displaced 'Others'. The concepts and categories employed by realism exclude women and distinctly feminine experiences since these are deemed to be non-political and 'outside' of the proper realm of study in IR.

Feminists have been concerned to explore the implications of representing a male experience (through the abstraction of sovereign man) as the human experience. The masculinized conception of sovereign man has been, for the most part, drawn from the intellectual fathers of realism: Thomas Hobbes and Niccolò Machiavelli. In Machiavelli, sovereign man was an abstraction, but one that was underpinned by the figure of the warrior, prince or modern-day practitioner of Realpolitik. Machiavelli was, arguably, the first thinker to shift the ground of political theory away from a central concern with justice to issues of power and autonomy. In what was, perhaps, Machiavelli's best-known work, *The Prince*, he sought to advise the ruler who could not base his rule on traditional authority on how to get power and how to keep it. Machiavelli's ideas would later appeal to the sceptical mood of the post-Second World War era and to scholars who believed that their role was to provide prudent advice to statesmen based on an understanding of the realities of power, rather than to speculate about how the world might be differently organized.

Hanna Pitkin has argued that Machiavelli displayed an understanding of self-government and of citizenship that was intimately connected with his sense of what it was to be a man. To be a man one had to be self-reliant, autonomous, avoiding dependence on others. Similarly, what mattered for the security and glory of the state was autonomy which was related to masculine traits. Women were excluded from the citizen body because they constituted a threat to men both personally and politically. Women were both a sign of man's original weakness and a threat to his self-control. Women were a potential source of conflict and division among men. More importantly, perhaps, they represented competing values, they could draw men out of the public realm. Thus, women were presented as subordinates, dependants and also subversive of the male-dominated political order.[4]

The feminized 'Other' in realism

Realists have not reflected on how this (inherited) conceptual baggage, specifically how the conceptions of power, autonomy, sovereignty and world order, are gendered. Most have been content to take the masculinized nature of world politics as yet another natural and immutable 'fact'. In contrast, feminists have called for reflexivity on just such matters, pointing out that the use of gendered imagery in realist texts is highly significant. Thus, feminists have focused not on the 'objective facts' of an anarchic, dangerous world, but rather on how dominant discourses in IR have worked systematically to create a conception of international politics as a realm characterized by ever-present 'threats' and 'dangers' and, in this way, present the world as disorderly and hostile.[5] In realist texts, the political community (nation-state) has been constructed as a community of men whose power and autonomy is predicated upon the ability to control and/or dominate those 'outside'. The realist conception of the autonomous state has been juxtapositioned against images of anarchy or a disorderly international 'state of nature'. The use of such imagery has to be seen in terms of a deeply rooted fear of the 'feminine'. Thus, Ann Runyan has argued that:

Whether the state has been viewed as continuous with nature, or juxtaposed to nature, its metaphysics has read order, unity, and an intolerance of difference, into both nature and the body politic. This has lead to a suppression and exploitation of all those things defined as 'natural' (including women) and that do not fit into the designs of the white, Western man and his state.[6]

While Machiavelli did not explicitly personify nature, the masculine world of human agency in history and autonomy was juxtapositioned against the world of women and relations of dominance and dependence. The 'feminine' in Machiavelli represented the 'Other', that force opposed to the masculinized world of order and discipline. The founder of the republic personified most completely the autonomous self-governing man.[7] Pitkin has argued that the masculine world of order and *virtù* was haunted from behind the scenes by female forces of great power. Fortuna was a woman, a force that threatened the overextended state or overambitious ruler and the male world of order, law and liberty.

Like Machiavelli, Hobbes's thought has to be seen in the context of an age characterized by great social change and political instability. Modern science challenged the idea that sovereigns ruled by virtue of divine right and the notion that the social and political order reflected a unified moral order. In order to explain the origins of the state and sovereign power, Hobbes posited the existence of a 'state of nature' in which all enjoyed a natural liberty but in which life was nasty, brutish and short because of man's desire to dominate and oppress others. Hobbes argued that all human beings were essentially self-regarding hedonists who sought to achieve their own ends with little regard for others. Only the desire for self-preservation allowed the setting up of a sovereign body to secure the conditions necessary for civilized life. However, while men might be persuaded to give up their natural liberty for the protection of the sovereign state, the international realm would remain a war of all against all, since the conditions that forced men to give up their natural liberty for security in the 'state of nature' could not be realized in the international realm.

While Hobbes is often presented in realist texts as having described the condition of human beings without government, the state of nature was 'a strange world where individuals were grown up before they were born', a world where 'wives, sisters and mothers did not exist'.[8] Hobbes's state of nature was structurally sexist, denying the historic role played by women as child-rearers and childbearers. Hobbes's thought must be seen in the historical context of profound social changes that were leading to the progressive loss of power among actual women. Hobbes recognized that the political order was patriarchal, but justified male rule on the grounds that, when erecting the sovereign state, men institutionalized their advantage over women. Rights were accorded to citizens but women and children were outside the realm of justice, could not exercise power nor provide for their own defence. The social and political order was then inherently and explicitly patriarchal.

The 'manliness' of international politics

In realist texts the patriarchal nature of the social and political order has seldom been explicit but, nevertheless, the assumption has been deeply embedded in realist texts. For example, in *Politics Among Nations*, Morgenthau argued that the starting point for theorizing about IR was the 'nature of man'. Morgenthau based his theory upon a distinctly Hobbesian view of human nature that proceeded from the central belief that man's behaviour was essentially driven by bio-psychological drives to create society. The drive to live, propagate and control was a power struggle. Morgenthau did not discuss gender relations as such but he did argue that the tendency to dominate was an element of all human associations from the family, which was necessary for the propagation of the species, to the state.[9] While Morgenthau made no explicit reference to women, one might infer with justification that he assumed politics to be a male-dominated activity and patriarchy to be necessary for social order, since he argued that social institutions (including the family) were necessary to channel the natural aggression of man. Moreover, the subordination of women was an inevitable consequence of the unequal power struggle and was also 'natural' in so far as it was deemed 'necessary'. In Morgenthau's view, politics was any activity or process that established the control of man over man. Morgenthau left undiscussed sexual relations and parent–child relations but, since he argued that all relations were essentially based upon self-interest, it might be assumed that women submitted to male rule because it was prudent to do so.[10]

Realists represent political order and political institutions as inherently fragile and precarious. Political order has to be reinforced by social institutions and symbols of national honour, unity and strong leadership. Carr saw the personification of the state as a device designed to encourage the exaltation of the state at the expense of the individual. The state was associated with pugnacity and self-assertion. Through the state the individual sought strength through combination with others. According to Carr, for the individual his national community meant 'the expression of a transferred egoism as well as altruism'.[11] If a man was strong he could play a leading role, while 'if he was weak he could find compensation for his lack of power to assert himself in the vicarious self-assertion of the group'.[12]

Morgenthau similarly believed that since in a society only a few would realize their aim (of power and domination), the majority sought to achieve their ends indirectly through identification with the state. According to Morgenthau, 'when we are conscious of being members of a powerful nation we flatter ourselves and feel a great pride'.[13] Social institutions might restrain aspirations for individual power but 'the nation encourages and glorifies the tendencies of the greatness of the population' and 'the emotional attachment of the nation as the symbolic substitute for the individual then becomes ever stronger'.[14] The masculinized imagery and language of realism has sometimes been highly explicit. Inis Claude argued that realism was a test of the intellectual virility and manliness of the field. The realist could look at the grim realities of power without flinching, while one who rejected this reality was 'cowardly' or 'soft'. According to Claude, 'a self-respecting realist could advance the proposition that the balance of power contributed something virile and vigorous like the protection of the national interest, but would be embarrassed to state that it contributed to something as lacking in intellectual masculinity as peace'.[15]

Teasing out the hidden assumptions about gender in realism is undoubtedly useful in exposing the social conservatism of realist thought; but beyond that, does it matter? Realists might no doubt respond to feminist criticisms by arguing that the patriarchal nature of state power is not discussed explicitly because it is not relevant to understanding relations between states. Furthermore, given that women have historically been excluded from political power and today remain heavily under-represented in the 'high politics' of statecraft, it could be argued that realism does in some senses present an accurate picture of the world. Once the 'maleness' of international politics and the patriarchal nature of state power is acknowledged, is it not the case that realism presents an accurate picture of the 'real world'?

However, feminist critique goes beyond exposing the masculine bias in realist writings. Feminist critique thus goes beyond the unspoken assumptions about the position and social roles of women and men in realist theory to a deeper analysis of the ways in which ideas about gender are constructed and used to legitimize and perpetuate inequalities and also raises fundamental challenges to realist knowledge claims. The ideology or discourse of realism constructs a particular model of the world that then serves to justify and perpetuate the kind of social and political order it describes. These issues will be revisited in the next chapter in relation to ruminations on what international politics might be like if 'women ruled the world'.

THE CONSTRUCTION OF BOUNDARIES AND IDENTITIES

Contra realism, the sovereign state cannot be ontologically privileged. Sovereignty is not an objective, settled condition of statehood, but a form of legitimation whereby power is converted into authority. The principle of sovereignty legitimizes the state's claim to be the primary political community to whom citizens owe loyalty.[16] The realist orthodoxy thus privileges the 'nation-state' not only as the only significant form of sovereign political authority and primary form of political organization, but also as the locus of collective identity. Deeply ingrained in realism is the largely taken for granted assumption that distinctive nation-states are the primary source of political community and so are of moral worth. Historically, the structure of political communities, including nation-states, has assumed gendered forms. The problem with realist (and neorealist) discourse is that both the historical specificity of political communities and the gendered forms that they assume is not questioned.

The gendered nature of political community

To recap briefly, feminists have pointed to the gender bias in realism but also criticized realist discourse because of its tendency to present historically contingent features of world order, such as the sovereign state, as 'given'. In the realist construction of the 'state as purposive actor', the state is given a concrete identity through the fusion of the sovereign state with a nationalist construction of political identity. In realism the 'imagined community'[17] of the nation-state is privileged as the single irreducible component of identity and human attachment and thus reduces questions of identity in International Relations to identification on the part of individual citizens with the nation-state. The assumption that the state in some senses embodies the collective identity and will of 'the people' reduces all aspects of social relations which play a role in shaping identities, including violence and conflict for example, to relations between sovereign states. The concept of the 'national interest' as a central organizing concept in International Relations relies upon the assumption that our identification with the nation overrides all other dimensions of social and political identification.

A great deal of work on security in International Relations – discussed at greater length in chapter 5 – defines its purpose in terms of understanding how the distinctive identity of 'human collectivities' called nation-states can best be protected. The 'national interest' is in essence about the preservation of the political expression of the nation, the sovereign state, and the defence of the nation from 'foreigners' who threaten its political and territorial integrity and its distinctive identity. Thus realism is predicated on certain ideas about place and identity (the nation/state) and serves to draw rigid boundaries between what is 'inside' and 'outside' and what is 'domestic' and 'foreign'.

Conflating the concepts of state and nation reinforces the idea that there are clearly demarcated boundaries between what is 'inside' and what is 'outside' the state. This in turn allows International Relations to impose a nationalist logic of identity on world politics.[18] However, the assumption of stable and homogeneous identities that underlies the use of the nation-state as the basis for political identity in International Relations is highly problematic. Critics of the realist orthodoxy argue that the state should be seen in dynamic rather than static terms. The boundaries of the nation-state do not embody eternal truths, but are made and remade by state practices, through powerful representations of 'national interests' and through received narratives on identity and on political space and place (territory).

Feminist work has highlighted the complex ways in which gender is deeply implicated in the carving out of political spaces, the construction of identities and the demarcation of the boundaries of community in practices of 'state-making'. Feminists see war, foreign policy and other instruments of statecraft as the means whereby the boundaries of political and moral community are demarcated, often in ways that have different implications for men and women. Processes of 'state-making' involve the institutionalization of gender differences. Women are controlled in different ways in the interests of demarcating identities. States are involved in regulating what are often held to be 'private' decisions, concerning, for example, marriage and the legal status of children. In this way the boundaries of the national community are drawn and reproduced.

States, nationalisms and identities

Feminist analysis raises questions about how identities are formed and transformed and about how power operates in the construction and ascription of identity. Historically, the creation of state boundaries in Europe was closely linked with the rise of nationalism as a powerful ideology and political force. The nation-state was seen as a form of political organization that allowed for the creation of 'centralized political institutions supported by a homogeneous national identity' and as such established 'a reasoned stable space for human improvements'. The constitution of the nation-state served to link political space to the creation of boundaries.[19]

Ideas about gender, sexuality and the family have been and continue to be of great symbolic import in the construction and reproduction of national identities and state boundaries and in ensuring the cultural continuity of specific communities.[20] Nationalist ideologies are based upon the idea that the imagined community of the nation is 'natural' because, irrespective of difference, there is a natural bond between members of the national group.[21] However, the nation is not a natural entity but is constructed. Essential in the process of establishing a sense of identification with the nation and inculcating a nationalist consciousness has been the telling of a particular story about the nation and its history.[22] Feminist scholarship has shown the relevance of gender relations in our understanding of the construction of the nation and underlined the significance of women, sexuality and the family as symbols in the reproduction of the nation and its boundaries. They have also explored the significance of gendered symbolism and imagery that is employed in story-telling about the nation and its history.

Benedict Anderson's account of nationalism emphasizes the importance of kinship. The nation is held to be something to which one is naturally tied. Indeed, it is not uncommon to find that the nation is depicted as the 'motherland'. The power of nationalism lies in its appeals to a sense of belonging – of being at home. The association of women with the private domain of the home and family reinforces the powerful imagery involved in merging the idea of national community with that of the selfless/devoted mother. This automatically triggers the response that one should ultimately be prepared to come to her defence or die for her.[23] Mosse has suggested that the sense of belonging and attachment is actually centred on male bonding. As such, it has special affinities for male society. This special affinity for male society legitimizes male domination over women.[24]

Nira Yuval-Davis and Floya Anthias have noted a 'janus-faced' quality in nationalist discourse.[25] On the one hand, it presents itself as a modern project that melts and transforms traditional attachments in favour of new identities. However, as Massey and Jess argue, 'nationalist constructions of political identity are in a sense always reactionary'.[26] The 'mother' of the nation is the unchanging point of reference, which is grounded in a complex net of social conventions, structures and practices. The idea of the nation is constructed out of an invented inward-looking history, a cult of origins. In this way, the fusing of nationalist political identity and the nation-state confers on women a 'place' within the social and political order, but it is a place that takes women prisoner.[27]

It is not uncommon to find that the nation is depicted as a woman. This deeply ingrained image of the homeland as a female body whose violation by foreigners requires citizens to rush to her defence is a powerful image in nationalist ideology. This depends upon an image of woman as chaste and dutiful.[28] Not only is nationalism couched in terms of 'love of country' but also, within this imaging of the nation, women serve as the repository of group identity. National identity is equated with ideas about gender, parentage and skin colour. Women not only bear the burden of being the mothers of the nation but their bodies may also be used to reproduce the boundaries of the national group, transmit its culture and become 'the privileged signifiers of national difference'.[29] It is because women embody the symbolic values of chastity and motherhood that incidences of rape in the armed conflicts that frequently accompany independence struggles have to be seen as political acts through which the aggressor attacks the honour of other men and through this breaks the continuity of the social order which it is women's responsibility to uphold.[30]

Power in the construction of identities

Thus when we think about processes of social identification we need to be sensitive to the operation of power in the ascription of identities.[31] In concentrating on the imagined community of the nation and nationalist constructions of identity, feminists have demonstrated that taking for granted the primacy of this concrete, familiar and seemingly 'unproblematic' example of collective identity disguises how power relations are implicated in the construction and ascription of identity.[32]

The struggle to create nation-states as political communities involves the institutionalization of gender differences. As the political map of the world this century has been drawn and redrawn, political spaces called nation-states have been carved and the boundaries between 'insiders' and 'outsiders' demarcated. Women have participated in struggles for national independence and self-determination[33] and in so doing have often challenged and transformed the 'authentic identities' that nationalist discourse often seeks to preserve and reproduce.[34] When participating in struggle, women have not only desired emancipation from foreign domination; they also, often implicitly, sometimes explicitly, challenge many of those same 'authentic' cultural traditions that have historically legitimized patriarchal relations. The participation of women has often constituted a direct challenge to the privileged position of men within the social order and, to some degree, resulted in fluidity in social relations.[35]

However, the possibilities for achieving advances in the status of women as a group have been constrained by the discourse of nationalism. It is not unusual to find that women who have actively campaigned for women's rights have been stigmatized and accused of betraying the nation. The desire to achieve changes in the position of women has sometimes been portrayed as a betrayal of cultural or national identity. Chatterjee has argued that the relationship between the 'women's question' and nationalism is inherently problematic. The problem arises because one politics is taken over and spoken for by another. When the imagined community of the nation is authorized as the most authentic unit of collective identity, men are often in positions of power and so able to define its meaning.[36]

Furthermore, women's protest must be seen in the context of pre-existing political organizations and socio-economic structures. Women frequently have a 'domestic orientation' to a lifestyle devoted to the home and family relations. Men, on the other hand, have a 'public orientation' to a lifestyle concerned with extra-domestic matters of economic, political and military import. While the distinction between domestic and public orientations should not be seen as a distinction between political and non-political spheres of activity, women's power is more diffused and individualized outside the bureaucratic structures of society, while men's power is more coordinated within an institutionalized framework. Women's protests also have to be understood not only in terms of pre-existing political organizations and socio-economic structures, but also in terms of the 'internalities' of political protest. In many ways women's own political powers are derived from their 'domestic orientation'. Thus, motherhood can come to be seen as a national duty and act. This seems to be especially true of older and less-educated women. Where women assert themselves in a political role as women they may be well received, even honoured, but once they step outside the boundary of the home and domestic roles they are often subjected to rough treatment in male-orientated societies.[37]

Women's political struggles do not occur in a vacuum but are determined by the goals and methods of wider social movements and wider power structures. The pursuit of 'interests' implies access to institutions that already in some sense embody male dominance and patriarchy. Callaway and Ridd have argued that institutionalized power is for the most part controlled by men and that where women enter the public domain they generally do so within a male-ordered framework.[38] For these reasons it is extremely difficult to politicize the 'women's question', and consequently it is easily and coercively spoken for by the discourse of nationalism.[39]

When gender relations are introduced into the analysis of nationalism, it encourages us to reassess nationalist political movements and to ask whether nationalism is 'progressive' or 'liberating' and, if so, from whose perspective. As the forces of nationalist struggle have drawn and redrawn the political map of the world this century, carving out political spaces and demarcating the boundaries between 'insiders' and 'outsiders', what has motivated women who have participated in nationalist struggles and what have been the consequences for the world's women? To what extent have women achieved lasting changes in their status? Asking questions of this kind raises further questions about how power relations operate and how existing social and economic conditions constrain the possibilities for achieving advances in the status of women as a group.

The participation of women in nationalist struggles

The mobilization of people in the cause of national liberation can open up spaces for women to challenge dominant conceptions of national tradition and culture and create new identities for themselves. However, at the same time, it demonstrates how the existing power relations limit the possibilities for long-lasting change. For example, in the case of the struggle for Zimbabwean independence, married women were partly motivated to support ZANU because cadres punished men who were found guilty of inflicting violence against women.[40] In other examples drawn from Africa, women frequently participated because they wanted to gain access to education, employment or mobility.[41]

The Nicaraguan revolution of 1979 opened up many opportunities for women to expand their horizons and this in turn had an important effect in legitimizing new roles and identities for women. Women were 'no longer silent drudges' but found spaces to create new identities and saw 'doors opening on the world'. The Nicaraguan experience was unique because women themselves pressured the Sandinista regime to move from a position of subsuming women's specific interests to what were seen as military and economic priorities, to incorporating women's demands as an intrinsic part of the revolution.[42] Women also played a central role in the Frente Sandinista para la Liberación National (FSLN). The symbol of the Nicaraguan Women's Association included a profile of a woman's head crossed by a gun, illustrating the central role played by women in the struggle. Women also provided vital civilian support, hiding Sandinistas, setting up first-aid posts, carrying messages, gathering information, providing food, sewing uniforms and providing transportation. Participation gave women confidence and a sense of worth, and as women took part in public life they gained consciousness of their oppression.[43]

In national independence struggles in India, both 'internal' and 'external' factors played a role in shaping the goals of the independence movement and so shaped the struggle for women's emancipation. According to Jayawardena, the struggle for national independence coincided with moves towards secularism and a broader concern with social reform. Jayawardena has argued that in India struggles for emancipation took place against a backdrop of nationalist struggles aimed not only at achieving political independence and asserting national identity, but also at 'modernizing' the country. As nationalist aspirations grew, the local bourgeoisie struggled against both imperialism and internal pre-capitalist structures. The bourgeoisie appealed to people in terms of both cultural identity and in terms of its desire to promote reforms aimed at education, scientific, technological and industrial advancement. In this context women's emancipation struggles became an essential and integral part of nationalist struggle because the status of women became a popular barometer of 'civilization'. Jayawardena suggests that while efforts were made to 'westernize' and educate women within the confines of patriarchal traditions, women often made their own demands. It was impracticable to launch slogans that claimed to be universal and to mobilize around these banners for political causes without oppressed groups taking up issues on their own behalf. Women wanted emancipation from certain social customs that were detrimental to them. Women demanded equality, entered the professions and demanded suffrage.[44]

Nationalist revolutions are certainly not watersheds for women. Even where women's emancipation have been openly declared to be integral to revolutionary struggle, changes in the status of women have often proved to be short-lived. It seems that the degree to which women achieve significant and lasting changes in their status or conditions of life depends in part on other factors, particularly class. Harris argues that in the Nicaraguan case the revolution certainly changed the idea of what middle-class women should be, and quite clearly some women saw their lives as transformed. However, in the post-revolution period, some women saw no difference in their day-to-day lives from what they had experienced under the previous Somoza regime. This might be explained by the ways in which women have been mobilized in support of nationalist movements. Harris's study of Nicaragua suggests that despite women's role in the struggle, the male-dominated army saw that women needed to be better educated because they were needed to fulfil administrative and logistical positions, rather than because it was a means to achieve general and lasting changes in their status.[45]

Existing power relations mean that men are able to interpret the meaning of certain actions. As Helie-Lucas has argued, 'if a man carries food to armed fighters over long distances he is acknowledged as a fighter, while if a woman does it she is "helping" the man in her natural way of nurturing'. Even in 'times of struggle, women are confined to the kinds of tasks which will not disturb the future social order'.[46] Power relations also shape how the struggle to redefine women's place is interpreted. It is not unusual to find that women who actively campaign for women's rights are stigmatized and accused of betraying the nation. The desire to achieve changes in the position of women can easily be portrayed as a betrayal of cultural or national identity. The struggle for changes in the position and status of women that flow from the fluidity in social relations and changing identities can be portrayed as betrayal. Feminism might be cast as a 'foreign' ideology that alienates women from 'their' religion, 'their' culture and 'their' family responsibilities, on the one hand, and from revolutionary struggle on the other. Calls for 'women's liberation' have been frequently and conveniently described as a product of western capitalism and of no relevance to women involved in national struggle in the non-western world. Where there are marked inequalities between women, this can be used to reinforce the view that feminism is a middle-class ideology of no relevance to poor women. At times of conflict when the nation is held to be under attack, it is particularly difficult to counter the accusation that women are betraying their cultural traditions and the greater interest of the national good. In the case of Algeria, for example, 'the overall task of women during liberation struggles was symbolic'.[47] Faced with colonization, 'the people had to build a national identity based on values of one's own traditions, religion, language and culture' and 'women bore the heavy role of being the keepers of this threatened identity and they paid a heavy price for accepting this role, because it is difficult to criticise the nation at times of struggle'.[48]

GENDERED CITIZENS

Within the realist orthodoxy, the nation-state is seen as the fundamental territorial and political boundary that separates and divides human beings.[49] If the sovereign state is taken to be a historically specific form of political organization and constituted authority, then it is appropriate to ask whether and how the structure of this political community has assumed gendered forms. Citizenship structures relations between 'insiders' and excluded 'others'. To be a citizen is to enjoy the rights and privileges granted by the state that are not accorded to outsiders. As such citizenship constitutes 'a space within a discourse on politics that institutionalizes identities and differences by drawing boundaries, in terms of both membership and the actual political practices associated with membership'.[50]

As the above discussion suggests, nationalist struggles for self-determination have sometimes brought positive benefits to women in terms of extending citizenship rights. However, nationalist discourses often draw upon cultural values from some imagined past. The search for national identity might involve harking back to a national culture destroyed or suppressed by the experience of foreign domination. Thus while nationalism may reconstitute the political order on a radically different basis, women cannot be the total negation of tradition. It falls to women to become the guardians of national culture, indigenous religion and family traditions and these same traditions and values are used to justify imposing particular constraints on women's activities, thus keeping women within boundaries prescribed by male elites.[51] Thus, while nationalist aspirations for popular sovereignty might stimulate an extension of citizenship rights, clearly benefiting women so the modern state can serve in this sense to facilitate progressive gender politics, it is clear that nationalism has a special affinity for male society and legitimizes the dominance of men over women. National identity is frequently articulated as a form of control over women and, to a great extent, this infringes upon women's lives as enfranchised citizens. Where women's rights are achieved during struggle, they can always be 'sacrificed on the altar of identity politics in another time'.[52]

For these reasons, the integration of women into the modern state often follows a different trajectory to that of men. Gender is central to the construction of the boundaries between the 'public' and 'private' realms, a process that has been central to the exclusion of women, historically, from citizenship.[53] The construction of women as 'dependants' who are identified only in terms of their relationship to men, as wives and mothers, plays a role in limiting rights of citizenship. Citizenship is frequently denied to the husbands and children of women who have married 'out'. Certainly, 'no nation state in the world has granted women and men the same privileged access to the resources of the nation state and claims to nationality frequently depend upon marriage to a male citizen.'[54]

Citizens and warriors

A further way in which the concept of citizenship might be 'engendered' is by highlighting the historical connection between citizenship rights and the duty to take up arms in defence of the state. In western political thought, discourses on political community and citizenship have been heavily militarized and profoundly gendered. Masculinity, virility and violence have been linked together in political thought through the concept of the 'warrior hero'. Hartsock claims that Eros and power have been connected since the ideal of public virtue first took theoretical form in ancient Athens in an all-male political community. In Greek thought the battlefield was inhabited only by men who achieved either glorious victory or death.[55] Hartsock sees the entire history of western thought on citizenship as being dominated by the themes of masculinity, the warrior ethic and death. Drawing upon feminist standpoint theory, Hart-sock contends that men's fixation with war arises from their need to affirm their manhood, a process that requires an ongoing and constant effort to distinguish themselves from women, a psycho-sexual drama in which masculinity is forged, affirmed and reaffirmed.[56]

Historically, political loyalty has been conceived as the disposition to act and speak in the interests and defence of the state and the nation. The ultimate test of one's loyalty has been the willingness of the individual to defend the state, particularly in times of war. Citizenship has been linked to an obligation to defend the state and this linkage has, in turn, been used to justify 'second-class' citizenship for women, deemed unsuited to the role of protector.[57] The linkage between military participation and citizenship has provided another justification for the exclusion of women from the public realm and has provided a strong justification for the subordination of women to male rule. Women have been excluded from citizenship through masculinist constructions of politics and 'further excluded through the close association of citizenship with bearing arms'. This has had important consequences for women who have historically been removed from the realm of justice, denied rights and subjected to patriarchal forms of authority.

In return for granting rights to male citizens, the state makes certain demands, the most important of which is to require, or compel, citizens to play an active role in the defence of the state. Stiehm has argued that there are thus different categories of citizenship, depending upon whether the individual is among the 'protectors' of the state or one of the 'protected'.[58] The linkage between the state, political loyalty and combat has meant that men have enjoyed a particular and privileged status, while women have been excluded from citizenship rights.[59] Historically women's citizenship has been mediated through the patriarchal family structure and women's primary duty has been held to be bearing and raising children. The first loyalty of the 'good woman', therefore, has been to her family and particular children, not directly to the nation or to humanity.[60]

In the United States of America in the 1980s, the National Organization of Women (NOW) demanded the integration of women into combat roles. This led to debates about the degree to which participation in combat roles could be used as an effective tool to advance the position of women. Liberal rights feminists argued that if fighting was necessary to defend values, then these same values should be seen as female as well as male, or as 'human' values. Moreover, obtaining the right to fight would address the problem that women faced in terms of their 'second-class citizenship'. Quite apart from issues of citizenship and women's rights to equal treatment and equal opportunities, liberal feminists pointed out that economic and other benefits accrued to men who serve.[61] Stiehm contended that women's entry in equal numbers and as full equals would change the military. If women and men shared the risks and responsibilities as 'defenders', the asymmetrical relation between protector and protected, and the ideology of violence which this permitted, would be broken. Acts of violence could no longer be carried out by the male military with an 'on-behalf-of' mentality.[62] However, critics of the 'right to fight' campaign accused liberal analysis of being theoretically rootless and the NOW campaign misguided. According to Elshtain, 'in its deep structure, NOW's legal narrative is a leap out of the female/private side of the public/private divide basic to Machiavelli's realism and straight into the arms of hegemonic man whose sex linked activities are valorised thereby'. Paradoxically, 'NOW's repudiation of "archaic notions of women's role" became a tribute to archaic notions of men's role'.[63]

CONCLUSION

This chapter has covered the feminist critique of the deeply masculinist assumptions embedded in realist concepts and in the image of an anarchic and dangerous world propagated in realist discourse. Through critiques of the IR orthodoxy, feminists have addressed in concrete ways issues of bias and exclusion in IR theory.[64] Feminist critiques of gendered discourses in IR have also illustrated how socially produced and bounded knowledge has set the parameters for how we have thought about the institutions of the state and the practices involved in 'state-making'. Feminist scholarship in IR has moved beyond critiques of the orthodoxy in IR theory, investigating the gendered processes at work in the practice of international relations, notably in the construction of identities and boundaries. In their efforts to understand and explain the exclusion of women from rights of citizenship, feminist theorists have pointed to the delimitation of the state's proper sphere through the active codification and policing of the boundaries of the public and the private.[65] In the interest of demarcating identities and constructing boundaries, states have historically engaged in practices with profound implications for women's citizenship in so far as they have worked to institutionalize male privilege.[66] Today, women are breaching what has previously been an exclusively male bastion by participating in increasing numbers in active military service and in combat roles specifically. In so doing, women are challenging that historical link between citizenship, combat and distinctly masculine identities. The masculinity of war is explored further in the following chapter.

FEMINIST PERSPECTIVES ON WAR AND PEACE

INTRODUCTION

This chapter provides an overview of feminist perspectives on war and peace. Wars have been and continue to be central to the struggle to carve out territorial spaces, forge collective identities and to mark out the boundaries of political communities. IR, a discipline born out of the experience of war, has understood war in social and political terms, resulting from social conflict and connected to the construction of political identities and the pursuit of 'national interests'.[1] Gender has rarely been seen as relevant to the analysis of war. Similarly, IR scholars have expressed no curiosity about the near male exclusivity of the military, believing this to be a consequence of 'natural' gender distinctions and differing characteristics and capabilities between men and women.

Work is now appearing on gender and war. Joshua Goldstein has argued that gender can be and should be employed in IR to understand 'real world issues of war in and between states'.[2] Adam Jones has also sought to make men as men visible in the study of conflicts.[3] Goldstein and Jones argue that gender can be viewed as a *variable* that might be integrated into a social constructivist or mainstream analysis of war. Feminists eschew the integration of a 'gender variable' into the study of war in favour of elucidating the multifaceted ways in which masculinities and femininities have been constructed and reproduced in warfare.

The first part of this chapter takes the near exclusively male nature of war, particularly in respect to combat roles, as a starting point for understanding the centrality of gender to war. The 'War on Terror' is afforded separate attention in the second edition because it serves as a contemporary illustration of how gender, and specifically the protector/protected division, continues to be used to legitimate war and national security policy. In the third section of the chapter, the focus of discussion turns to the military as a core institution of the state – the coercive arm of state power. Women have never absented themselves from war. Indeed, wherever battles are fought women have supported the military engagements of men. There are numerous examples of forceful women who have led the troops into war in a symbolic, if not physical, sense. Therefore, the fourth section of the chapter turns to the role that women play, in both material and ideological terms, in support of the military system, of militarization and of war.

In the fifth section, the focus turns to the relationship between war and peace. In both realist and liberal approaches to IR, peace has been largely understood in negative terms; that is to say that peace has been held to be a condition among states character-ized by the absence of war. Realists argue that in an anarchic international system, peace is at best a temporary or fragile condition. In contrast, liberals hold out much hope that international institutions and international law might provide the conditions that facilitate diplomacy and supply a mechanism for the pacific settlement of disputes. Liberal idealists invest much faith in the power of public opinion and the commitment to peace among civil society actors in overcoming the prevalence of war in international relations. However, neither realists nor liberals have made gender central to their understanding of peace.

If historically war has been associated with men and masculinity, peace has long historical associations with women and the 'feminine'. Whether or not women are indeed more peaceful than men is a moot point. Indeed, given the constructivist ori-entation of most feminist scholarship in IR, it would be surprising to find support for such essentialist claims among feminist scholars. Nevertheless, feminist standpoint theorists, such as Carol Gilligan, Nancy Chodorow and Dorothy Dinnerstein,[4] have argued that the women/peace nexus is a useful point of departure in developing a critique of conventional approaches to war and peace and in moving feminist discourse to 'centre stage rather than being relegated to the periphery' in narratives on war and peace.[5]

THE MASCULINITY OF WAR

Masculinity has been and continues to be linked to combat in complex ways, but it cannot be explained in terms of men's 'natural' capacity for violence and aggression. Few men who take part in war can be said to 'make war'. Most fighting men are foot soldiers sacrificed in the service of grand campaigns they do not design, about which they are not consulted and which they rarely fully comprehend. Yvonne Roberts has argued that for young British working-class men serving in the Gulf, military service provided a route out of the 'crisis of masculinity' that besets those robbed of the pros-pect of following their fathers and grandfathers into traditional, masculinized jobs, and who had few qualifications and few alternative prospects.[6] Furthermore, reports have shown that a large number of male recruits cannot bring themselves to fire weapons even when under attack.[7] It is certainly a mistake to assume that all men necessarily benefit from the making of war. Men make up the majority of casualties in situations of conflict. In the former Yugoslavia, tens of thousands of men were selected for death or imprisonment purely on the basis of their gender.[8] Moreover, women's *innate* peacefulness is as mythical as men's *natural* proclivity towards violence.[9] Women are certainly capable of violent acts (although women in general perpetrate far fewer violent crimes than men) and women, like men, have shown that they are prepared to take life in self-defence.

It is not necessary, however, to rely upon essentialist ideas of men's natural aggression or women's inherent peacefulness to make an argument for the relevance of gender to understanding war. Gender is a system of meaning that can be manipulated to encourage both men and women in their support for war. Appeals are made to masculinity to encourage men to take up arms in defence of their country, ethnic group or political cause and in defence of 'their' women. In the former Yugoslavia, women were assigned the mythical roles of 'Mother Juvoica' (the mother who sacrificed nine sons and her husband to the homeland, without tears) and 'Daughter of Kosovo' (the daughter who tends injured soldiers).[10] The holding up of women as symbolic bearers of caste, ethnic or national identity can expose them to the risk of attack.[11] Moreover, women often 'lose out through the political manipulation of gender ideology as part of the process of militarisation'.[12] It is not uncommon to find that at such times women's human rights are eroded and restrictions are placed on the mobility of women. While men's seeming capacity for dominance, aggression and violence is not natural and women are not, by nature, submissive, passive and peaceful, the myths surrounding men and masculinity and women and femininity are both pervasive and powerful.

Today, women are entering the military in increasing numbers and are more likely to take part in active combat than in previous times in history, a fact evidenced by the numbers of women who have taken part in the recent conflicts in the Gulf region, including the war in Iraq in 2003.

However, there continues to be strong resistance to women in combat roles among military and political elites and among wide sections of the public generally.[13] Often this resistance is couched in terms of a 'threat to military preparedness' or on the grounds that women are unsuited to the rigours of military life, or because only men have the requisite courage and honour to defend the state. The justification for excluding women from combat roles has also been couched in terms of women's maternal instincts that mean women are instinctively unable to kill. There is little or no evidence to support this contention. It has also been argued that men's natural inclination to protect women will distract them from the task in hand of defeating the enemy, or that women will disrupt the male bonding process vital in developing trust among comrades in the face of battle.[14]

These beliefs remain pervasive among academics too. The necessity of maintaining the male exclusivity of combat was a prevalent theme of Francis Fukuyama's article on 'Women and the Evolution of World Politics' that appeared in the influential journal *Foreign Affairs* in 1998.[15] Fukuyama asserted that the emerging gender gap in support for (US) national defence spending was evidence that women were, indeed, more peaceful than men. He also pointed to evidence of a growth in female influence in western societies, reflected in, among other things, women having a greater degree of political power.[16] However, Fukuyama cautioned that greater gender equality and the demise of the male protector/female protected model of gendered relationships might ultimately be a cause for concern rather than celebration, since we continue to live in a world where 'toughness and aggression in international politics' was necessary. Moreover, the military must maintain combat readiness, which necessitated sex segregation lest the male-bonding process be disrupted.[17]

Even if one were to accept that, while not natural, particular male and female identified gender traits and roles mean that men more so than women are suited to the life
of soldiering, this can be contested. As Charlotte Hooper has argued:

The job of soldiering has been traditionally characterised as a manly activity requiring the
'masculine' traits of physical strength, action, toughness and capacity for violence. Officers must
evidence resolve, technical skills and logical, tactical and strategic thinking. But such jobs could
be equally characterised as requiring the traditional 'feminine' qualities of obedience and submis-
sion to authority, attention to dress detail, and the repetition of mundane tasks.[18]

While the masculinity of war might be a 'myth', it is myth that plays a vital role in
sustaining both women and men in their support for violence. If gender differences are
not natural, these powerful myths 'seem to be the most certain proof of the necessity
of maintaining the all-male nature of warfare'[19] and so have to be otherwise explained.
The key to understanding the continuing resistance to women in combat roles lies not
in understanding the innate characteristics of men and women as such, but in understanding gender as a set of cultural institutions and practices that constitute the norms
and standards of masculinity and femininity. Gender is a 'system of meaning', a way
of thinking that shapes 'how we experience, understand and represent ourselves as
men and women'.[20] Thus, a man who cries easily cannot avoid in some way confronting that he is seen as less than fully manly by other men, and indeed by many women.
Similarly, an aggressive and incisive woman cannot avoid having her own and other's
perceptions of such qualities being mediated by the discourse of gender.[21]

The link between particular constructions of (socially acceptable) masculinities and
combat is a core component of the ideology of patriarchy that in turn justifies the
superiority of men in the social order.[22] While 'masculinity' is not all of a kind[23] – the
violent masculinity of the squaddie would not be acceptable in the officer – nevertheless, in the armed forces there is a deliberate cultivation of a 'dominance-orientated'
masculinity, that necessitates learning to control fears and domestic longings that are
explicitly labelled feminine. Ruddick argues that boot camp recruits are 'ladies' until
trained in obedient killing.[24] Only then do they become 'real men'.

'Effeminate' young soldiers are frequently the victims of bullying because of the
prevalent intense loathing of homosexuality that exists among both the officer corps
and regular soldiers in the armed services (homosexual men have either been excluded
or required 'not to tell' because they represent a direct challenge to this dominant
conception of what it is to be 'manly').[25] Carol Cohn[26] argues that the debate about
the role of gays in the military is often presented as one regarding issues of morale,
good order and unit cohesion, arguments that are very similar if not identical to those
made in the debate about allowing women into combat roles. However, these issues
do not fully explain the intensity of emotion in the debate. What is really at stake here,
according to Cohn, is the need to maintain the institutions of heterosexual masculinity.
According to Cohn 'An important attraction of the military to many members is the
guarantee of heterosexual masculinity. That guarantee is especially important because
the military provides a situation of intense bonds between men, a much more homo-
social and homo-erotically charged environment than most men otherwise have the
opportunity to be in.'[27] This gives rise to a paradoxical situation in so far as the military is at once 'an institution that constructs and upholds the most rigid stereotypes

of hegemonic masculinity but at the same time provides a context that allows men to transcend some of these limits, notably the rigid constraints that typically prevent men from bonding with other men.'[28]

There is an extensive literature that has also shown how women who serve in the military find themselves under pressure to remain 'feminine'.[29] Where women have entered the bastions of male privilege in militaries they have frequently found that the myth that military women need protection has made it easier for men to be persuaded of their 'protector' role, and this in itself has made it difficult for women to gain acceptance on the same terms as men. Where women have been admitted to the military in wartime, usually in response to manpower shortages, it has been in the face of strong resistance. Pierson argues that the outward expression of women's place in the system could be summed up by the term 'femininity' and that 'through dress, deportment, mannerisms, expression, "femininity" both signified and maintained women's difference from, deference towards and dependence on men and prevailing definitions of womanhood'.[30]

It is likely the inclusion of more women in combat roles has more to do with a fall in the number of young men who are ready and willing to sign up for armed combat than a fundamental shift in societal attitudes towards the proper roles of men and women, and changing attitudes among male elites in the military particularly.[31] In a commentary on the role of women in the Iraq war that appeared in the British press, Roberts noted that, despite the increasing number of women serving in the armed forces, femininity continued to be linked to 'home and hearth' with women most highly visible in their roles as sweethearts, victims and among the protected. The British military, for example, refused to reveal just how many women were serving in the Gulf conflict. This portrayal of the relationship between women, men and war was then essentially propaganda. She pointed to the way in which traditional machismo surfaced when the war machine required it and highlighted the continual marginalization and often invisibility of women serving in the Gulf conflict.[32]

The increasing number of women in combat roles notwithstanding, the ways in which women have been incorporated into the military suggest that it has been done in a manner that does not challenge the view that the military is a predominantly male institution. Women employed in militaries are usually disproportionately engaged in administration or in a variety of support services. Cynthia Enloe has argued that as long as women can be represented as inherently or intrinsically non-combative, and so objects of protection, their labour can be mobilized by governments and strategists without fear that such mobilization will shake the social order in which 'women are symbols of the hearths and homes that the armed forces claim to be defending.'[33] It also means that it is always possible for the moves to incorporate women to be reversed at a later stage.

THE 'WAR ON TERROR'

Mary Kaldor argues that in the late twentieth century and early twenty-first century, international violence is no longer only violence between sovereign, territorial bounded nation-states. Kaldor uses the term 'new wars' or 'post-Westphalian wars' to describe new trends in conflict, conflicts that tend to be more prolonged and less decisive and increasingly involve non-state actors. In 'new wars' it is difficult to distinguish clearly between civilians and combatants and 'insiders' and 'outsiders'. International terrorism is an example of the new forms of pervasive violence that characterize the contemporary international landscape.[34]

However, as with 'old wars', traditional gender roles surface during periods of militarization when efforts are made to mobilize public support for violence. The ideological representation of men and women as heroes (protectors) and victims (protected) was a central feature of the 'War on Terror' in the wake of the attack on the World Trade Center in New York on 11 September 2001. Asking the questions *where did all the women go* and, more to the point perhaps, *why did all the women go*, serves to open up further questions about the ways in which men and women were represented in traditional roles in discourses on 9/11 and subsequent efforts to rally the US nation and indeed the rest of the world behind the War on Terror.[35]

Media coverage of the immediate aftermath of the attack on the Twin Towers focused heavily on the heroism of the emergency services. From a feminist perspective, it is telling that the media coverage of 9/11 was characterized by the near complete absence of those women who participated in the rescue and recovery operation. There were female heroes at Ground Zero. Terri Tobin, a police department veteran, had concrete lodged in her skull, shards of glass in her back and a fractured ankle as she pulled three people out of the rubble and helped evacuate an apartment building. She later gave up her place in an ambulance so that a photographer with multiple fractures could be transported to hospital.[36] The invisibility of women did not go unnoticed by women in the rescue services. For example, Captain Brenda Berkman of the New York Police Department commented:

I was immediately struck by the total invisibility of women in the media coverage of the rescue and recovery efforts in New York. Women rescue workers found that our own agencies were even ignoring our presence at the countless funerals for our co-workers. This picture of an all male rescue effort was not only historically inaccurate but threatened to discourage young women from considering careers in the emergency services.[37]

In the aftermath of 9/11 the male hero was afforded a central place in the project to foster national solidarity.[38] A popular image of the attacks was the depiction of *Our Towering Heroes* that likened the image of the World Trade Center to the bodies of a male fire fighter and a male police officer.[39] The depiction of men in political discourse and in media representations of the heroes of 9/11 did not conform to the usual stereotype of masculinity. The 'new military heroes' were both 'tough and tender'. Men were allowed to display stereotypical feminine traits. Men were permitted to cry in public, to openly demonstrate their deep sorrow and anguish in the face of destruction, death and loss. The warrior was now 'sad and tender and because of that, the warrior could be brave too'.[40] The 'new warrior' and 'new man' were perhaps a reflection of the degree to which stereotypical ideas of masculinity have been challenged and have changed in the West in the late twentieth century and how US culture has become accustomed to less militarized ideals of masculinity.[41] Nevertheless, the story of post-9/11 heroism was told in a way that affirmed conventional understandings of what it was to be a man and, moreover, the depiction of the hero depended on similarly conventional constructions of women and femininity. For example, one of the men who had been a passenger on the plane that was hijacked and flown into the Pentagon in Washington was a gay man, Mark Bingham. However, media coverage of his story of bravery failed to acknowledge his sexuality, because it 'didn't fit in'.[42]

Feminist commentators on 9/11 have argued that the 'front line' might be understood as both a physical and symbolical location where identity politics are played out. Female firefighters were on the 'front line' in a military sense, but also in a feminist sense, since their presence challenged public perceptions of what women could be and do. In so doing, women in the front line on 9/11 challenged the boundaries between public and private.[43] Writing women out of dominant narratives of 9/11 reasserted that boundary and reaffirmed the 'public' and the 'front line as masculinised domains; spaces where women (and gay men) did not "fit in" '.

Overwhelmingly women were portrayed as victims of aggression perpetrated by 'other' men. A great deal of attention was focused on those widowed and orphaned by the hijackers/suicide bombers, women who were thereby afforded the status of 'moral icons'.[44] 'Victimization' became a powerful reason to go to war. It was not only American women that were presented as victims in need of protection, but also Afghan women. First Lady Laura Bush and Cherie Blair, the wife of the British Prime Minister, were marshalled in the cause of generating support for the subsequent intervention in Afghanistan. Laura Bush stated that 'the fight against terrorism is also a fight for the rights and dignity of women'.[45] The veil or burqa was represented in the West as a symbol of oppression and evidence of the 'irrational barbarian' of the Taliban regime, a regime that gave succour to al-Qaeda.[46] While not denying that Afghan women were subjected to brutal treatment at the hands of the Taliban regime, focusing on the burqa only as an index of the oppression of Muslim women without listening to what Afghan women had to say about the meaning of the veil in the construction of religious and cultural identity served to silence Afghan women.

At the same time, George Bush seemed to have great difficulty listening to those same women that he was ostensibly seeking to 'liberate'. The Revolutionary Association of the Women of Afghanistan (RAWA) argued that fundamentalism was an 'abomination of Islam', but nevertheless initially called for aid rather than direct intervention in Afghanistan, arguing that the Taliban must be overthrown by internal uprising. Later RAWA supported intervention, but only by a multinational peacekeeping force. Their opposition to western intervention was on the grounds that it would create hatred and resentment of US imperialism and allow terrorist and fundamentalist groups to flourish in the future.

RAWA also urged the US not to support other fundamentalist regimes that denied women their most basic rights, citing US support for the Mujahadeen, General Zia-ul Haq in Pakistan (who allowed thousands of religious schools to spring up which became the breeding ground for the Taliban) and the Northern Alliance (who have an anti-democratic agenda and who have subsequently enjoyed great sway in post-conflict Afghanistan).[47] The US put its commitment to women's participation in post-Taliban Afghanistan on record at the UN. However, the Administration has subsequently been criticized on the grounds that it could have done more to ensure that women were granted the same rights as men in Afghanistan's proposed constitution (drafted without the participation of women).

In the project of building national solidarity, feminist voices were ignored or dismissed. Feminist discussions were 'placed on the backburner, considered unimportant'.[48] While individual US feminists read and responded to 9/11 in different ways, they agreed on the irony of George Bush claiming that the bombing of Afghanistan would liberate Afghan women.[49] As Drucilla Cornel stated, 'RAWA convinced me that bombing of the devastated people of Afghanistan would not solve problems of terrorism, but would only bring more suffering to those who could not flee to the hills – women, children and 500,000 disabled orphans (as estimated by UN).'[50]

The attacks on New York and Washington and the subsequent War on Terror further illustrate the centrality of gender in boundary-drawing practices and the importance of gendered images and symbolism in the depiction of the 'body politic' (see chapter 3). The events of 9/11 'violated and shattered the confidence of the US in the total security of its territorial body'.[51] Hitherto, the United States had not experienced the violation of its territorial boundaries directly. The closest the US had come to experiencing a direct attack had been the bombing of its naval fleet at Pearl Habor during the Second World War and unsurprisingly the memory of that incident was 'cited over and over again after 9/11'.[52] Consequently, the 'dominant moral imaginary of the US' has been 'shaped in part by fantasies of impregnability and invincibility', an imaginary that can scarcely be conceived as gender-neutral.[53] Unsurprisingly then, powerful gendered images of violation and penetration were characteristic of media representations of 9/11. In the run up to the intervention in Afghanistan, in one cartoon, Osama bin Laden was depicted as being sodomized by a US bomb with a picture of the Twin Towers in the background; a 'frightening statement' on how militarized masculinity 'conceives of sexuality as lethal penetration'.[54]

The military and the state

The military is one of the central institutions of the state; the coercive arm of state power. While feminists have failed to develop a single, agreed, definition or understanding of the gendered nature of the state,[55] the creation of states and the consolidation of state power has gone hand in hand with the institutionalization of gender relations of inequality.[56] Moreover, 'the personnel of the state are divided in visible, even spectacular, ways, along gender lines. Not only does the state arm men and disarm women, but also the diplomatic, colonial and military policies of major states have been formed in the context of ideologies of masculinity that put a premium on toughness and force.'[57]

In political discourse, the state is often presented as clearly separated from civil society, just as the 'public' and the 'private' have been regarded as distinct realms. However, many traits of the modern nation-state that emerged in the seventeenth and eighteenth century can be traced to military institutions and, moreover, as states have altered to meet the needs of their armed forces, societies have changed to meet the new demands of the state.[58] According to Roberts, in the seventeenth century military discipline became the model for a well-ordered civil society and the state began to intervene in areas of life once regarded as 'private'.[59]

The creation of armies and empires has involved the historical embedding of violent masculinity in the state.[60] Bob Connell argues that it is often difficult for us to see beyond individual acts of violence – or in this case beyond the individual acts of violence committed by personalized states as actors – to a structure of power. Yet all acts of violence are deeply embedded in power inequalities and ideologies of male supremacy. State-sanctioned violence is legitimized through the use of concepts like 'autonomy' and 'national interest', concepts that in turn rely upon masculinized notions of rationality as a technique of control. As Connell puts it, 'if authority is defined as legitimate power, then the main axis of the power structure of gender is the general connection of authority with masculinity'.[61]

Sara Ruddick has pointed out that both the practices and ideology of the state are strongly masculinized.[62] Not only is the world of generals, negotiators and chiefs of staff still a man's world, but also it is usually men who make battle plans, invent weapons and supervise their construction.[63] Furthermore, as Cynthia Enloe has argued, state power is exercised by policy-makers and law enforcers, who are mostly men.[64] Across the world it is men who predominate as police chiefs, spies, judges, politicians and governors who construct a peacetime order guaranteed by the threat of violence.[65] States 'destroy on a mass scale' and 'to do this requires masculine toughness which becomes institutionalised'.[66] In the 1980s, the feminist anti-war movement often treated the state's military apparatus, especially nuclear weapons, as an expression of male aggression and destructiveness. Hegemonic masculinity does not just manifest itself in the military, but in the inner core of the security establishment. In the nuclear defence establishment, a 'language of warriors' – a 'techno-strategic rationality' – is shared by armers and disarmers, chiefs of staff and chief negotiators. War is about masculinity and heroism, 'wimps and women'.[67]

Militarism

Analyses that go beyond the military and the institutions of the state generally, to elucidate the ideological and material connections that hold the entire complex together, necessarily involve some discussion of militarism. Militarism can be defined as an ideology which values war highly and, in so doing, serves to legitimize state violence. Militarism is not merely an ideology, but also a set of social relationships organized around war and preparation for war, and so occurs during periods of both war and peace. Militarism denotes a state of affairs when any part of society becomes controlled by or dependent upon the military or military values. In this way virtually anything can become militarized – toys, marriage, scientific research, university curricula, motherhood.[68]

Enloe argues that what is distinctive about feminist theorizing about militarism is that it posits gender – that is, the social construction of masculinity and femininity – as a critical factor in the construction and perpetuation of militarism and therefore the possible reversal of the process. Male employees in weapons factories may work against their own class interests because they perceive themselves as doing important 'men's work'. The patriarchal assumption that they are doing men's work then reinforces the militarization and the hegemony of the 'military industrial complex' in ways that may be crucial for the maintenance of such a militarizing alliance.[69] Enloe argues that whether tracing militarization or demilitarization as social processes, one must chart how women and men in any particular historical setting comprehend what it means to be 'manly' and what it means to be 'womanly'. Government and military officials are affected by their own perceptions of 'manliness' and 'femininity' and design policies to ensure that civilians and soldiers relate to one another in gendered ways that ease the complicated process of militarization.[70]

Connell has argued that the structure of 'gender power' works to privilege men at the expense of women in general. He has identified a core to gender power that includes hierarchies that work through the forces of institutionalized violence, found in the military, the police forces and prison services, which he calls the coercive arms of state power. Connell points to the hierarchy of the labour force in heavy industry and the hierarchy of high-technology industry, to the planning and control of the machinery of the central state, and to the working-class milieux that emphasize physical toughness and men's association with machinery as integral parts of the structure of gender power. The first and second components of this core are connected through the military industrial complex, from which women are largely excluded. These are tied together through the ideology of masculinity, authority and technological violence. However, Connell argues that the connection with the fourth component is the crucial link in understanding the sexual politics of the whole, because it is this connection that gives a mass base to militarist beliefs and practices.[71]

Women also contribute to the militarization of society in both material and ideological terms. Women play a vital role in encouraging men to 'act like men'. Women have been incorporated into war in many roles: as a pretext for war, as wives and prostitutes who provide for warriors, as entertainers, as victims, as sympathetic nurses, spies or castrating bitches.[72] But in all these many and varied roles the incorporation of women has served to reinforce the masculinity of war and justify militarism. Indeed, feminist opposition to the incorporation of women into the military has centred on the argument that integrating women will have the effect of increasing the militarization of society as a whole and so undermine the work of peace movements and women's movements. The result will be to reaffirm the inferiority of women and women's experience, destroy the feminist tradition of non-violence and increase the militarization of society as a whole.

WOMEN IN THE MILITARY SYSTEM

Women have always participated in the 'military system' by providing indispensable support services, though such women have been frequently dismissed as mere 'camp followers'. In the seventeenth century, as the armed forces (in western states) changed, it became more difficult for women to follow armies. At the same time, official policy statements made it clear that women were regarded as a disruptive influence, a diversion that jeopardized male loyalty and obedience. Where women were attached to companies, usually in their capacity as soldiers' wives, they were deemed to have a moral obligation to subservience to both military institutions and to individual men.[73] Enloe claims that contemporary military wives, and other women who provide vital support services for those involved in combat roles, are the modern-day 'camp follow-ers'.[74] While contemporary army wives are apt to be less subservient to male dominated militaries – often complaining that they feel trapped and that they feel that their lives are controlled by the army[75] – many still 'lean over backwards to avoid offending male sensibilities'.[76]

Goldstein argues that war both shakes up and reinforces gender stereotypes and gender expectations.[77] It is unsurprising to find then that, where women have been involved in the servicing of the war industry, this has not played a decisive role in improving the status of women. With the advent of mass warfare and mass conscrip-tion, the franchise was granted to lower-class men in many western countries and, indeed, women too were often rewarded for their contribution to the war effort by being granted the right to vote. But despite participating in much greater numbers and in a wider variety of roles in the workforce during wartime, women in Britain did not achieve lasting changes in their economic status and social roles.[78]

Historical studies show that prejudices surrounding women and attitudes towards their role at home and work remained remarkably consistent over the first half of the twentieth century. In Britain in both the First and Second World War periods, conven-tional sex roles were put under strain, as women did far more 'men's jobs', but at the end of the war, women returned, if not to the home, then to more conventionally feminine jobs.[79] Undoubtedly women's participation in war efforts was an important instrument of radicalization and served to delegitimize, to some extent, dominant norms. It seems, however, that when it came to organizing women's employment both government and the trade unions were careful to ensure that women's incursion into men's jobs was not permanent and would not shake up family life after the war. As men enlisted, women were drafted into the labour force. Women were also desperately needed in munitions factories. However, trade unions were reluctant to welcome women into skilled trades and, while there was a desperate need to increase the supply of women to the labour force, at the heart of government there was a reluctance to introduce any policy that would change the conventional role of women, even at the height of war. According to Braydon and Summerfield the war made men think again about what women could do at work, but it did not alter their belief that women alone were responsible for the home life of the nation.[80]

CHALLENGING THE WAR/PEACE DICHOTOMY

While the distinction between war and peace, and between the battlefield and the domestic arena, has been central to political discourse, in reality this distinction has never been clear-cut. Feminist work has not only challenged the distinction between the 'war front' and 'home front', but also the war/peace dichotomy. The distinction between the protectors and the protected has served to obscure the nature of warfare by perpetuating the view that there is a clear division between the war front – a mas-culinist domain in which masculinity is affirmed in the heroic actions performed on the battlefield – and the 'home front' – a feminized realm of domesticity, care and peace. Indeed, the very idea of the 'home front', which has been very much part of the language of twentieth-century warfare, is indicative of the industrialization of war.

This in itself transformed the earlier distinction between the 'front' and the domestic arena.

Feminists have challenged the war front/home front distinction by uncovering the unknown testimonies of women who have suffered greatly in war but whose suffering is unrecorded. While most commentaries view war as a discrete phenomenon arranged by diplomats with neat beginnings and endings and/or concentrate upon the political or strategic objectives, or the heroics of the battlefield, feminists have recounted women's testimonies and post-war stories and so highlight the 'unboundedness' of war – unbounded in the sense that wars have no neat beginnings and endings. Women who bear the burden of picking up the pieces at the formal cessation of hostilities have come to see that wars do not simply 'end' with the signing of peace treaties. Women are left to deal with the task of rebuilding the physical infrastructure, along with men, but they must also cope with the terrible physical, psychological and emotional damage that people suffer. As carers, the lives of women are also greatly complicated. Women are often left with sole responsibility for the welfare of the elderly and disabled relatives as well as children. Women and children constitute on average 70–90 per cent of refugee populations, although the smaller percentage of male refugees frequently gets disproportionate access to food, clothes, land, jobs and legal identity papers, water, livestock and tools.[81]

Moreover, the central importance of women's bodies in reproducing group identity renders women vulnerable to specific forms of violence in armed conflicts, from which until relatively recently women had no form of protection or redress (see chapter 5). Women are frequently the targets of sexual violence from the enemy in war. The idea that women are part of the 'spoils of war' remains a part of the militaristic concept of the soldier's 'right to women'. Rape in warfare does not occur as an isolated incident. Feminists involved in the peace movement have long argued that rape should be viewed as an accepted part of the code that governs the fighting of wars rather than as an individual act of wrongdoing. Moreover, some feminists have argued that in warfare it is always difficult to distinguish between rape and war prostitution.

However, rape and sexual violence against women in wartime is not only a crime perpetuated by 'the enemy'. Women are also more likely to be subjected to violent attack from men in their own communities at times of heightened aggression. The distinction between the protectors and protected has been challenged by feminists because it obscures the connection between war and other forms of violence. The feminist understanding of violence in warfare, particularly war rape, once again emphasizes the connections between manhood and nationhood, between masculinity, militarism and violence. As Stiehm argues, 'protectors usually control those whom they protect'[82] and, as Jan Pettman notes, 'the protector/protected relationship makes women vulnerable to other men's/states' violence'.[83]

THE WOMEN/PEACE NEXUS

Women peace activists often invoke the 'natural' peacefulness of women. For example, the early suffragettes used the idea of biological difference to present arguments in favour of women's suffrage. They argued that maternal urges made women different from men, but that women's peacefulness was evidence of moral superiority rather than inferiority.[84] Others, while rejecting essentialist accounts of apparent gender differences, have noted the close association with peace and the 'feminine' and have argued that the experience of maternity on the part of the vast majority of women, the obligation to care that threads through women's lives and women's historical exclusion from public power mean that women do have a special relationship to peace.

Certainly, there is a long history of women's activism in peace movements. In the nineteenth century, the spaces and locations available for women to organize politically were severely circumscribed, as were the range of issues on which women were considered able to voice an opinion. Peace was deemed to be one subject that women might legitimately speak about. The Olive Leaf Circles that brought together three thousand British women in the 1850s to discuss ideas about peace are an early example of women's political activism.[85] By the nineteenth century, growing affluence, increased leisure time and the expansion of education to upper-class and middle-class women, created a group of women who shared in a culture rooted in domesticity.[86] Victorian social values and the liberal state denied women much public space to carry out political work, forcing women peace activists to work on war and peace issues in the private sphere of the home.[87] However, while largely confined to the home and domestic sphere and the issue of peace, women activists developed awareness of themselves as political actors and set about establishing links with like-minded women.[88]

Explicit linkages were often made between motherhood, peace and women's rights. For example, the women's suffrage movement proclaimed: 'let us do our utmost to hasten the day when the wishes of mothers shall have their due weight in public affairs, knowing that by doing so we hasten the day when wars shall be no more.'[89] The Women's International League for Peace and Freedom, a pacifist organization founded during the Women's Peace Congress at The Hague in 1915, brought together women of all races, nationalities and social classes to work for disarmament and the abolition of violence as a means of resolving disputes. Members believed that, by helping to bring about non-violent social transformation, they would also help to bring about social, economic and political equality for all people.

By the early twentieth century, it was evident that women involved in transnational political activity not only identified as women, but as 'Germans, or Egyptians, pacifists or socialists, Christians or Jews'.[90] However, amidst this diversity, motherhood continued to serve as a unifying idea. Since all women were perceived to be potential mothers, motherhood functioned as a unifying interest that transcended barriers of race, class and religious differences among activists. Women were often portrayed as 'guardians of new generations', rather than defined in terms of their relationship to particular children and families. Through their activism in the peace movement women forged solidarist projects and mobilized in the interests of generating wider political and social change (see chapter 9).

Throughout the twentieth century, women across the world continued to mobilize as peacemakers. For example, Nobel Peace Prize winners Betty Williams and Mairead Corrigan were motivated to protest for peace when three small children were killed and their mother seriously injured in Northern Ireland in August 1975. This initiative eventually mushroomed into marches supported by over 100,000 people as the local community 'began to imagine a different way of solving conflict'.[91] Today, the Women in Black: Women's Solidarity Network Against War, an organization that started out as a protest against the war in (former) Yugoslavia, has forged transnational linkages with feminist and peace networks throughout the world in order to establish 'a network of solidarity against war'. Women in Black see the causes of ending war and ending all forms of violence and discrimination against women as intimately connected.[92]

Women's political activities are often closely associated with the domain of their everyday realities. Women's anti-war demonstrations typically involve bringing private pain into the public realm. In demonstrations outside Greenham Common in the UK in the early 1980s, for example, women wove ribbons of life, including photographs of children, and messages around the 'camp of death'.[93] This idea has found echoes in the calls by 'moral feminists' in the 1980s and 1990s for the inclusion of women in government elites because the inclusion of women would change the foreign policy of states.[94]

Feminist discourse too has often emphasized human connectedness, dialogue and cooperation over dominance and violent confrontation. The work of Dorothy Dinnerstein, Carol Gilligan and Sara Ruddick, perhaps, best exemplifies this school of thought.[95] Dinnerstein claims that feminism means mobilizing the wisdom and skills with which female history has equipped women and focusing them on efforts to change the world. She claims that women are constantly forced in practice to rediscover the necessity of speaking for peace because they are not represented in places where decisions about war are taken. Therefore, if women do not speak for peace they will be excluded from speaking on all life and death questions that face the species. Sometimes this leads to the conscious and subversive use of women's traditional place as mother and 'Other', but at the same time it demonstrates that women are refusing to stay on the margins. In this way, by taking a more powerful place in the political arena, feminist peace activists are changing the terms in which public discourse is conducted.[96]

Because feminists, generally, start from the conditions of women's lives, and because they see many forms of violence, unhappiness and distress, they define peace in terms of people gaining control over their lives. Feminist peace activists claim that for women the 'oppressors' are found among immediate family or lovers. In this view, not only is war part of women's daily existence, but also war, violence and women's oppression all grow from the same root – patriarchy. Similarly, non-violence is not just about the absence of war, but about a total approach to living, a strategy for change. At Greenham Common women learnt how to protest effectively and assertively by confronting the police and military, but at the same time their action was deliberately non-violent. The women at Greenham tried to work in supportive ways, sharing tasks, skills and knowledge. In drawing upon a diverse range of views among the women in the camp as a source of strength, peace activists privileged 'women's culture and practice' that they saw as necessary in defeating the 'warring patriarchy'.[97] Enloe argues that women's peace movements in general deliberately avoid forms of organization that are top-down and valorize qualities of equality, spontaneity and connection. Women who took part expressed the need to withdraw from what they perceived as a patriarchal system that perpetuated militarism, because it could not be sustained without women's cooperation.[98]

Of course, not all feminists share the views of Gilligan, Dinnerstein, Ruddick and other standpoint thinkers who champion the women/peace nexus. Chapkis, for example, contends that such essentialist arguments about masculinity and femininity are not only limited as a basis for organizing opposition to militarism, but also danger-ously counter-productive and personally self-defeating.[99] Micaela di Leonardo has argued that any reinvigorated image of women as more peaceful will have disastrous consequences for the women's movement, while Janet Radcliffe Richards has expressed deep concern with the position that women are either by nature or socialization more peaceful than men, because this plays into the hands of those who would keep men and women in separate spheres and limit women's equality. She points out that male chauvinists have always used the idea of 'difference' to discriminate against women.[100]

There is some empirical evidence that suggests that women – in the West at least – are less likely to throw their support behind governments who are mobilizing for war or other forms of intervention. However, it seems that liberal feminists are correct in warning that championing women's 'special relationship' to peace can provoke political backlash, as is evidenced from the earlier discussion of Fukuyama's 'If Women Ran the World'. That said, campaigning for the 'right to fight' is equally problematic from a feminist perspective, since this simply ends up justifying state-sanctioned violence and reinforcing received narratives on politics and war.

Conclusion

While eschewing essentialist conceptions of gender, feminist perspectives on the mili-tary and on war and peace point to deep and profound connections between the construction of masculinities, femininities and state-sanctioned violence. Moreover, NOW campaigners apart, feminists generally support the idea that challenging domi-nant gender stereotypes goes some way towards challenging the ideology of militarism. As long as ideas about masculinity can be manipulated to encourage men to kill and be killed and while ever women continue to accept, or fail to resist, certain construc-tions of femininity and womanhood, they will not be able to challenge the gender ideology upon which the military is built. Moreover, militarist ideology has very real consequences in so far as 'it gives rise to a view of community both in theory and in fact obsessed with revenge and structured by conquest and domination.'[101] This would be no easy task if it were only a question of changing ideas or challenging dominant discourses on war and peace, but it is made all the more difficult by the material, concrete structures that underpin the interconnected military system and 'gender system'. Moreover, liberal strategies that promote women's equality, while disregarding deeply embedded gender inequalities and deeply ingrained gendered ideologies, are unlikely to do much to promote peace. As Stiehm acknowledges, even if women were to participate in combat roles, and were accepted, it would not solve the problem of their relation to other states' 'protectors' and 'protected', a relationship which feminists should be concerned to problematize.[102]

One might be highly sceptical of the degree to which values can be seen as essentially male or female. Nevertheless, for many feminists the proper question to ask is how both women and men might strengthen institutions and processes that will help to build peace-orientated communities that recognize the common humanity and worth of all human beings.[103] As the horrors of war continue to blight human life in the twenty-first century, there may be good reason to support all efforts to radically rethink both war and peace in order to achieve a more stable and secure world for human beings as a whole.

Re-Visioning Security

Introduction

Like so many of the concepts used in the study of International Relations, 'security' is essentially contested. A broad definition of security might be 'a state of being secure, safe, free from danger, injury, harm of any sort'[1] but few International Relations scholars would accept such a pervasive definition. Indeed, many would argue that such a state of being is neither possible nor desirable, pointing out that an element of danger will always be part of human existence. In 'mainstream' IR, therefore, security has been understood in terms of the protection of national communities from violence – actual or potential. Feminist approaches to security problematize the state as 'protector' and guarantor of security and expand the security agenda beyond the high politics of military security.

This chapter is divided into four sections. The first two cover feminist critiques of 'orthodox', especially realist, approaches to security. Feminist perspectives on security challenge the view that the nation-state is the only significant form of political community. Turpin and Lorentzen, for example, point out that problems of environmental degradation, poverty, population growth and sustainable development are both global concerns and security issues.[2] Security is not viewed purely in terms of threats or actual acts of violence from excluded 'others', but in terms of the economic, political, social or personal circumstances of individuals.

The third section turns to the subject of how security might be re-visioned when viewed from feminist perspectives. There are a number of distinctive ways in which feminists have contributed to the re-visioning of security within IR. Along with critical theorists and constructivists of many persuasions, feminist scholars, such as V. Spike Peterson, have challenged the idea that the nation-state is the mainstay of security by encouraging a radical rethinking of dominant conceptions of identities and boundaries in which traditional approaches to security have been framed.[3] There is a literature that assesses the 'impact' on women's security when resources are channelled into military expenditure justified in the name of national security. The gendered power structures, social institutions and values that underpin the 'national security state' have also attracted the attention of feminist scholars.

The last section discusses the concept of human security. One does not have to be a feminist to embrace a broad conception of 'human security', but there is a great deal of overlap between feminist interests and concerns and the human security approach. For example, feminists point out that the fate of women is a crucial determinant of the fate of whole societies and countries. The achievement of global security is tied up with the need to improve the status of women around the world. The degree to which women have control over income and resources is a major factor in determining the nutritional status of children throughout the world.[4] While frequently ignored, 'women's work' makes an enormous contribution to the global economy (as elaborated in the following chapter). Women are not only usually the main providers of food, fuel and water in many societies, but often the main sustainers and developers of whole communities. Yet, ideas about the 'private' and 'natural' roles of women serve to render invisible women's contribution to security and also distort our understanding of many of the most pressing problems facing the world today.

THE STATE AND NATIONAL SECURITY

During the Cold War period, realist and later neorealist assumptions and perspectives dominated thinking about security in IR. While realists argued that ultimately the problem of security was rooted in man's aggressive nature, in neorealist discourse anarchy was deemed to be the central problem. The problem of anarchy arose from the constitution of the state-system, the central problem that states had to overcome. The insight of neorealism was that, in the absence of any central sovereign power, nation-states must ultimately look to themselves to provide security for their citizens. Security was seen in terms of the overriding need to ensure the survival of human collectivities called nation-states.[5] Thus, both realist and neorealist discourses on security privileged the state and nationalist constructions of identity and foregrounded relations between insiders and outsiders, citizens and foreigners. Those outside the bounded community of the nation-state were apt to be viewed as 'threats', either actual or potential, to the citizen body.

Security was, therefore, defined as a guarantee of safety. This necessitated political arrangements that made war less likely, facilitated negotiation and dialogue among states, rather than belligerence, and which allowed a tentative and unstable peace among states.[6] 'National security' denoted 'all purposes of defence, in effect the preparation for belligerence in order to defer or deflect it.'[7] The achievement of security depended ultimately upon military power. Indeed, such power was seen as the essence of security in times of intense conflict. There was a strong sense in realist writings that national security issues, particularly in times of war, offered a sense of shared political purpose. As Ann Tickner argues, it was, perhaps, for this reason that military budgets were least likely to be cut and contested by politicians of all kinds.[8] Certainly, from this perspective, citizens were willing to make sacrifices, or sacrifice themselves, in the name of national security. Moreover, the primacy of the state and nation was not justified purely in terms of an unreflective nationalist sentiment. Whatever the shortcomings of the nation-state, it is the best form of political community that human beings have devised in the modern age and so of moral worth.

Realists and neorealists defined peace in negative terms. That is, peace was viewed as the absence of war. In classical realist thought, peace and security were achieved by shifting alliances that preserved a balance of power among states. Efforts to achieve security through disarmament, development and respect for human rights, from a realist/neorealist point of view, were laudable but ultimately utopian aspirations. Since states operated in an essentially 'anarchic' international system, in the final analysis state survival and international order could only be secured through a stable balance of power. Neorealists argued that hegemonic states dominate international institutions and, in this way, 'managed' international security and so the security order was ultimately built upon and reflected the realities of power in the international system.

Not all significant contributions to the literature on security rested on realist or neorealist assumptions. Barry Buzan's *People, States and Fear*, for example, developed an approach to security that shared the state-centric assumptions of realism, but also drew upon some ideas central to the English school, which stressed the importance of norms in international relations. He argued that in a 'mature anarchy'[9] states, secure within themselves might recognize and uphold international norms and in this way strengthen international security. However, the security of the individual was 'inseparably entangled with that of the state'.[10] So from this perspective too, individuals were not the appropriate starting point for thinking about security because most threats to individuals arose from societal issues and the principal role of the state was to protect and preserve the social order and protect individuals from 'the invasion of foreigners and injuries to one another'.[11] Buzan acknowledged that building up military strength incurred costs to society and that these were not distributed equally among individuals or social groups. Furthermore, the state might in some circumstances constitute a threat to the people living within its sovereign jurisdiction. Buzan argued that the 'maximal state' might oppress its citizens, while the 'minimal state' might be weak and fail to resolve disputes between citizens and so fail in its duty to protect and uphold societal order.[12]

The concept of interdependence between states, arising from historical associations or geographical proximity, was also highlighted in the security literature. Interdependence gave rise to 'security complexes' or 'security subsystems'[13] in which the security of one state was closely, inextricably even, linked with the security of other states. Buzan presented a fairly sophisticated analysis of the connections between individual, state, regional and global security. However, the nation-state remained the central linkage in this chain of security.

Some of the work on security during the Cold War period recognized an intersubjective dimension to 'threats' and danger in the international system, in so far as perceptions were held to be important to understanding the dynamics of arms races and other security dilemmas. Jervis, for example, argued that attempts to achieve military security by building up levels of armaments were likely to fuel fears and suspicions among neighbouring states and so encourage a 'spiral of international insecurity'.[14] Here too the primacy of the state was rather taken for granted.

CRITIQUING STATE-CENTRIC APPROACHES TO SECURITY

In the Cold War context, discourses on security were heavily coloured by the ideological conflict between the 'superpowers'. Yet, during this period in history, most military conflicts actually took place in the Third World. Furthermore, the state-centrism of much of the security literature belied the reality that it was becoming increasingly difficult to distinguish clearly between 'domestic' and 'international' conflicts. It was the changed political circumstances of the post-Cold War, in conjunction with the openness of theoretical debates in IR in the 1980s and 1990s that encouraged a radical rethinking of approaches to security.

Postpositivists in IR began to develop a critique of realism/neorealism and state centrism, both on the grounds of problems of reductionism and in terms of the conception of the state as a concrete entity or actor with interests and agency. Critical theorists – in a broad sense – and constructivists were inclined to view the state in dynamic rather than static terms, as a 'process' rather than a 'thing'. The 'state' did not exist in any concrete sense. The state was a creation. The state was made by processes and practices, such as diplomacy and foreign and defence policies. The making of the state involved the construction of boundaries and identities that differentiated between the 'inside' and the 'outside'.[15]

Contemporary globalization, discussed further below, also encouraged a radical rethinking of the concept of 'security'. A debate emerged about whether it was appropriate to take the state as the fundamental 'referent' of security. Discontent with the 'orthodoxy' in IR ultimately led to the emergence of a school of 'critical security studies' that challenged the fundamental assumptions of realism and neorealism, questioned state-centrism and argued for radical new approaches to security[16] that were sorely needed to address central problems in contemporary international relations. The resurgence of nationalisms and inter-ethnic conflicts across the post-Cold War world put issues of identity firmly back onto the agenda of International Relations.[17] At the same time the agenda of world politics had changed radically. Population growth, large-scale migration, poverty, global recession, global warming, pollution and the rapid and indiscriminate use of the world's natural resources along with widespread human rights abuses increasingly came to be viewed as 'threats' to the future well-being and security of humanity as a whole. It was not surprising, therefore, that the state-based, war-dominated understanding of the world was subjected to a multi-pronged assault.

Critical security studies

Keith Krause and Michael Williams argued that discontent with the ontological and epistemological assumptions of realism/neorealism in particular were a central factor in opening up a wide-ranging debate about what security now meant, whose security mattered and how security could best be promoted or achieved. Unlike realists/neorealists who tended to emphasize the enduring and intractable problems generated by anarchy, critical security studies emphasized possibilities for change, agency and emancipation. Security could be defined in various ways, depending on the most immediate threats to the survival of the person. Thus, the Women's International Peace Conference in Halifax, Canada, in 1985 defined security in various ways, depending on the most immediate threats to the survival of the person. From this perspective 'security' meant freedom from threat of war certainly, but also safe working conditions, freedom from the threat of unemployment or an economic squeeze on foreign debt that was resulting in the impoverishment of millions of people across the world. Participants at the conference agreed that the security of some could not be built on the insecurity of others. As will be elaborated below, feminist thinking about security starts out from the circumstances and needs of people and stresses that security is not just about the absence of threats or acts of violence, but the enjoyment of economic and social justice.

Below – and in the following chapter – the relevance of gender to security and international political economy are discussed at greater length. First, however, it is useful to set out the two broad schools of thought that emerged within critical security studies: constructivism and critical theory. While there were and remain important differences between these two schools, what they had in common was a concern with the processes through which individuals, collectivities and 'threats' were constructed as 'social facts'. This was a radical departure from earlier approaches to security in that both schools questioned the supposed 'objective' threats to the state that were 'out there' in the real world.[18]

The role of elites in constructing threats was given more attention. David Campbell argued that the construction of 'threat' was integral to the construction of state identity and worked to legitimate state power.[19] Jean Elshtain argued that the problems of war and the difficulties of achieving security in the so-called 'anarchy' of the international realm should not be seen as problems which were rooted in the compulsions of interstate relations as such. Rather, they arose from 'the ordering of modern, technological society' in which political elites sought to control the masses by the implementation of the mechanism of the perfect army. Elshtain argued that to see war as a continuation of politics by other means was to perpetuate the 'military model' as a means of preventing civil disorder.[20] This seemingly explains why 'threats' in discourses on security were always located in the external realm and why citizenship had come to be viewed as synonymous with loyalty to the nation-state and the elimination of all that was 'foreign'.[21] Critical and constructivist approaches problematized the relationship between nation-states, citizens and excluded Others and questioned the claims of sovereign states, along with the 'powerful sway of received narratives' on security.[22] In the 'making' of the state the construction of the hostile 'Other' – who was threatening and dangerous – was central to the making of identities and the securing of boundaries.

Within what was rapidly becoming an increasingly influential school of social constructivism in IR, social interactions were seen to produce and reproduce certain social structures and worked to shape actions, identities and perceptions of interest. It follows from this that security could not be conceived of as an 'objective condition' and, moreover, the object of security, or referent of security, changed over time.[23] As Thomas Diez argued, it is necessary to ask therefore, how is the object to be secured constituted. Is the referent, for example, a state, nation or social group?'[24] This in turn led to an 'emphasis on interpretative methods that examine the actors' understandings and possibilities for agency in a changing social world'.[25] Social constructivists shared with postmodernists and some schools of feminism a concern with practices of 'Othering' that were central to the construction of identities and were similarly concerned to widen the concept of security beyond the nation-state and military threats.

To challenge the discourse of national security was to 'recognise the powerful sway of received narratives'.[26] As Elshtain argued, to challenge received narratives was to recognize that the concepts through which we think about security, war, peace and politics got repeated endlessly, shaping debates, constraining the consideration of alternatives, reassuring us that things cannot really be different.[27] As such, the received narratives of the orthodoxy 'put our critical faculties to sleep, blinding us to the possibilities that lie within our reach'.[28]

The implications of gender inequality for theorizing security

Inequality, structural violence, militarism, maldevelopment and human rights abuses are not only relevant to our understanding of the multiple insecurities which people face, but profoundly affect the process of conceptualization and theorization too. When Cynthia Enloe asks 'what does it mean to theorize state-sanctioned violence?', she reminds us that all too frequently theory is separated from human activity. However, when trying to make sense of security, for example, it is important to look at the implications of theorizing as an activity and not just at the resulting theories. When we think about the activity of theorizing, we understand that hegemonic domination is not just a question of the social relations of inequality, but is also about the production of knowledge and the formulation of concepts and ideas that set the parameters for how we think about 'security'. It is also, crucially, about the ability to be heard.[29]

Enloe argues that 'rethinking' security is not just a question of adopting a global, rather than narrowly conceived national perspective. Nor is it simply a question of broadening our definition of security to embrace a range of new issues and concerns. It is also about the capacity of people to articulate their fears and insecurities and present new 'visions'. In this context feminist perspectives do not simply make a contribution to our understanding of security, but are rather central to the 'reconstructive' project. However, as Enloe maintains, women need 'a room of their own' to theorize. Women need space, resources and physical security. Enloe claims that the more a government is preoccupied with what it calls 'national security', the less women experience the physical security necessary for theorizing. Enloe goes on to say that, similarly, women who question their own subordination are often perceived as 'threats' to national security and it is precisely those women in the world with the most pressing need to discover the underlying causes of war, militarism and peace who have the least capacity to write down their thoughts.[30]

FEMINISTS (RE-)VISIONS OF SECURITY

The state as a 'barracks community'

In critiquing dominant conceptions of security in International Relations, feminists to some extent echoed the arguments of non-feminist critical thinkers. Given the feminist interest in gender in the construction of dominant conceptions of identities and boundaries in IR, discussed at length in earlier chapters, this is unsurprising. However, feminist scholars have also been concerned to show what is lost from our understanding of security when gender is omitted. As was noted in chapter 4, feminist theorists have demonstrated that in much western political thought the conception of politics and the public realm has been constituted as a 'barracks community', a realm defined in opposition to the disorderly forces that threaten its existence. This same conception of politics has been constructed out of masculine hostility towards the female 'Other'.[31] Criticism of the 'right to fight' campaign, in part, focused on how the politics of access was at odds with a feminist interest in challenging militarized and gendered conceptions of security and the legitimization of state violence. Feminists argued that violence should not be viewed as a specific and limited act, but as part of a complex that involved institutions and the way they were organized.

In chapter 1, it was acknowledged that the notion that women necessarily share a particular perspective or have common interests founded in their essential difference from men was problematic. Nevertheless the legitimacy of feminist standpoint positions was also defended on the grounds that, in so far as part of the feminist IR agenda was to empower women as subjects of knowledge (see chapter 2) in the interests of advancing a political project of emancipation, standpoint could serve as the point of departure in rethinking security. The starting point for feminist standpoint re-visions of security has been the development of a distinctive critique of dominant conceptions of political community and citizenship. Feminist standpoint offers an alternative view of the relationship between citizens of particular states and excluded Others. Carol Gilligan, for example, has argued that while the state is not a mother and citizens are not children, nevertheless the ideals of reciprocity inherent in an ethics of care can be used to forge political relationships of mutuality and respect in the midst of particularities, and in so doing has provided a fundamentally different conception of community and citizenship.[32] Taking the profound socio-sexual processes involved in the construction of boundaries between self and Other as a starting point also leads to a critique of rigid notions of autonomy and separation in the construction of identities and boundaries, emphasizing instead interdependence and connectedness.[33] The reconception of key concepts in IR, such as autonomy and power, constituted the basis of Ann Tickner's feminist revision of security.[34] Similarly, centring women's experiences of conflict that are usually marginalized or omitted in mainstream approaches to security provides a starting point for developing a feminist standpoint. As is evident from the discussion in the previous chapter, this would involve addressing all types of violence, including violence in gender relations.

National security/women's security

A second feminist approach to security starts out from the particular problems and insecurities experienced by many women, addressing the wider social impact of military expenditure. Some feminist economists have been concerned to demonstrate that military expenditure imposes particular costs on women as a group. Since one of the most prominent feminist strategies has been to push women towards equal economic opportunities, access to jobs, equal wages, similar career possibilities and equal economic protection in the form of pensions, unemployment insurance and so on, it is pertinent to ask what impact does military expenditure have on women in all of these areas.

During the 1980s, at the height of the second Cold War, perceptions of 'threat' from the hostile communist 'Other' dominated national security debates. Billions of dollars were poured into the United States military. In 1984 there were approximately 200,000 women in the US military involved in active duty forces. In 1985 42 per cent of all enlisted women were black. That is four times the proportion of all American women. It is clear that women who joined up did so because they saw it as a way of improving their social position and benefiting from the economic rewards attached to military service.

However, feminists argued that the statistical evidence could be read in a completely different light. It could well be that the militarization of American society was, on the one hand, opening up new opportunities for women to enter the military but, on the other hand, it was increasing the vulnerability of precisely those women who were precariously positioned in the economic system.[35] Between 1980 and 1985, increased military spending had a big impact on welfare and social spending as domestic social programmes and support to low-income families, often female-headed, was drastically cut. The feminization of poverty became a significant phenomenon with 34.6 per cent of all female-headed households falling into the official category of 'poor'. This figure increased to 50 per cent among black and Hispanic female-headed families.

Beneria and Blank's work demonstrated how women as low-paid workers and single mothers were less likely than working-class men to derive benefit from increased military spending. Outside of the number of people directly employed by the military, military expenditure had an impact on the number of people hired to work in factories that produced military hardware. Military expenditure also had an impact on the amount of resources diverted from other areas of the economy because expenditure on weapons did not have the same 'multiplier' effect as expenditure in other areas. That is, military spending did not transmit economic growth to other areas of economy in the way that expenditure on other goods did. Thus the renewed arms race in the early 1980s exacerbated the economic insecurity of women.[36] Even where women found employment in the 'military industrial complex', they were frequently paid less than men and had less job security than men in the same industry.[37]

Feminists have drawn attention to the costs of high levels of military expenditure to women across the world. Feminist economists argued that increased expenditure on the military, either directly or indirectly, was defeating the aims of the wider feminist movement to improve the status and position, health, welfare and security of women as a group. Beyond the United States, it was even more evident that high spending on militaries, arms and military research was a gender issue. At an international level, rising military expenditures put countries under severe strain. The higher the levels of military expenditure worldwide, the less resources were spent on food and welfare. Feminist economists argued that this illustrated the need for a broader social analysis of the effects of military expenditure on women as a whole.[38]

Feminists also argued that the transfer of resources from the military to the civilian sector of the economy would in all countries reap social and economic benefits for all people, but especially women. Resources devoted to arms expenditure could be spent on health, education and development, and in this way the most vulnerable people would derive immediate benefits. For example, the amount of resources devoted to the research and development of weaponry, all in the name of national security, also strongly affected the overall pattern of scientific research. It was argued that women's health needs in particular would be better served by scientific research concerned with the development of nutritional supplements and safe methods of family planning than on armaments. Furthermore, the massive use of resources and capital to fund the military depleted the resources available to support social, health and education spending.[39]

In the early twenty-first century, at a global level, conflicts are on the increase. In 1960, there were estimated to be ten major wars under way. By 1992, this figure had risen to 50, ten of which had started since 1985. Over the last century, conflicts have followed a disturbing trend, with the increasing involvement and killing of civilians. The escalating violence has been interpreted by some as more than a temporary interruption to development, a sign that development and the assumption of the universality of social progress on which it rests are in crisis.[40] Arms transfers do not cause wars, but they do exacerbate conflict and divert vital resources from development projects that would benefit the world's poorest peoples. Countries that go to war may have legitimate security needs, but the costs of meeting these needs often have a huge impact on the provision of goods and services such as education and health care in developing countries. For example, seven developing countries currently spend more on military than on health and education combined: Oman, Syria, Burma, Sudan, Pakistan, Eritrea and Burundi. Fourteen developing countries spend more on the military than on both health and education taken individually: Saudi Arabia, Jordan, Turkey, Sri Lanka, Iran, Cambodia, China, Ecuador, Nigeria, Rwanda, Angola, Guinea-Bissau, Ethiopia, Sierra Leone. Twelve developing countries spend more on the military than on either education or health: Macedonia, Laos, Morocco, Lebanon, Egypt, India, Armenia, Zimbabwe, Uganda, Yemen, Cameroon and Nepal.[41]

The UN Charter requires all member states to 'promote universal respect for, and observance of, human rights and freedoms' in order to achieve 'economic and social progress and development' and 'to promote the establishment and maintenance of international peace and security with the least diversion for armaments of the world's human and economic resources'.[42] Many states have also ratified the International Covenant on Economic, Social and Cultural Rights that commits signatories to contribute to the progressive realization of these rights through international assistance and cooperation. The United Nations recognizes that women make a significant contribution to development (see the following chapter). For example, the literacy of women is an important key to improving health, nutrition and education in the family. However, gender disparities in economic power-sharing are a significant contributing factor to the poverty of women. The Women's International League for Peace and Freedom has suggested that global military activity may be the most serious worldwide polluter and consumer of precious resources. This is compounded by the fact that poverty is induced and increased by high levels of government expenditure on weapons and the arms trade. The debt crisis in the 1980s was in part caused by Third World expenditure on arms, in spite of the desperate need for development.[43]

The Millennium Development Goals (MDGs) agreed in September 2000 by all 189 UN member states commit the international community to halving extreme poverty and hunger, universal primary education, reducing child mortality and promoting gender equality and the empowerment of women. The target for achieving these goals is 2015. However, this target has little hope of being met while resources are diverted from this task by inappropriate arms transfers.[44] By 1994, it was estimated that one-fifth of the developing world's debt was due to arms imports. The 1993 Organization for Security and Cooperation in Europe (OSCE) *Principles Governing Conventional Arms Transfers*, the 2000 OSCE Document on *Small Arms and Light Weapons* and the 2002 Wassenaar Arrangement *Best Practice Guidelines for Small Arms and Light Weapons* all set out the foundations for taking sustainable development into account in arms transfers. However, in very many cases exporting governments are failing to respect the commitments they have made. In 2002, arms deliveries to Asia, the Middle East, Latin America and Africa constituted 66.7 per cent of the value of all arms deliveries worldwide, with a monetary value of nearly US$17 bn. The five permanent members of the United Nations Security Council accounted for 90 per cent of those deliveries.[45] James Wolfensohn, the former president of the World Bank, has argued that there is a 'fundamental imbalance' with the world spending US$900 bn on defence and only US$325 bn on agricultural subsidies and US$50 bn–US$60 bn on aid. The countries of Africa, Latin America, Asia and the Middle East hold 51 per cent of the world's heavy weapons.[46]

Security Council Resolution 1325

Women's political activism at the United Nations (covered in greater detail in chapters 7, 8 and 9) has fostered a greater awareness of the specific kinds of violence that women suffer both in times of war and in post-conflict situations. Women's groups and feminist movements have made significant progress in elevating violence against women to a global issue. As the UN Secretary-General Kofi Annan declared, violence against women is 'perhaps the most shameful human rights violation. It knows no boundaries of geography, culture or wealth. As long as it continues, we cannot claim to be making real progress towards equality, development, and peace.'[47]

While there is some way to go before feminist perspectives are integrated into the thinking of the UN, rape is now recognized as a political act rather than an act of individual transgression and this has led to the recognition of rape as a war crime.[48] The Outcome Document of the Beijing Plus 5 Review, which took place in New York in 2000 (further discussed in chapter 8), was presented as a triumph in so far as it represented a 'hard-won consensus' to criminalize violence against women and saw measures to strengthen the prohibition of violence against women. The Outcome Document strengthened the language of Beijing Platform for Action (BPA) in a number of specific issue areas and called on governments to take comprehensive measures to eliminate violence against women in whatever form it took.

During the period 1998–9, the sections of the BPA dealing with violence against women in post-conflict situations began to be implemented and the Special Committee on Peacekeeping Operations took on board the requirement to mainstream a gender perspective into all activities and strategies concerning conflict prevention, conflict resolution and peacekeeping. Recent UN initiatives spurned by Security Council Resolution 1325 along with the Secretary-General's Report on 'Women, Peace and Security' have led to concrete measures to eliminate violence against women, including a detailed review of the impact of armed conflict on women and girls, suggesting that there is now a growing awareness at least of the particular problems that women face in both conflict and post-conflict situations.[49]

In relation to peacekeeping, the UN code of conduct has provided a useful tool for deterring violations, but more measures are needed. Christine Corrin has argued that translating international resolutions into legislation and training can challenge and change the realities of violence suffered by women, but this in itself is an enormous task. Agendas for mainstreaming can become sidetracked by training exercises that do not always recognize the political issues of changing power relations between women and men.[50] Moreover, it is evident that women and children continue to be exposed to persistent violence in times of crisis, despite having the protection of international humanitarian law.

Corrin argues that the under-resourcing of NGOs on the ground is also an impediment to progress. Resources devoted to addressing women's needs and interests remain negligently low.[51] In unequal power situations, women's interests and needs are likely to be continually marginalized. Problems also remain with regard to how women and women's groups are incorporated into strategies to address violence against women in a variety of contexts. The work of grass roots organizations made up of local women is vital to the success of mainstreaming strategies in conflict situations, conflict resolution and peacekeeping. Yet, such groups are not always centrally involved in policy and decision-making. For example, Corrin argues that few Kosovo women were involved in decision-making and even fewer appointed to key decision-making positions in the wake of the conflict. Moreover, no account was taken of their participation in wartime (at home and in refugee camps) or their key involvement in reconstruction processes locally and regionally.[52]

HUMAN SECURITY

It was stated above that critical security studies have problematized the dominant conception of identities and boundaries characteristic of traditional approaches to security. This in turn has generated new visions of security that are sensitive to questions of race, ethnic identity, political status, class and, of course, gender and to problems of poverty, inequality, development and the denial of human rights. It is not just within academic discourse that state-centric conceptions of security have been challenged. The concept of human security has been very influential in the policy-making at the United Nations.[53] As the name implies, human security embraces people as a whole. The achievement of human security necessitates building new institutions to provide security for 'human society'. This has been articulated in narrow terms as the need to provide an adequate level of food, health care and other social and economic resources to meet basic needs. A more expansive conception of human security goes beyond a basic needs approach, to include all that is needed to live a dignified life as a human being, beyond the minimum needed for survival.[54]

Gender inequality and security/insecurity

When security is viewed outside the nation-state context and in terms of the multiple insecurities that people face, the argument that what is really needed is a global perspective on security becomes persuasive. Neoliberal discourses on globalization stress the benefits of open trade and market competition in spreading wealth and increasing welfare around the world. However, in the drive to secure profits, the 'benefits' and 'opportunities' of globalization have not been shared equally. Consequently, globalization has resulted in 'a grotesque polarisation between peoples'.[55]

Increasingly International Relations scholars are turning their attention to the security implications of resource depletion, global warming and other ecological 'threats' to the survival of human kind.[56] Constructing global conceptions of security, therefore, involves some engagement with global political economy and development processes. Problems of ecological degradation are inextricably linked to poverty and maldevelopment. Often environmental degradation and resource depletion are presented as problems caused by overpopulation and poverty among 'backward' Third World states. The poverty and maldevelopment of much of the so-called Third World cannot be separated from the wider global political and economic context. Similarly, the achievement of peace, economic justice and ecological sustainability is inseparable from overcoming social relations of domination wherever and however they are manifested.

Nowhere can the linkages between gender inequality, poverty and security/insecurity be more graphically illustrated than in the unfolding tragedy of HIV/AIDS in Africa. It is now recognized that there is a direct correlation between the low status of women and the violation of women's human rights and the transmission of HIV/AIDS. The results of ongoing research indicate that cultural practices and beliefs are important in understanding aspects of the HIV/AIDS pandemic. For example, culture goes some way in explaining why Africa is the only region in the world where more women than men are infected by HIV/AIDS. The failure of governments to address head-on issues of gender inequality has also been cited as reason why it has proved so difficult to halt the spread of HIV/AIDS. However, social and cultural practices and governmental failures by no means fully explain the extent of the problem in Africa – and elsewhere – or why it is women are disproportionately affected. The statistical link between gender and poverty is compelling. Of the estimated one billion people across the world living in abject poverty, the majority are women. Poverty combined with gender inequality has a huge impact on the nutritional status of women and children that is also a crucial factor in the HIV/AIDS pandemic.[57]

Food security

Women are vital providers of security for whole communities, a fact that is evidenced by UN initiatives that make gender central to our understanding of food security.

Access to food is crucial in ensuring human security, but in many parts of the world finding enough food to eat is part of the struggle of everyday existence. There is considerable evidence that during times of food scarcity it is women and children who suffer most. However, hunger is not so much a consequence of under-supply, but a consequence of the way that food is distributed and of problems of access or entitlement.[58] The move to cash-crop production and export-led growth, often as a condition of structural adjustment, has sometimes decreased the levels of food available to local populations (see chapter 6). Environmental degradation is similarly tied up with structural adjustment, which often increases pressures on land use, encouraging the exploitation of marginal land.

According to FAO estimates women produce more than 50 per cent of the food grown worldwide. In addition to their crucial roles in food production, women contribute to food security in other ways. For example, efforts to protect biodiversity necessitate the inclusion of women since it is generally women who process and prepare food. Women also provide for the basic needs of the household in their capacity as wage earners. As will be further elaborated in the following chapter, when women have direct control over income, they tend to spend it on the well-being of the family, particularly on improving the nutritional security of the more vulnerable members.[59] Recognition by the international community has taken the form of initiatives like the United Nations' World Food Programme, which has the declared intention of making food a more effective tool for women's advancement and improved employment prospects and health.[60]

Jeanne Vickers has argued that the very worst consequences of an insecure and militarized world are felt by that particular group long recognized by the international community to be central to achieving a genuinely secure world: women. According to Vickers, authentic food security depends to a large extent on women who are responsible for 80 per cent of all agricultural production in developing countries, yet own hardly any land, find it difficult to get loans and frequently are overlooked by agricultural advisers and projects.[61] It is precisely in these areas that the UN is concerned to bring about change. V. Spike Peterson and Ann Sisson Runyan also point to UN initiatives as important in recognizing women not as 'victims' but as having a role to play in achieving security through development.[62]

Human rights approaches

Ultimately human rights are based on a particular conception of human dignity and a belief in the inherent moral worth of individual human beings. When human rights are made central to security, the focus of the debate about security shifts away from state survival, towards the promotion and protection of human dignity. There is a long history of liberal thought and internationalist sentiment within International Relations which has stressed the need to transcend 'power politics' and govern relations between peoples on the basis of moral principles and according to what is 'right' and 'just'. This has in turn led to the promotion of international law, international institutions and human rights.

Many liberals take the individual as a bearer of rights as the fundamental referent of security. Liberals believe that, irrespective of race, gender, class, religion, ethnicity or nationality, human beings have basic human rights. Liberals often argue that we cannot achieve truly comprehensive and global security, either in theory or in practice, unless we recognize that security is fundamentally a question of human rights. Indeed in a global age when the nation-state as the basic form of political community is subject to multiple challenges, human rights might be the only fruitful way of approaching security.

States are obliged to uphold and advance human rights. These obligations arise ultimately from Article 1 of the UN Charter and subsequent conventions on civil and political rights and economic and social rights. Liberals believe that all people have a basic right to life, liberty and the pursuit of happiness and so maintain that civil and political rights should be viewed as basic human rights. Many liberals support the view that all human beings need economic and social security and so these things should be recognized as fundamental human rights too. However, while virtually every state in the world has accepted that people do have human rights in principle, just which categories of 'rights' should be recognized as 'human rights' has been the subject of intense political, ideological and, more recently, religious and cultural conflict.

Liberal feminists too stress the importance of not only civil and political rights, but also economic and social rights in achieving security, and have argued that women's human rights must be recognized as central to achieving genuine security. Article 1.3 of the UN Charter pledges states to promote human rights without respect to race, ethnicity or sex. In more recent years there have been more systematic attempts to codify the human rights of women. Women's human rights are the subject of chapter 8 and so will not be covered in detail here; suffice to say that there are objections to the human rights approach to women's security, including the objection that human rights are based upon rational interest, egoism and the defence of property, and that non-Western traditions which see the individual as part of the social whole and emphasize human dignity and development are more fruitful starting points for developing alternative conceptions of security.

People-centred approaches

There are affinities between feminist revisions and 'people-centred approaches' to security. People-centred approaches argue for the equal importance of all people and their security needs and stress the importance of focusing on the collectivities in which people are embedded. Feminists engaged in the project of challenging state-centric and militarized conceptions of security have also taken the specific circumstances of people, rather than 'citizens', as a starting point for thinking about security. People-centred approaches are able to show how when the 'person' is a woman, gender hierarchies and inequalities in power constitute a major source of domination and obstacles to the achievement of genuine security. Ken Booth has argued that we cannot have comprehensive security until people, rather than citizens, are recognized as the primary subject of security.[63] This approach does not, however, view the individual in abstract terms as the bearer of rights, but rather in social and cultural contexts. Threats to the 'person' are viewed in the context of membership of collectivities. To focus on the person is not to suggest that all people are equally vulnerable, however. Indeed the strength of this approach is that it simultaneously highlights the equal importance of all people and their security needs regardless of race, class, gender or formal political status and highlights the multiple sources of insecurity which particular groups of people face according to their specific circumstances.

People in general and women in particular are not only vulnerable to the threat of direct violence, but also indirect or structural violence. Structural violence occurs where the economic insecurity of individuals is such that their life expectancy is reduced. Structural violence consists of the denial of food and economic security to the degree that the health and well-being of the individual is jeopardized. While structural violence affects poor people irrespective of gender, poor women and girls tend to suffer most. In poor countries, when there is a squeeze on already scarce resources, women and girls are first to feel that squeeze and feel it most keenly.[64]

CONCLUSION

Adopting feminist perspectives on security not only challenges the view of the military as a defender of a pre-given 'national interest' but also suggests that the degree to which people feel or actually are 'threatened' varies according to their economic, political, social or personal circumstances. Rethinking security, therefore, involves thinking about militarism and patriarchy, maldevelopment and environmental degradation. It involves thinking about the relationship between poverty, debt and population growth. It involves thinking about resources and how they are distributed. It is to some of these issues that the discussion now turns.

THE GENDER DIMENSION OF INTERNATIONAL POLITICAL ECONOMY

INTRODUCTION

In chapter 5, poverty, inequality, maldevelopment and the denial of human rights, or at least basic needs, were identified as central to understanding how secure or insecure people feel or actually are, according to their specific circumstances. It follows, therefore, that the study of gender in IR must necessarily embrace the dynamics of international political economy; that is, systems of production, the distribution of resources, how wealth is spread across national boundaries and the linkages between international, national and local economies.[1] The study of International Political Economy (IPE) covers both the domain of economics, the system of producing, distributing and using wealth and the realm of politics, 'the set of institutions and rules by which social and economic interactions are governed'.[2] The International Monetary Fund, the World Bank and the World Trade Organization are influential actors in international affairs and so the decision-making processes and policies of these bodies are relevant to this domain of study. Moreover, the activities of multinational corporations that engage in production and exchange activities in many different countries and NGOs are of interest to IPE scholars.

Feminist scholars who work on international political economy are similarly concerned with the interplay of economics and politics in world affairs. However, feminists argue that activity that takes place in the household or private domain is also economically significant, while politics is understood as the exercise of power broadly conceived and includes (gendered) power relations within both the public and private domains. Feminist international political economy includes a critique of mainstream approaches. In the first part of this chapter, feminist critiques of the mainstream once again serve as a point of departure. This section also introduces the key ideas and concerns of feminist IPE and outlines the main feminist approaches in IPE. In the middle section of this chapter, feminist analyses are further developed and applied in the study of contemporary globalization. The third section of this chapter focuses specifically on development.

Making gender visible

The first feminist works in IPE were mainly concerned with highlighting the processes of marginalization or exclusion inherent in key concepts and conceptual mapping processes in mainstream texts. Hitherto, much of the work that had been done in IPE not only conceptualized the economic realm as separate from the political sphere, but also posited a clear separation between the economy and the social and familial realm. This was based on a 'common-sense' view of what constituted 'political' and 'economic' activity. As Christine Sylvester argued, there was 'a hidden gender to the field that affects how we think about empirical political economy'.[3] By concentrating on the impersonal structures of states and markets, it was not possible to see how women's activities have been demoted to the private sphere. Moreover, the way the field of IPE was constructed rendered invisible 'a set of social and economic relations characterised by inequality between men and women'.[4]

This invisibility was a consequence of the way in which distinctions had been drawn between public and private activities. Approaches that focused on the interactions between states and markets drew a clear distinction between public activities, centred on the production of goods and services that were sold in local, national and international markets and purchased by individuals, families or economic enterprises, and private activities carried out within the domain of the family and the home. In economics, for example, the household was often taken to be the basic unit of consumption, rather than a unit of production. Familial relations were not included within the purview of analysis.

A major problem in mainstream IPE highlighted by feminist scholars was the invisibility of unpaid labour. With the rise of the modern state and the birth of capitalist market economies, the public/private divide was drawn in such a way that the public world of work and the 'informal economy' of the home and domestic labour came to be seen as clearly separated. Participation in the labour force and the inclusion of production in measurements of global economic activity was defined only in relation to the market, or to the performance of work for pay or profit. The construct of the housewife worked to privatize women's work and disguise the economic significance of housework by constructing this activity as not 'real work'.[5] One might add that it was also impossible to see that women and men entered into the formal economy as bearers of a gender identity. Thus, as Ann Tickner pointed out, ignoring gender distinctions hid a set of social and economic relations characterized by inequalities of power.[6]

While IPE had largely been confined to telling stories about 'men, states and markets',[7] feminist analysis in international political economy sought to develop new definitions of the 'economic' and the 'political'. This was not simply an academic issue. Feminist work developed alongside campaigns by activists in the women's movement to accord proper value to work in the home.[8] Furthermore, the exclusion or invisibility of gender had concrete consequences in so far as the exclusion of unremunerated work and the person performing it (usually a woman) distorted the data that was used in the policy-making process, especially, though not exclusively, in relation to development policies.

The feminist economist Marilyn Waring argued that policy makers only accorded value to those activities that were marketable. Consequently, the impact of cuts in public spending that worked to shift the burden of care back to the 'community' resulted in an additional burden for women, who were already working up to 18 hours a day, on tasks that were both paid and unpaid. Women not only bore a 'double burden' of paid and unpaid work, but also suffered the insult that their contribution was not recognized and their problems were not addressed in policies ostensibly designed to help 'workers' and 'carers'. Waring argued that this pointed to the need to rethink commonly used concepts such as Gross Domestic Product to take into account the contribution that women's work made to wealth generation and also to the welfare of communities.[9]

Distinctions between what is considered public and what is thought to be private are deeply embedded in the 'common sense' of everyday life, particularly in western societies. There is a tendency to forget that the line between the public and the private can be and has been drawn in different ways and is apt to shift as certain issues and activities are politicized and de-politicized in different societies and in different historical periods. For example, conflicts over access to resources or income between husbands and wives in the home are not generally held to be 'political' even though the distribution of resources and income can generate conflict between family members and has real consequences for the material well-being of men and women.

Feminist critiques of mainstream approaches

If the first aim of feminist IPE was to make gender visible, a second aim was to raise ontological, epistemological and methodological questions and issues in the field. As one might expect from the earlier discussion of theory and methods within the social sciences and IR particularly (see chapter 2), feminists have challenged the supposed 'objectivity' of knowledge claims and 'value-free' theories in IPE. In what was at the time an influential work, Roger Tooze and Craig Murphy highlighted the problems inherent in rationalist and positivist approaches to IPE that shut off any discussion of ontological, epistemological and methodological questions in the field.[10] As elaborated elsewhere in this text, critical theorists – in the broad sense of the term – start out from the position that the subjectivity of the social science should be recognized and historical modes of analysis and explanation encouraged. In this way, the importance of the subject, who positions herself or himself politically, assesses the social and political significance of institutions and practices and infuses her or his own actions with social and political meaning, is made central to our understanding of 'theory'.

Ann Tickner argued that one should be wary of the gender bias of the model of 'Rational Economic Man' that underpinned both neorealist and neoliberal institutionalist analyses in IPE.[11] Sylvester similarly claimed that the rationality assumption prominent in mainstream IPE derived from the deep, unexamined cultural expectation that men were supposed to be motivated by calculations of instrumental interests.[12] The concept of rational man or, more specifically, 'Rational Economic Man' was based on the idea that the individual human being was a rational, self-interested, maximizer of utility. This ignored the role of human emotions and feeling as motivating factors in human behaviour.[13] 'Rational Economic Man' was a construct that extrapolated from behaviour associated with bourgeois man and was then used to represent humanity as a whole.[14]

The construct of 'Rational Economic Man' was first evoked as the basis for liberal explanations of the workings of the economy and appeared with the rise of capitalism, when a variety of human passions were subordinated to a desire for economic gain.[15] As Tickner argued, this was also a time when definitions of 'male' and 'female' nature and social roles were constructed around the division between 'work' and 'home'.[16] In raising epistemological issues concerning the association of reason with knowledge and reason/knowledge with the masculine, feminist IPEs sought to introduce gendered subjects and gendered subjectivities into IPE and thus challenge the 'states and markets' orientation of much IPE scholarship.[17]

Feminist scholars argued that there was an urgent need to develop new theoretical and conceptual tools of analysis and identify possible new research trajectories that would elucidate the gendered nature of political economy.[18] To remedy the deficiencies and pitfalls of positivism and rationalism, Tickner advocated alternative understandings of the field that were not 'embedded in a masculine epistemology'.[19] Tickner believed that feminist analysis could and should go 'beyond an investigation of market relations, state behaviour and capitalism' to 'understand how the global economy affects those on the fringes of the market, the state or in households'.[20] Tickner was explicit about the normative goal of feminist IPE: 'to build a more secure world where inequalities based on gender and other forms of discrimination were eliminated.'[21]

FEMINIST APPROACHES IN IPE

As one might anticipate from the earlier discussion of the diversity in feminist thought, there is no singular feminist approach in IPE. The differences between feminisms are set out at length in chapter 1 and will be only briefly revisited here. Liberal feminists are primarily concerned with locating women empirically within the field.[22] While limited in scope, empirical research on women in the world economy has uncovered significant inequalities between men and women in terms of rates of pay and command and control of financial resources generally. Gender makes a difference in terms of job security or insecurity and in experiences of discrimination in the workplace. Marxist feminists concentrate on gender inequalities that are embedded in international political economy.[23] Marxist feminists emphasize the role of material structures in supporting and reproducing unequal social relations. Gender inequality is seen to have its roots in the 'privatization' of women's productive and reproductive labour power, the control of women's sexuality and the subordination of women to male authority through a range of patriarchal institutions. From this perspective gender is understood as a social relationship of inequality that is sustained and reproduced in the material relations that exist between men and women and also by states and international institutions that formulate and implement policies relating to social security, welfare and pensions, inheritance, labour legislation, taxation and so on. Critical feminists are similarly concerned to analyse 'how female subordination is created and sustained both nationally and internationally'.[24] However, more emphasis is placed on ideas and ideologies that value men more highly than women, and that justify and perpetuate gender inequalities.

Poststructuralist feminists focus on the ideational realm in IPE.[25] While discourses on gender matter in so far as they will influence the distribution of resources and power in specific societies, one should not work from a prior assumption that women are always disadvantaged since dominant understandings of gender might confer a certain amount of social power on women in specific societies. Much poststructuralist feminist scholarship eschews 'grand theory' in favour of local studies and cross-cultural analyses of patriarchy, focusing on the complex and historical interplay of sex, race and class. In addition, rather than stressing common interests among women, poststructuralist IPE highlights the instability of female – and indeed male – identities and the active creation and recreation of women's needs. Gender must be 'read contextually since gender relations and their representations refer always to other social and cultural relations that are embedded in particular histories and geographical places'.[26] In so far as it is increasingly difficult for people to live in any place that is socially, economically and culturally isolated from the wider world, poststructuralist IPE has an international or global dimension. Poststructuralist feminists working in the field have also produced insightful work on the construction of knowledge in IPE, exposing the gendered imagery that is used to construct the meaning of 'order' and 'chaos' in relation to global financial markets, for example.[27]

GENDER AND GLOBAL RESTRUCTURING

IPE and globalization

International Political Economy necessarily engages with debates concerning globalization. Globalization has no privileged disciplinary context and no one commonly accepted definition, but it is widely agreed that the concept refers to a number of dynamic processes that have collectively combined to produce an ongoing, worldwide interconnectedness.[28] Economic globalization particularly has facilitated trade and investment flows and this, combined with the growing sophistication of computers and telecommunications, allows financial actors to operate in markets across the globe. In consequence, it is increasingly difficult for states to successfully regulate international financial markets.[29] Globalization has been held to have led to a 'rolling back' of the state and the retreat of the welfare state specifically.[30] The expansion of communication technology has also facilitated the growth of transnational pressure groups and policy-networks as non-governmental organizations have forged links to policy makers in national governments and international institutions.[31]

A number of commentators have noted the continuities between contemporary globalization and the earlier period of the expansion of modernity and capitalism, a process driven initially by colonialism and imperialism.[32] In the post-Second World War period, modernization strategies, adopted by national governmental elites in developing countries across the world and by international development agencies and the World Bank, typically sought to promote industrialization, technological innovation, consumerism and a move to market economies. As elaborated below, in recent years, the move to market economies has been encouraged through neoliberal ideologies that stress the benefits of unfettered markets.

In the so-called 'first wave' of literature, there was a tendency to universalize the concept of globalization.[33] Globalization was understood to have uniform and similar effects across the world. The second and third waves of the globalization literature have, however, paid more attention to the uneven impacts of globalization and stressed the specificity of different forms or modes of capitalism within the context of an overarching global framework. The contemporary literature is also much more likely to emphasize the 'various processes that interact – often in highly complex and contingent ways – to produce the phenomena variously referred to as economic, political, social and cultural globalization'.[34] This literature has produced more detailed empirical studies that have revealed uneven and differential impacts across countries,[35] on rural and urban populations and on specific social groups. In the contemporary literature on globalization, more emphasis has been placed on 'discursive or ideational processes in the mediation of globalising tendencies'.[36]

Marianne Marchand and Ann Sisson Runyan prefer to employ the term 'global restructuring', rather than globalization, because this term conveys more powerfully a series of dynamic and interrelated economic and political processes that have worked to generate both structural transformations in the global economy and changes in internationalized social relations. Certainly, the increasing influence of transnational corporations, the growing complexity of the global division of labour and the intimate relationship between debt, development and environmental degradation are all integral parts of the ongoing process of interconnectedness characteristic of 'globalization'.[37]

The first phase of global restructuring can be traced to the 1973 oil crisis when big companies in the West resorted to international subcontracting to survive. In the wake of the second oil crisis in the late 1970s, many enterprises in the North, who faced large increases in production costs, combined with economic recession in many western markets, introduced new forms of technology in the production process to save on labour costs, or began to shift the labour-intensive parts of production process to the global South where labour was cheap. In the 1980s, as big business emphasized the importance of managerial flexibility and decentralized production, corporate strategies in the West sought a more flexible workforce to undermine the power of trade unions.[38] However, the knowledge-intensive parts of the production process remained located in the West.[39]

Following the breakdown of the Bretton Woods system, there was a shift towards the adoption of neoliberal or neo-classical economic policies across the world, although the degree and extent to which this occurred varied from region to region and between countries. Neoliberalism places emphasis on the deregulation of markets, particularly labour markets (achieved by weakening the influence of organized labour) and export-led growth strategies, in generating economic growth and development. The shift to export-led growth strategies and policies to attract inward investment led to the setting up of Export Production Zones or Export Processing Zones and Free Trade Zones in many developing countries. The shift to export-led growth strategies, along with the privatization of sectors of the economy previously under state control and efforts to attract new foreign investment, combined to create investment opportunities for multinational corporations, particularly in the global South.[40]

In the wake of the collapse of communism, developing countries – or at least dominant elites within developing countries – perceived 'no alternative' to western capitalism and increasingly adopted neoliberal or neoclassical growth strategies. In the former Soviet Union and throughout Eastern Europe there was a move to market economies, while in India and Pakistan and China, an ostensibly 'communist' state, economic policy became increasingly directed towards trade liberalization and market-led economic reforms. Similarly throughout Africa and the Middle East, more countries moved to market economies because this was seen (by elites at least) as a route out of poverty.[41] Many developing countries were keen to attract new jobs and investment, believing that the arrival of multinational corporations (MNCs) heralded the dawn of new opportunities for economic growth and development.[42]

Gendering globalization

Feminist scholars have investigated 'the interconnected material, ideological and discursive dimensions of globalisation' and offered 'more complex sightings or conceptual renderings of global restructuring'.[43] As such, feminist scholarship has made a considerable contribution to the contemporary globalization literature. Again, there is no one feminist approach to globalization, but all feminist IPE scholars share 'a commitment to a broader definition of globalisation than a narrowly economic one that can include the social, cultural and ideational dimension'.[44]

Feminists have produced empirical work that has highlighted the changing experiences of women and men in local, national and global labour markets. Swasti Mitter has claimed that restructuring in the 1980s had a profound effect on the composition of the workforce. The process encouraged the growth of a 'new proletariat' in both the North and South, with women ghettoized in assembly-line work with poor pay and prospects. The 'feminization' of the workforce was a significant phenomenon in many regions of the North previously characterized by heavy industry. Mitter argued that in areas where traditionally unionized industries such as coal and steel had previously thrived, the male workforce frequently had a reputation for radicalism. For this reason, employers in growth industries preferred to employ the wives and daughters of, for example, ex-miners and ex-steelworkers.[45]

In the 1980s big business also invested more and more in hi-tech research and automation and computer-integrated manufacturing systems. This investment was aimed at replacing skilled labour. However, in some labour-intensive industries it was not always cost-effective to invest heavily in technology. This was particularly the case where there was a supply of cheap female labour because women made the most flexible robots of all.[46] In both Europe and North America, in the garment industry, for example, employers who felt threatened by the restructuring of the global economy but who could not relocate abroad moved to feminize their workforce and this resulted in the re-emergence of sweatshops and home-working.[47] This phenomenon was replicated in a number of other industries, including electronics, toy manufacturing and food processing.

Nevertheless, 'masculinity' continued to be identified with the claims of 'breadwinner' status, and this provided a justification for paying women less, even though male unemployment was actually increasing. Women were frequently paid between 20 and 50 per cent less than men in comparable jobs,[48] a discrepancy justified both by the idea that women and men had innate capabilities and on the grounds that men needed to support families but women did not. Pearson and Elson argue that women's role in the family is socially constructed as a subordinate role. Females do the work that is required to nurture children and men, work that appears private and personal, while men represent women and children in the wider society. It is this representative role that confers social power on men. The gendering of the breadwinner role as essentially male means that it is easier to dismiss women workers in times of crisis. Flexible workers who are absorbed in phases of expansion can be thrown back into dependency when crisis sets in. Women are the cheapest and most vulnerable of the waged labour force and are thus open to high levels of exploitation. Thus, the organization of global production depends upon a multifaceted power structure and the profitability of mobile global capital continues to thrive on the politics of class and gender.[49]

A further significant aspect of global restructuring in the 1980s was the increasing numbers of part-time and home-workers. The rise in home-working in the West was also a direct manifestation of 'flexible-manning' business strategies. Mitter and van Luijken claimed that women constituted the majority of home-workers, because everywhere women constituted the poorest sections of society. They claimed that there was a marked similarity between home-working and housework. These activities were largely performed by women and remained invisible. However labelling home-working the 'informal sector' of the economy misrepresented the numbers involved. It was not outside or parallel to the formal sector, but was rather an integral part of the global market economy.[50]

As the least unionized and poorest paid of all workers, women were particularly vulnerable to the market policies that characterized global economic restructuring in the 1990s. Where women were encouraged to take up roles in the paid sector, it was still the case that on average they earned 30–40 per cent less than men for comparable work. In transition economies, there was evidence that women in particular lost their jobs as these economies 'adjusted' to the rigours of the global marketplace. Women also took up the burden of care that results from cuts in the social sectors.

In developing countries, women were heavily concentrated among the labour force in Export Production Zones. The centrepiece of IMF strategies in the 1980s and 1990s was export-led growth combined with 'structural adjustment'. Governments set aside territory specifically for the use of factories producing goods for the global market. In Asia, in the 1980s, women made up 85 per cent of workers in Export Production Zones. In other areas, the figure for women workers was typically around 75 per cent.[51] So, while the shift to Export Production increased employment opportunities for women, women were employed on less favourable terms than men, enjoyed less job security and were more likely to encounter problems of harassment and unfair dismissal. For example, it was not uncommon for women workers to be dismissed if they fell pregnant.[52] While there is some evidence that the 1990s saw a 'remasculinization' of the workplace,[53] women remained concentrated in the lowest-paid jobs.

Dianne Elson and Ruth Pearson claim that the provision of women for such jobs was encouraged because it could be viewed as a way of involving women in the development process.[54] World-market factories producing components for the electronics industry, for example, were usually owned or partially owned by subsidiaries of Japanese, North American and European multinationals. These were particularly important in the development of the global trade in consumer goods. When deciding where to locate, a crucial factor was the availability of a suitable labour force, defined in terms of low cost and high productivity. In the twenty-first century women remain the cheapest and most productive of all workers.

Paid employment takes women out of the home, of course, and gives women some measure of independence. However, studies show that many states support an unequal sexual division of labour or sanction below-minimum wages for women workers. Where women do work or earn money income, it does not necessarily create the same sort of power in the household. Allocation mechanisms within the household embody important ideologies that render non-comparable the work that men and women do and the income that they earn. Women's attempts to translate paid employment into financial independence are often thwarted by lack of access to capital, inadequate education and training and because women carry an unequal burden of family responsibilities. Moreover, global restructuring can work to 'privatize' women's labour and, consequently, result in a loss of power and autonomy. As noted above, a phenomenon of contemporary globalization has been the 'rolling back' of the state and welfare services. It has been women who have most often taken up the burden of care that has resulted from such cuts.[55]

Mackintosh argues that the sexual division of labour embeds and further perpetuates female subordination. The gendering of particular social roles is likely to be most rigid in areas crucial to social relations of human reproduction and that generally incorporate male dominance and control of women's sexuality. Once the sexual division of labour is established it takes on a life of its own and creates a national division of labour between men and women that can be exploited by employers. According to Mackintosh, the increase in the part-time and flexible work that is an integral part of the global economy reflects the constraints of women's domestic role and so is an economic expression of the marriage contract.[56] Swasti Mitter similarly argues that the patriarchal values promoted by the state and family in both North and South places women in a position of subjugation. Thus if gender hierarchy and subordination are rooted in the institution of marriage or the privatization of the 'household', they become embedded features of the wider economic structure and, so, the global economy.[57] The specific form taken by the sexual division of labour is perpetually being transformed and recreated as economic and social change occurs, but it is hard to challenge.

As is clear from the earlier discussion of masculine breadwinners and feminine housewives, the ideational dimension is relevant to understanding the differing experiences of male and female workers. The importance of the ideational dimension of globalization is also evidenced in neoliberal discourses on globalization that stress the opportunities that globalization provides. To some degree, women – particularly highly educated, highly skilled women – have been empowered through paid work, gaining access to an independent source of income, for example. However, neoliberal development strategies have generated both 'winners and losers', measured according to income inequality, poverty and access to economic opportunities. Social relations of (gender) inequality are seemingly embedded in and perpetuated by global economic and political processes, allowing women and men's labour to be incorporated and rewarded differently in national economies and in the international economy. Moreover, women often find that opportunities to work only result in a 'double burden' of both paid and unpaid work, or indeed a triple burden if reproductive and care activities are taken into account.[58]

Women might be favoured over men in certain jobs – in textiles or in the microelectronics industry for example – because women are held to be 'naturally' dexterous, possessing the 'nimble fingers' needed to sew on buttons or process computer chips. However, this perception that women have certain skills or capacities does not necessarily translate into real advantages for women over men because women's skills are defined in an ideologically biased way, that is as natural rather than learnt, and so not rewarded.[59] Even in highly developed OECD economies where 'structural' changes – the decline of heavy industry and manufacturing for example – have seemingly generated new 'opportunities' for women, there exist significant disparities in rates of pay and promotion prospects for men and women respectively.[60]

A further aspect of international political economy that has attracted the interest of feminist scholars has been the rapid growth of sex tourism, or prostitution, often linked to economic transition and the expansion of the tourist industry particularly. As Jacqui True notes, increases in prostitution, trafficking in women and the objectification of women's bodies in a thriving pornography industry have accompanied the move to market economies in the former Eastern bloc.[61] In a number of countries tourism has become an important earner of foreign currency. In Thailand, the Philippines, the Caribbean, West Africa and Brazil, the growing sex industry has been linked closely with the expansion of tourism and inextricably tied to the problems of debt and development strategies.[62] In the Caribbean and Latin America, for example, the impact of the high rates of migration and the drain on resources – both of which have been attributed to structural adjustment – is closely associated with increases in child prostitution and sex tourism, while in the Asian Pacific region the negative impact of structural adjustment and migration is also associated with an increase in the trafficking of women.[63]

Sex tourism does not just involve women, although it is overwhelmingly women who are drawn into this particular form of prostitution – frequently women who have been displaced as a direct consequence of 'development' strategies. Nor can prostitution be viewed as solely driven by the expansion of tourism. Nevertheless it is conditioned by the demands of a stratified global market and the impact of development policies that are themselves conditioned by global economic processes.[64] Truong has suggested that prostitution is itself becoming a globally traded commodity. The growing integration of the tourist industry that links countries, hotel chains and package-holiday firms is a crucial enabling factor that allows spare capacity in airline seats and hotel beds to be matched with the demand for esoteric sexual services. It is, Truong claims, no accident that Bangkok and Manila, both major cities that have experienced massive growth in prostitution in recent years, are also both major centres for multinational corporations and regional centres for global organizations. Increasingly the issue of prostitution needs a global analysis.[65] Enloe argues that sex tourism is both a part of the global political system and the global economy and the fact 'that it is not taken seriously says more about the ideological construction of seriousness than the politics of tourism'.[66]

GENDER IN DEVELOPMENT

As is evident from much of the discussion above, development must be viewed in a global context. In contemporary IPE, rather than imagining the world to consist of a number of separate countries moving in the same direction towards modernization and progress, a single arena of development is now recognized. This is not to say that the local and specific context in which development policies and strategies are formulated and implemented is irrelevant – far from it – but the development process in individual countries is nevertheless profoundly shaped by international institutions and regimes, by trading patterns and global investment flows and also by prevalent ideas about what constitutes 'development'.

Ideas about what constitutes development, and policies ostensibly designed to achieve modernization, are conditioned by dominant ideologies that assume that the western experience provides the model for the 'developing' world. The production of knowledge about 'development' is itself a historical process that is conditioned by the socio-political, economic and cultural context in which it takes place. Historically, 'development' has been driven by dominant western perceptions of the needs and circumstances of people in 'underdeveloped' countries.[67]

After more than four decades of attempts to promote the development or 'modernization' of the poorest countries of the world, many find that their relative prosperity has declined. The world recession that followed the oil crisis in 1973 resulted in both deteriorating terms of trade and fewer trading opportunities that further exacerbated the problems of poorer states. Many Third World states are now so deeply in debt that new loans are devoted almost entirely to the servicing of old ones. At the same time the Third World's share of world trade is steadily falling and in many 'developing states' levels of infant mortality and malnutrition are rising.[68] Much of the blame for the crisis that currently affects many countries has been laid squarely at the door of previous models of development.

There is an extensive literature that has documented the often negative impacts of development on women particularly.[69] Development strategies frequently reflect ignorance about the role of women in many societies and are not sensitive to how prevailing gender relations both influence and are influenced by the impact of development strategies. Ignoring or, at least, misunderstanding the nature and significance of gender in development has meant that, in the past, trickle-down strategies have benefited only those at the top of the social ladder. Since women in all states tend to be clustered at the bottom of the socio-economic scale, falling national income tends to disproportionately affect women. When the household is taken to be the basic 'unit', another kind of bias is introduced. Around the world, approximately one-third of all families are supported by women. As was stated earlier, in many cases assumptions about gender relations and the model of the male breadwinner role have served to deprive women of access to land and resources. The idea that women are dependants can serve to deny women access to pension rights or employment. It might also encourage the view that women should be recipients of welfare rather than incorporated into the policy-making process. Throughout the developing world, but particularly in Africa, women are heavily concentrated in subsistence agriculture. Here, the degree to which women are denied access to land has been highlighted as a significant barrier to women's full participation in development. Even though women are often the main farmers, they are still frequently ignored when development schemes are designed and implemented. It is simply assumed that men, and not women, are farmers. Furthermore, because the value of women's work is overlooked, the introduction of new technologies may not significantly benefit women.[70]

The western assumption of a harmonious family unit also disguises the fact that conflicts of interest can exist within the family group. Men may have very different interests in cash-crop production, for example, and so be willing to sell the rights to forestland to timber merchants. This can deprive women of not only the means to grow food but also the means to provide for their energy requirements. It has been claimed that a major cause of the current crisis in food self-sufficiency that affects many Third World states is a consequence of the neglect of the needs and interests of the majority of women farmers. 'Progressive' farmers are selected for schemes and subsistence farmers are disadvantaged. Since subsistence farmers are often also small traders who produce a surplus for sale, when they are forced out of production the local community loses a vital source of food supply that had previously helped to meet seasonal and regional shortfalls. It is clear that the widespread hunger that exists in many parts of Africa is not simply a consequence of the failure of crops, or cultural practices, but connected to the global power structures and global economic processes.

Structural adjustment policies

Whitworth argues that feminist analyses in IPE should be directed towards an understanding of how hegemonic structures and institutions perpetuate gender relations of inequality.[71] There is now a growing literature on the 'governance' of the international/global economy. Governance refers to a range of institutions and mechanisms of governance that shape the domestic policies of states over a range of issues and areas. The capacity of governments to control events within nation-states has been influenced by the flow of power away from domestic institutions to supranational entities like the IMF and regional bodies like, for example, the European Union. Governance also incorporates an analysis of the networks that link civil society actors (notably NGOs) with formal decision-makers. Governance can be understood in terms of mechanisms, norms, discourses and practices that underpin policies that facilitate globalization.

The debt crisis has much heightened the power of both the IMF and the World Bank in their relationships with developing countries and transitional economies particularly. Indeed, Ankie Hoogvelt has described the IMF as having 'a degree of economic intervention in the debtor countries which has matched, and perhaps exceeded, the direct administration of bygone colonial governments'.[72] The IMF's management strategy in relation to individual indebted countries typically involves new lending and debt rescheduling, combined with domestic austerity programmes. These measures have been operationalized as Structural Adjustment Programmes (SAPs), the main elements of which are privatization, cuts in government spending, tax-cutting measures and the devaluation of national currencies. SAPs rest on a generally optimistic 'Bretton Woods paradigm' that holds that globalization will benefit all and eventually remove poverty. However, there is evidence that SAPs are exacerbating problems of poverty and leading to cuts in education and health care. The overriding impact of structural adjustment has been to undermine efforts to provide for basic needs in many poor countries. Thus, SAPs are also held to undermine the political stability of many developing countries because governments are unable to provide for the basic welfare of their citizens.

A gender analysis of structural adjustment policies illustrates the ways in which the burden falls most heavily upon the most vulnerable groups in society. Female labour is assumed to be 'infinitely elastic', expected to 'stretch', to work harder and for longer hours, in order to compensate for cuts in public services.[73] This takes no account of the way that the sexual division of labour and women's roles within the household constrain their activities within the labour market.[74] Structural adjustment promotes increased efficiency by shifting productive resources into the market sector, and particularly into exports. In reality this approach often simply shifts the cost of care from the paid to the unpaid economy, further exploiting women's unpaid time and labour.

In many developing states, agricultural produce is often the first thing singled out for increased exports. Produce grown for export uses land that could be used to grow food for domestic consumption. Therefore, increased cash-crop production for export frequently leads to increased domestic food shortages. Since women are usually responsible for providing food for children and adult men, women have to deal with the problems of food shortages. Cuts in social expenditure also result in a disproportionate loss of women's jobs.[75]

Micro-finance

The World Bank has played an increasing role in devising and implementing SAPs in developing countries. In recent years, the World Bank has tended to favour micro-credit or micro-finance schemes to overcome the exclusion of poor groups, especially women, from the development process and to go some way towards alleviating global poverty. Micro-credit/finance has been embraced because it is seen as a way of extending financial services to the poor, while also ensuring that development continues to be promoted through largely free-market mechanisms. Micro-credit/finance appeals to both policy makers and NGOs, since both the eradication of poverty and the empowerment of women are identified as core Millennium Development Goals[76] advanced by the United Nations.

Supporters of micro-finance argue that it will generate a '"virtuous upward spiral" of economic, social and political empowerment'.[77] However, research on the impact of micro-credit has uncovered mixed effects with regard to the empowerment of women. On balance, micro-finance programmes appear to have led to some changes in gender roles, increased women's mobility and empowered women to some degree through the increased knowledge they gain of life outside the household.[78] However, critics of micro-credit argue that genuine empowerment requires that gender be mainstreamed in all economic policies, including development policies. Offering poor women only 'micro'-credit serves to perpetuate their marginalization.

The gender politics of governance

There is, of course, opposition to neoliberal globalization. United Nations development agencies have called for 'adjustment with a human face'[79] in which basic levels of education, health care and nutrition are protected, although the UN has fallen some way short of criticizing neoliberal development strategies. Indeed, many developing countries complain that goals agreed at UN conferences on poverty eradication, social progress and equality are undermined by economic liberalization, structural adjustment, debt and a decline in aid flows.

Transnational women's NGOs have challenged the neoliberal economic development paradigm that the IMF and World Bank promote and that, they argue, is responsible for the accelerating rate of female poverty in developing countries particularly. Criticism from the UN and from an increasing number of civil society groups has led to changes in the rhetoric of the World Bank in recent years. Since the Beijing Women's Conference in 1995 (see chapters 7 and 8), the World Bank has endeavoured to engage development NGOs on policy issues. However, it is debatable how far there has been a real shift in World Bank policy.

Critics argue that the World Bank has engaged selectively with NGOs and that those most critical of both the IMF and the World Bank have tended to be marginalized or excluded from the process of negotiation.[80] Economic globalization and structural adjustment have rather undermined the possibilities for more democratic decision-making. The World Bank has worked to maintain the status quo, while 'alternative' paradigms, such as the one put forward by transnational feminist networks like DAWN,[81] while enjoying support among activists in grassroots organizations have received little support from national governments or bilateral aid agencies that continue to work within the neoliberal model.

CONCLUSION

This chapter has sought to map out and elucidate the gendered nature of international political economy. In so doing, it has highlighted the differentiated impact of globalization, global restructuring and development and the negative impact of these processes on women specifically and poor women particularly. However, as is evident from the discussion above, one should not assume that women are ever the victims of global economic and political processes in which they are caught up, but over which they have little control. Feminist theorists have not only sought to challenge international political economy and globalization, but have also offered new visions of what development should or might entail. These alternatives seek to empower not only women but to realize a better life for all peoples. The United Nations has been an important site of struggle for women's rights and women's needs in the global economy and in the development process. This politics of gender in development is the subject of the following chapter.

PROMOTING WOMEN'S STATUS AT THE UN: GENDER IN DEVELOPMENT

INTRODUCTION

From its inception, the United Nations (UN) has played a role in promoting the status of women throughout the world. Much of the UN's work in this area has sought to promote women's rights. Women's human rights are afforded separate attention in the following chapter. Efforts to promote the legal status of women (rights) are likely to fail unless problems of poverty, hunger and illiteracy are addressed and so the UN has also sought to promote women's status through the development process.

This chapter focuses on the role of the UN in promoting women in development across the world. As elaborated below, the work of the United Nations cannot be viewed in isolation from the wider ideological and political context in which it operates. Similarly, the project to 'advance the status of women' has, at different times, been tied up with political and ideological conflicts, notably between the western world that has sought to promote a liberal, secular agenda, and parts of the global South that have resisted what they have perceived to be the imposition of western values on the rest of the world. The politics of North/South, and also East/West relations during the Cold War period, have also been highly relevant to understanding the politics of what might broadly be described as the transnational women's movement.

The first section of this chapter assesses the role of the UN in the context of a politically and ideologically divided world, focusing particularly on the major developments during the UN Decade for Women (1976–1985). This section sets out what might be considered the achievements and also the disappointments or failures of that period. The second part of the chapter is devoted to the politics of Women in Development (WID) specifically. The problems and potentialities of the project of forging solidarity among diverse women's groups and feminist organizations are set out in chapter 9. However, some consideration is given to this topic in the final section of this chapter too, because in many ways it was the postcolonial feminist critique of the Women in Development agenda that stimulated serious reflection on the diversity of women, women's 'status' and 'women's needs' and the implications of diversity for feminist politics.

THE UNITED NATIONS AND DEVELOPMENT

The international politics of development

In some respects, the UN can be seen as the successor to the short-lived League of Nations, an organization established after the First World War that collapsed in the 1930s. The UN was erected with the cooperation of the Soviet Union and later won the support of many countries that had previously been colonies of major powers. Despite differences in ideology, the United States (US) and Soviet Union were able to agree on most substantive issues to do with the structure and operation of the organization of the UN in the immediate post-war period. That said, the US emerged from the Second World War as the single most powerful state in the world and the newly established UN was heavily dependent upon the United States, since it provided the lion's share of funding for its activities. It is a matter of debate whether the UN can be accurately characterized as nothing more than an instrument of US foreign policy, because developing countries have undoubtedly been important and in some respects influential actors at the UN. However, it would be uncontroversial to state that the US has exercised the greatest degree of political influence within this institution.

In the context of the ideological and political divisions of the Cold War, the United States was keen to promote modernization strategies that fostered growth and industrialization according to basically free-market principles. In the aftermath of anti-colonial struggles for self-determination, the influence of the West continued to find expression in liberal development strategies, promoted by bilateral linkages between newly independent countries and former colonial powers. The United Nations was also seen to have a vital role to play in 'modernizing' and supposedly 'civilizing' the Third World.

Advancing the status of women

The principle of sexual equality was written into the UN Charter largely thanks to the efforts of women's NGOs, many of which were based in Latin America, and high-profile women like Eleanor Roosevelt. In the early years of the UN's existence, the 'advancement of women' took the form of promoting civil and political rights, notably the right to vote, and focused on discrimination in nationality laws and in matters concerning marriage and the family.

During the first twenty-five years of its life, the Commission on the Status of Women (CSW), discussed at greater length in the following chapter, embarked on a programme of work that, in turn, stimulated action in favour of women by UN specialized agencies and other UN organs, including the provision of technical assistance to benefit women in developing countries.[1] By the 1960s there was accumulating evidence that women were disproportionately affected by poverty, while inequalities between men and women manifest in, for example, barriers to land ownership and access to credit perpetuated the low status of women in many countries. This was the origin of programmes that focused on women's needs in development, specifically agricultural work and family planning. The Commission also started to pay greater attention to the impact on women of scientific and technological advances in development programmes. In 1962 the Economic and Social Council (ECOSOC) called upon UNICEF to expand and strengthen its efforts to assist women in developing countries. The culmination of the work of the Commission was the eventual adoption by the UN General Assembly of the Declaration on the Elimination of Discrimination against Women in 1967 (again, this is covered in greater detail in the following chapter).[2]

Early theories of development placed emphasis upon the twin objectives of economic growth and 'modernization'. Modernization is a rather vague and ill-defined concept but it is usually used to describe a process characterized by interconnected economic, technological, industrial, social, cultural and political changes. Modernization is typically associated with industrialization, technological innovation, moves to a market economy, consumerism, improved levels of education, an expanding role for the state, the emergence of political pluralism, respect for civil liberties and rights and the establishment of democratic, as opposed to authoritarian, forms of government. The assumption that underpins modernization is that developing countries will eventually become more like 'modern' western states.

According to the UN's own history of events,[3] the period 1963–1975 saw growing awareness of women's role in development. In 1970 Ester Boserup published what has since been recognized as a groundbreaking work, *Women's Role in Economic Development*. In the early modernization literature, very little regard was given to the status and role of women. Kinship and family were held to be facets of social organization that were seen to be essentially outside the modernization process. However, Boserup demonstrated how 'women's work' was vital to the social and economic well-being of societies and, as such, added further weight and urgency to the CSW's mission.[4] At the same time, the concept of development was being transformed to embrace not only economic growth but also human needs for good health care, an adequate supply of food and an elementary level of education. The UN began to commission surveys and reports that documented the link between the low status of women, poverty, overpopulation, illiteracy, food shortages, malnutrition and poor health conditions.[5]

Developments at the CSW coincided with a wave of decolonization across the world that resulted in an expansion of the membership of the UN. As more newly independent countries joined, there was a change in the composition of the organization. The UN General Assembly became a vehicle through which the priorities and problems of mainly newly independent states, namely building legal and political institutions and achieving economic development, could find expression. However, during the 1970s debates within the General Assembly were increasingly characterized by North/South splits, as developing countries challenged the principles of 'embedded liberalism' built into all of the post-war international institutions and called for a New International Economic Order. From the mid-1970s onwards, the status of women became something of a barometer of civilization and progress in liberal modernization theory, but at the same time efforts to promote women's rights specifically became a political bone of contention between western states and countries that had previously been under colonial administration.

While developing countries accepted that development was unlikely to be successful unless women's status was improved, many countries argued that the prioritization of women's rights should give way to social welfare measures and legislation to protect women workers. Thereafter, the work of the CSW on women's rights continued quietly but increasingly the CSW became focused on overcoming obstacles to the realization and enjoyment of rights, notably poverty and under-development.[6] The struggle to establish the principle of equality between men and women similarly gave way to programmes that aimed to meet women's basic needs in the development process. Specialized machinery was established at national and international levels to achieve this objective.[7]

The UN Decade for Women

The 1973 Percy Amendment to the 1961 United States Foreign Assistance Act required women to be involved in decision-making bodies that dealt with aid and development issues. This measure prompted UN agencies, including the World Bank, the United Nations Educational, Scientific and Cultural Organization (UNESCO), the International Labour Organization (ILO) and the Food and Agriculture Organization (FAO) to set up special offices that concentrated on women's role in the development process. The 1973 Foreign Assistance Act subsequently spawned the Women in Development movement (WID). WID rested on two related convictions: first, that women were essential to the achievement of human development and that women were entitled to share in the benefits of development with men; second, that both women and men had a role to play in fostering social progress. Shortly afterwards, in 1975, the First United Nations Conference on Women was held in Mexico to mark the beginning of International Women's Year. As on many previous occasions, this initiative originated not with states but with NGOs and was subsequently taken forward by the CSW. By the mid-1970s, along with promoting equality and development process, a third issue had emerged: the role of women in achieving peace and disarmament. Thus the organizing themes of the first UN Conference on Women were 'Equality, Development and Peace'.

Documentation collected in advance of the first women's conference was valuable in identifying practices of discrimination against women in different parts of the world, in raising issues that required international attention and in identifying the key objectives of the World Plan of Action (WPA) adopted at Mexico. The WPA outlined short- and long-term measures for achieving the integration of women into the development process as full and equal partners and called for effective and sustained national, regional and international action to implement the Plan. The period following the Mexico gathering was subsequently designated as the United Nations Decade for the Advancement of Women (1976–85). A Second United Nations Conference on Women was held in Copenhagen in 1980 to review progress in implementing the goals set out at Mexico and to update the WPA adopted at the 1975 conference. An action programme was approved during the conference that prioritized education, health and employment.

However, the Copenhagen conference served to illustrate graphically how the work of the UN could not avoid becoming embroiled in the East–West and North–South conflicts. The 1980s were characterized by global economic recession and mounting debts among developing countries following a period of easy lending and reckless borrowing by western banks and developing countries respectively. World recessions hit the poorest and weakest countries and the most vulnerable individuals and social groups particularly. In the 1980s, high levels of indebtedness in countries across the Third World retarded the process of integrating women in development, since gender issues now received low priority among Third World elites and within the UN generally. Across the western world, governments not only championed free-market policies, but also stressed the role of the family, rather than the state, as the main provider of welfare. Development assistance among both bilateral and multilateral agencies was also rolled back during this period. Unsurprisingly, the resurgence of Cold War politics opened up divisions between East and West and North and South over the political aspects of the Plan of Action. The conference document was littered with references to Zionism and the need for women to denounce imperialism. Unsurprisingly, the conference failed to produce a consensus document.[8]

Despite the ongoing East–West and North–South tensions generated by the Second Cold War and the debt crisis respectively, the Third UN Conference on Women, held in Nairobi in 1985, produced an important document called Forward Looking Strategies for the Advancement of Women to the Year 2000 (FLSAW). The FLSAW was significant for a number of reasons. First, it highlighted the problems of women's double burden (documented in the previous chapter) and demanded equal access for women to land, property and credit. Second, reference was made to the need to include unpaid work in national accounts and in social and economic indicators. There were also allusions to the need to redefine the meaning of 'work'. Third, for the first time the issue of violence against women in the family was highlighted in an international document (albeit initially as an issue related to peace). Fourth, the UN Secretary-General was asked 'to establish, where they do not already exist, focal points on women's issues in all sectors of the work of the organizations of the UN system'.[9] Thus, the FLSAW shifted the emphasis from the promotion of gender-specific activities to a strategy of mainstreaming, that is, incorporating gender concerns into other areas of the UN's work as a matter of course rather than as 'add-ons'.

Some concessions were made to cultural sensibilities and to the practical problems that many developing countries faced in meeting their obligations. The FLSAW conceded that countries at different levels of development should be able to set their own priorities based on development policies and resource capabilities. The FLSAW document was not uncontroversial, with a number of delegations verbally expressing reservations, but by the end of the conference the FLSAW was adopted by consensus, thus avoiding what had happened at Copenhagen five years earlier.

Five years on from Nairobi, the Commission met to review the achievements of the objectives set out in the FLSAW. In the light of what was conceded to be 'disappointing' progress (the survey undertaken at the end of the UN Decade alluded to above suggested the relative status and position of women throughout the world had declined in the previous ten years), a decision was taken to convene a Fourth United Nations Conference on Women in Beijing in 1995. The major significance of the Beijing conference was that it shifted the emphasis of the UN's work back to the prioritization of women's human rights. As such, it is appropriate to leave detailed discussion of the Beijing Platform for Action (BPA) to the following chapter. Suffice to say that the Beijing conference also carried forward the 'women in development' agenda in so far as the BPA stressed the need for women to participate fully in economic and social development; the need to eradicate poverty and achieve sustainable economic growth; and the need to ensure women's equal right to land, property and credit, regardless of customary laws and traditional practices related to inheritance.[10] It also fostered agreement on the need for women's full participation in economic and political decision-making processes and advocated that national mechanisms be set up to achieve this end. After intensive lobbying by the International Women Count Network, governments were also required to carry out surveys to count the amount of time women spent performing vital, but largely unrecognized, work and include this data in satellite accounts.

Evaluating the women's conferences

In some respects the UN Decade for Women was a significant event. Governments were required to acknowledge in public their obligations towards women. Women's organizations gained some access to policy-making by insisting that women's offices were set up within development agencies, and this helped to legitimize the women's movement as an international actor. During the UN Decade a number of specialist organs were set up with the specific remit of advancing the status of women, including the International Research and Training Institute for the Advancement of Women (INSTRAW, 1976) that provides technical assistance and training programmes to support women in developing countries and the Development Fund for Women for the UN Decade for Women (UNIFEM, also established in 1976). These initiatives aimed to improve women's access to national policy makers. The WID literature that proliferated in the 1970s put the issue of women firmly on the international political agenda, highlighting inequalities in opportunity and the disproportionate contribution that women made to the development process. It also led to the first real attempts to look at how technologies could be developed and applied that would help to reduce the drudgery characteristic of much of the work of women. In addition, the UN women's conferences allowed women to travel, to meet and exchange ideas. The Mexico conference offered NGOs an international platform in the form of an NGO forum. NGO forums have subsequently been a feature of all the women's conferences. Some 6,000 NGOs attended the parallel NGO forum in Mexico. At Beijing some 30,000 people attended the NGO forum. Participants at the women's conferences have referred to these events as history's largest consciousness-raising session, in the sense that participants discovered that their problems were not unique, but shared by women all around the world.

FROM WID TO DEVELOPMENT AS 'EMPOWERMENT'

Since 1985 the WID approach has been subjected to considerable criticism. As noted above, the status of women around the world, as measured by a range of indicators, actually declined during the Decade, while to a large extent the failure of the UN Decade can be explained by the failure on the part of many states to implement UN recommendations (this is revisited in the next chapter).[11] That said, the WID idea might be said to have contained the seeds of its own failure. During the UN Decade, development policies were based on the underlying belief that the problems of Third World women were related to insufficient participation in the process of development. It has been argued that WID rested on a liberal feminist view that the problems of sexual inequality could be largely overcome if women were integrated into the public sphere. The aim of WID was to 'bring in' women, but women were already involved in the development process, although recognized only in their roles as visible producers whose commodities could be traded. The economic role of women as subsistence farmers, providers and full-time carers, the cornerstone of economic life, remained, therefore, largely uncounted and unrewarded (the subsequent successes of Beijing in this area notwithstanding). In the early period of the UN's work, development strategies targeted women to provide for their 'practical needs', what women needed in order to carry out the tasks allocated to them under the prevalent sexual division of labour.[12] Moreover, this top-down approach recognizes women only as objects of development, passive recipients of development assistance, rather than farmers, workers, investors and trade unionists.[13]

Furthermore, the WID approach ignored the broader context in which women-specific projects were inscribed. The possibility that increasing poverty amongst women, and the relative decline of women to men during the Decade, was the direct result of previous development policies was not considered. Contemporary neo-classical (or neoliberal) approaches to development, that became popular in the 1980s and 1990s, similarly emphasize the efficacy of the market in generating economic activity and distributing resources and assume that the benefits of growth will 'trickle down' to poorer members of society. However, all too often economic growth has only benefited a small elite. Many development strategies made the reform and restructuring of agriculture production a priority, but these measures often led to the displacement of women from the land that they had traditionally farmed.[14] Moreover, as is evident from the discussion in the previous chapter, modernization processes are profoundly influenced by global trade, by the operation of global markets, by transnational investment patterns and, increasingly, by a global division of labour.[15]

Critics argued that WID policy avoided and obscured issues of inequalities and power by presenting the issue of assistance to women as a purely technical exercise. It did not address the broader redistributional issues that assisting women raised.[16] Bringing women in increased women's productivity and overall workload, but did little to address the double burden of reproduction and the servicing of men's and children's needs. A second WID strategy focused on poverty. The aim of this strategy was to increase the employment and income-generating options of low-income women. By focusing on women's productive role, and ignoring their reproductive role, many income-generating projects assumed wrongly that women had free time and succeeded only in extending the working day of women and increasing their overall burden.

Allison, Ashworth and Redcliffe have argued that the central issue of gender inequalities was ignored in development policies. Men and women could not benefit equally from aid and development initiatives if they had different political rights, burdens of time and expectations and if women could not get access to credit and if the laws of inheritance and ownership discriminated against them.[17] In short, while the CSW had recognized the need to address all of these areas, actual development policies were rather limited in terms of their scope and aims.

From WID to GAD

Criticisms of the assumptions that guided the WID approach led to widespread calls among both academic commentators and activists for a different approach. The term 'gender and development' (GAD) was coined to describe an approach that was attuned to the degree to which women already participated in development, that sought to develop historical modes of analysis and was sensitive to the specificity of gender relations in particular countries and localities.[18] GAD also emphasized the importance of socially constructed ideas about gender and how these were shaped by development strategies.[19]

GAD aimed to promote gender-sensitive development strategies that recognized the 'triple role' of women, in production, reproduction, and as providers of care for the community. An 'equity approach' was formulated that aimed to meet strategic gender interests as well as to meet practical needs. Midway through the Decade, academic commentators on development and many NGOs began to shift the emphasis in development discourse and practice towards the need to transform gender relations. The need for strategies designed to meet strategic rather than practical needs derived from an analysis of the power relationships between women and men. However, GAD also sought to develop an analysis of gender in the economy and the state. GAD suggested that gender inequalities were a consequence of the way relationships between men and women were structured in the marketplace. This approach also emphasized differing interests between women and men within the family. The technical project of access as numerical inclusion was seen as insufficient to challenge the unequal allocation of values that sustained oppressive gender relations. The stress on gender, rather than women, was a reminder that men must also be the targets of attempts to redress gender inequalities and that their interests were also socially constructed and amenable to change.[20]

Gender and development challenged the view that the state was a neutral body. As feminists have long argued, 'part of the definition of the state and the delimitation of the state's proper sphere involves the active codification and policing of the boundaries of the public and the private'.[21] Furthermore, in many states those boundaries also 'delineate gendered spheres of activity, where the paradigmatic subject of the public and economic arena is male and that of the private and domestic is female'.[22] In this way, according to Goetz, by confirming and institutionalizing the arrangements that distinguish the public from the private, states are involved in the social and political institutionalization of gendered power differences. For example, states set the parameters for women's structurally unequal position in families and markets by condoning gender-differential terms in inheritance rights and legal adulthood, by tacitly condoning domestic and sexual violence, or by sanctioning differential wages for equal or comparable work.

From GAD to WED

Challenges to the notion that development means economic growth have been given a boost in recent years by a growing awareness of the impact of growth on the environment. In more recent debates, the emphasis has shifted from WID and GAD to 'women, environment and development' (WED). A growing number of commentators and activists have called for a new approach that challenges dominant conceptions of development and calls for a greater understanding of the crucial role that women play in managing the environment.[23]

The dominant models of development (modernization and neoliberalism) emphasize the need for economic growth; indeed, growth is the main indicator of 'progress'. These models neglect almost entirely the degree to which development is sustainable because they fail to recognize the environmental consequences of development and the inherent limits to growth.[24] When nature is viewed as a resource that is there to be exploited, growth is frequently accompanied by environmental destruction. For example, the dash to growth in many countries has resulted in massive deforestation through commercial exploitation and cash-crop production. Deforestation leads to soil erosion that in turn affects rivers and local water supplies. The exploitation of the earth's resources continues to fuel economic expansion in the West where nations comprise 22 per cent of the world's population but use 70 per cent of its energy and are responsible for two-thirds of carbon emissions and 90 per cent of chlorofluorocarbons.[25] Development strategies that rely on energy intensive modes of production and transportation are spreading throughout the world. The enormous growth in the world's population will put enormous pressure on the world's resources and on the environment. Population size and the need for fertility control are all important gender issues, of course, and are recognized as central to combating global environmental degradation. However, the real issues that need to be addressed are poverty and inequality.

Development as empowerment

At Nairobi, NGOs from developing countries became much more visible and active in generating their own vision of what 'development' might mean to poor people and poor women particularly. The movement Development Alternatives for Women in a New Era (DAWN) was particularly important in re-visioning development as empowerment. At the heart of this 'empowerment' approach was an insistence that race, class, the legacy of colonialism and the position of countries in the international economic order were important sources of inequality. Moreover, the dominant understanding of the causes of 'underdevelopment' or 'maldevelopment' reflected imbalances of power within and between nations rather than the presence or absence of resources. Therefore, women had to challenge oppressive structures simultaneously and at different levels. Similarly, feminist analysis needed to integrate the social, cultural and political dimensions of development into economic analysis. Empowerment also conceptualized power differently – placing much less emphasis on increasing women's status relative to men and more on the capacity of women to increase their own self-reliance and internal strength.[26]

THE POLITICS OF GENDER IN DEVELOPMENT

The postcolonial feminist critique of WID

Policies to promote development challenged the view that outside intervention in the areas of family relations or 'cultural practices' was always unjustified. Indeed, certain cultural practices were identified as impediments to women's advancement and desirable social change. Unsurprisingly, development strategies that aimed to advance the status of women were apt to be viewed with suspicion by government elites in some countries. Activists within the WID movement who lobbied for the advancement of women were sometimes accused of 'interfering with culture' or even 'cultural imperialism' by nationalist men from Third World countries.[27] Attempts to use international organizations to improve the status of women were often resisted on the grounds of sovereignty or culture.

The claims of culture do not necessarily trump the claims of gender equality. Moreover, the norm of sovereignty changes over time in line with state practice. However, it was not only (male) political elites that criticized the WID.[28] In the 1980s, criticism emanated from feminist groups and intellectuals within developing countries. GAD did much to expose some of the weaknesses in the WID approach. However, postcolonial feminist commentators went much further, developing a thoroughgoing critique of the WID discourse and challenging the entire strategy of development and modernization, since that was seen as an imposition by western states and western-dominated institutions on the so-called developing world.

The WID approach appeared to accept the underlying assumption of liberal modernization theory in so far as social structures, institutions and cultural practices were deemed to disadvantage women in the developing world. The WID project rested on an assumption that western women were more 'advanced' or 'liberated' than women in developing countries and, moreover, largely accepted that the basis of development lay in a diffusion of capital, technology and values from the West. Both of these assumptions were questionable.

Feminists and activists in postcolonial countries began to question the very notion of 'advancement' inscribed in western economic and political projects.[29] Processes of colonization and decolonization involved unequal economic exchanges that produced and reproduced inequalities in the international economic order. 'Modernization' and 'development' were not, then, likely to result in the 'advancement' of women nor in developing countries 'catching up' with the West.

Moreover, even as the participation of more groups and NGOs from non-western societies grew, sceptics continued to challenge the very idea that the specific problems of particular groups of women could and should be addressed in a forum like the UN. Gayatri Spivak argued that UN development strategies accepted the underlying logic of the free market as the best distributor of resources and 'life chances', but in practice it only perpetuated inequalities. She claimed that the Beijing conference should be seen less as an event that produced an agenda for women's empowerment and more as a 'tremendously well organized ideological apparatus', used ostensibly to demonstrate the unity of North and South, when 'the North organizes the South'.[30] Spivak criticized the way in which NGOs were put together in the South to exclude the poorest women as self-critical agents. In her view, NGO forums, such as those that accompany UN conferences, afforded diaspora the opportunity to represent the 'South' and women from the 'North' the opportunity to matronize women from the 'South'.[31] Indeed, Spivak has been scathing in her criticism, arguing that 'serious activists' should stay away from the women's conferences because 'the real work was to be done elsewhere'.[32]

The notion that women were unified rested on essentialist notions of 'woman'. Mohanty castigated western feminists for naively positing the existence of a 'global sisterhood'.[33] The transnational women's movement was actually comprised of a loose and diverse coalition of women's groups, mainly from the West, who had dominated international political forums and spaces and pursued a western-led agenda. Women from the South had, in practice, little opportunity to articulate their own specific concerns and aspirations in those same sites.[34] Postcolonial feminists challenged the assumptions that western women were more 'advanced' or 'liberated' and that cultural practices and traditions were necessarily oppressive for women. Western liberal feminists were attacked for racism inherent in calls for the 'advancement' of Third World women. WID also ignored issues of power in the construction of knowledge. The WID literature was charged with being imbued with colonial discourse, in which 'Third World Women' were frequently represented as a monolithic group, or monolithic subject, who were passive and voiceless. Chandra Mohanty accused the 'hegemonic white women's movement' of colonizing the experiences of Third World women.[35] Moreover, despite the nuances of the GAD approach – the need for historical and cultural specificity in feminist analysis – it was subject to some of the same criticisms in so far as GAD rested on an unstated commitment to an emancipatory politics that, critics argued, was implicitly grounded in a western discourse of universalism, 'progress' and 'liberation'.

Postcolonial feminists claimed that their aim was to refine sensitivity to differences and encourage the toleration of the incommensurable. The deconstruction of identity, or scepticism towards the usefulness of 'woman' as a category of analysis, did not necessarily mean the deconstruction of feminist politics, although it did involve redefining feminist politics outside of the binary and sexual difference upon which it had historically been built.[36] The feminist and/or women's movement must resist the notion that political strategies entailed the mobilization of a homogeneous group with a common interest in realizing common goals. Since gender relations were embedded in wider power relations, the objectives and strategies of feminism were intertwined with very different cultural and socio-political conditions.[37]

While Spivak was deeply sceptical about the politics of transnational feminism and the UN women's conferences particularly, other postcolonial feminist commentators have recognized that women from the global South can and do play an important role in shaping the politics of transnational feminism and have been important actors in shaping debates within the UN context too.[38] Bulbeck has argued that since the UN Decade on Women, the sense that women share common oppression has been placed alongside a more comprehensive analysis of their differences.[39] If feminism is the political expression of the concerns and interests of women from different regions, classes, nationalities and backgrounds, then it has to be responsive to different needs and concerns as defined by women for themselves. However, women in the Third World endorse some development goals, for example, education, health care, wider choice and better renumeration of labour, even while holding different views on the nature of the problems faced by women and the solutions. While diverse, the transnational women's movement is built upon a common opposition to gender oppression and hierarchy and promotes a political agenda which aims to challenge all structures and relationships that perpetuate and reinforce the subordination of women everywhere. Ferree and Martin define a feminist organization as 'embracing collectivist decision-making, member empowerment and a political agenda of ending women's oppression'.[40] Individual women's NGOs may organize around specific gender issues. However, NGOs engage in a dynamic and reciprocal relation with the women's movement as a whole. Identification with a wider transnational movement gives NGOs a broader purpose, that purpose being the struggle for wide-ranging social and political change.[41] Rather than undermining the notion of a distinctly feminist political project then, there is a need to balance sensitivity towards cultural differences with the need for politics of solidarity predicated on women's shared problems.[42]

The diversity of 'women'

The impact of postcolonial and poststructuralist critiques of WID (and to some extent GAD) was such that it compelled feminists critically to reflect upon and rethink a number of presuppositions in feminist thought. The assumptions upon which feminist politics had been grounded historically were also questioned. An impassioned debate emerged about the significance of not only class but also race and ethnicity in under-standing gender relations. This, in turn, called into question the universal meaning of 'woman' as western feminists were forced to face up to their own exclusionary prac-tices which were resident, for example, in their conceptions of 'liberation' or 'emanci-pation'. Postcolonial feminist critiques of western feminism initiated a debate about 'difference' by raising issues about race and ethnicity. Postcolonial critiques also claimed to expose the pretence of a unified concept or category called 'women'.

As such, postcolonial feminism echoed many of the same themes that emerged in western academic feminism in the 1980s and which were alluded to in chapter 1, notably that 'difference described the human condition' and that 'women were many not one'.[43] Within the academy, a debate ensued on the aim of feminist scholarship and how it should be carried out. Differences among women within western societies were also the focus of attention. Valerie Amos and Pratibha Palmer, for example, argued that issues prioritized in the political campaigns of white bourgeois feminists had contributed to an improvement in the material situation of a small number of white, middle-class women, but this had often been at the expense of their Black and working-class sisters. Since Black women shared experiences with Black people gener-ally and with women in different class contexts, the only appropriate political response was to recognize the duality of experience and explore the range of political options available to Black women according to the social context in which this dualism was experienced.[44]

Poststructuralist feminist thinkers argued that research should concentrate on the historically and culturally specific experiences of different groups of women. Feminist work should not be abandoned, because it constituted a 'site of resistance' to hegemonic discourse and provided spaces for women to be heard. However, the universal and emancipatory pretensions of feminism should be scrapped. In turn their detractors claimed that this would merely produce empirical studies that would have nothing to say about how existing power structures could be transformed. In response to these charges of political quietism, poststructuralist feminist scholars attempted to reformulate feminist theory so that it became more focused on the political, theoretical, self-analysing practices that arose from the historical experience of concrete women. If one's history was interpreted or reconstructed from within the horizons of meaning and knowledge available in given historical moments, horizons that also include modes of political commitment and struggle, then some notion of agency might be salvaged.[45] Efforts to forge new forms of solidarity that are built upon and respectful of differences among women are the subject of chapter 9.

Conclusion

This chapter has provided an overview of efforts to promote women's status through the UN, focusing specifically on development. It is evident that the work of the UN cannot avoid being embroiled in wider political and ideological conflicts in international relations. In recent years the UN has put up some resistance to the imposition of neoliberal structural adjustment policies in developing states and transitional economies, but has fallen short of criticizing neo-classical development policies per se. This suggests, perhaps, that the work of the UN is profoundly constrained by the realities of power and political influence in the world.

Similarly efforts to promote the status of women through development have been caught up in the politics of North/South (and East/West) relations. Given the disappointing lack of progress, one might be sceptical of the ultimate usefulness of the UN as a vehicle for the 'advancement of women'. However, in defence of the UN and the women's conferences, they have played an important role in facilitating networking, providing the web that links NGOs, social movements and groups across national borders. The UN NGO forums have also provided a public and international space for women's voices. At the Beijing conference, women's human rights have (once again) become a focal point for feminist activism. Efforts to promote women's human rights are the subject of the following chapter.

WOMEN'S HUMAN RIGHTS

INTRODUCTION

The UN has played a key role in developing both a body of law and institutional machinery to promote women's human rights, notably through the Commission on the Status of Women (hereafter the Commission or CSW) established in 1946. The work of the Commission has helped to establish the principle among many, if not most, member states that women have human rights and has set international human rights standards for member states to adhere to. It is, perhaps, because human rights discourse enjoys legitimacy in many countries around the world that it has increasingly been embraced by NGOs as a potentially useful political tool that women might use in varied national and cultural contexts to challenge discrimination, or other harmful practices, that have hitherto served to reinforce the inferior/subordinate status of women.[1]

Since the end of the UN Decade for Women in 1985, there has been a proliferation of groups organized around the promotion of the women's human rights agenda. At the same time, gender 'mainstreaming' and efforts to implement specific measures outlined in the Convention on the Elimination of Discrimination Against Women (CEDAW) and other documents such as the Beijing Platform for Action (BPA) have institutionalized the link between (selected) NGOs and various bodies in the UN system and strengthened their capacity to have an impact on policy formulation, law-making and the implementation and monitoring of women's human rights at both international and national/local levels.

By the tenth anniversary of the Fourth United Nations Conference on Women in 2005, one could identify some clear gains in women's human rights. In his opening statement at the Beijing Plus 5 Review held in New York in 2000, the Secretary-General of the General Assembly emphasized progress in making violence against women an illegal act in almost every country (while also acknowledging that violence against women was still widespread).[2] And yet, despite these developments, it is evident that women's human rights continue to be contested in some countries around the world and, even where there has been agreement on which specific rights should be regarded as women's human rights, it seems that many governments have failed to follow through on their commitments.[3] The steps that have been taken have often been uncoordinated and somewhat perfunctory.[4] The slow progress in realizing women's human rights in practice has raised questions about whether human rights have been or can be an effective means of protecting/advancing the status of women.

The first part of this chapter traces the development of women's human rights at the UN, highlighting issues where there has been significant progress and also identifying areas where women's human rights are still contested. The second part of the chapter covers the debates on cultural relativism and the specificity of rights. The final section of the chapter considers whether rights discourse and a rights agenda is a useful political tool that allows activists to stake claims on behalf of women in specific societies and varied locations around the world.

PROMOTING WOMEN'S HUMAN RIGHTS AT THE UN

The commission on the status of women

The UN Declaration of Human Rights states that man is endowed with universal and inalienable human rights. As such, it is consistent with a humanist conception of the human subject and embeds a cosmopolitan view of how world society should be organized. The project to promote human rights across the world had been central to the Woodrow Wilson plan for a liberal world order in the aftermath of the First World War. In the post-Second World War period, in the aftermath of atrocities committed by the Nazi regime in Germany, human rights again occupied a central place in the UN's vision of world order. The UN Charter affirmed faith in 'fundamental human rights', in 'the dignity and worth of the human person' and in the 'equal rights of men and women and of nations large and small' and promoted and encouraged 'respect for human rights and for fundamental freedoms without distinction as to race, sex, language or religion'.[5]

Once established, the Commission assumed overall responsibility for all matters relevant to women. Much of the early work of the Commission involved extending rights already enjoyed by many men to women, including the right to vote, to have an education and to enjoy employment rights. During the 1950s and 1960s the Commission undertook a number of studies designed to elucidate the political, economic and social status of women around the world as a first step in devising action plans in favour of women that were to be taken up by other UN agencies. As Reanda points out, documenting gender inequalities and setting out measures to eliminate discrimination marked a historic change in political discourse since many issues previously thought private and steeped in custom and tradition began to be openly debated in an international forum.[6] This work was underpinned by a number of core liberal principles that included the right of women, along with men, to enjoy freedom and equality.

As noted in the previous chapter, the history of the Commission has revealed how political and ideological divisions have sometimes frustrated the execution of its brief and demonstrated how the struggle for gender equality has sometimes been submerged in global concerns. During the Cold War, Eastern bloc countries challenged the UN's human rights agenda on the grounds that the promotion of human rights (and women's rights specifically) was meaningless if discussed in isolation from the problem of poverty, the key concern of the vast majority of women around the world.[7] The prioritization of economic development over the entrenchment of civil and political rights in newly independent countries began to overshadow concerns with the legal and political status of women.[8]

Nevertheless, the women's rights agenda did not completely run out of steam. During this period, the European members of the Commission made efforts to keep the rights agenda on track.[9] In many countries women could be deprived of nationality and even find themselves stateless in the event of divorce.[10] The culmination of the Commission's work was the eventual adoption by the UN General Assembly of the Declaration on the Elimination of Discrimination against Women in 1967. Among other things, the Declaration called for the abolition of discriminatory customs and practices and in-equities in marriage and divorce. This led eventually to the development of CEDAW.

The adoption of CEDAW was one of the major achievements during the UN Decade for Women. Although subject to criticism for its weak language and provisions, at a minimum CEDAW articulated an international standard for what was meant by 'equality' between men and women, granted formal rights to women and also pro-moted equality of access and opportunity. CEDAW also recognized that rights could be meaningless unless attention was paid to the economic, social and cultural context in which they were claimed and called for changes in traditional gender roles, where these were deemed to perpetuate inequality and discrimination.[11] Initially CEDAW was slow to obtain signatories and was characterized by a large number of reservations entered by those states that did sign up. The continual refusal of the United States to sign up to and ratify CEDAW, along with the high number of reservations, undoubt-edly weakened its moral authority and legal force. However, many governments worldwide have now enacted CEDAW and have revised domestic legislation to con-form to the principles of the convention.

While the record of the Commission in promoting women's rights is somewhat chequered, it has undoubtedly played an important role in propelling issues previously regarded as private into the international public domain. Furthermore, the Commission has sometimes been able to overcome or negotiate the politics of nationalism, culture and competing ideological worldviews. A review of the key debates in the Commission has revealed that women members, while ostensibly representing the position of their governments, have often decried sex-based discrimination within their own societies and engaged in criticism of their own governments.[12]

When Mary Robinson, a notable campaigner for women's rights, was appointed the UN High Commissioner for Human Rights, she prioritized the task of mainstreaming women's human rights throughout the UN system.[13] The mainstreaming of women's human rights into other areas of the UN's work necessitates the coordination of UN programmes and so requires a centralized institutional mechanism to perform monitor-ing, evaluation and coordination functions. The Commission has fulfilled these func-tions. In serving as both a channel for proposals from NGOs and sometimes making use of the resources of locally based NGOs in the implementing process, the Commis-sion has also facilitated NGO participation in the process of mainstreaming. In so doing, the Commission has helped to legitimize the role of women's non-governmental organizations in national and international decision-making forums.[14] The terms of reference of the Commission include dealing with complaints of violations of women's rights. The Optional Protocol to CEDAW (discussed further below) will no doubt further enhance its role.

The Beijing conference

While all four United Nations' Conferences on Women have played a role in the development of women's human rights, the Beijing conference was particularly significant in that the need to further develop and embed women's human rights underpinned all of the critical areas of concern set out in the BPA.[15] The BPA affirmed the principles of freedom of choice for individual women and proclaimed that it was the duty of governments to promote and protect human rights of women by building on previous agreements and ratifying and implementing relevant human rights treaties. The BPA imposed on states, 'regardless of their political, economic, and cultural systems', an obligation to promote and protect all human rights and to address the violation of women's human rights in varied contexts.[16] The BPA also acknowledged the lack of substantive progress thus far in advancing women's human rights and called for the mainstreaming of gender issues into national and international policy-making bodies and processes.[17]

While the BPA does not have the status of international law (at best it is 'soft law'), in agreeing to the text governments made a public commitment to its contents, except on points where they made reservations. As will be elaborated below, this has proved useful to NGOs, in varied locations, in holding their governments to account when they have failed to meet their obligations. The Beijing conference also gave impetus to the drafting of an Optional Protocol to CEDAW that allowed women to make complaints about breaches of the convention.[18] A complaints procedure also meant that the implementation of the Convention could be monitored more effectively.

Some states continue to resist intervention in areas regarded as within the realm of family, culture and/or religion. However, in so far as women's rights in each of these domains has been brought into the public domain, states find that they are now compelled to justify their (in)action rather than assert a sovereign right to organize their domestic arrangements as they see fit. However, it should be noted that, while affirming the universal and indivisible human rights of women irrespective of the specific political, religious, cultural or familial context, the BPA also allowed a degree of discretion in how these broad principles would be implemented in deference to cultural sensibilities.

The role of NGOs in promoting women's human rights

NGOs campaigned to be involved in the implementation and monitoring process in respect to the BPA and CEDAW.[19] The earlier women's conferences proved to be useful learning experiences for NGOs, so much so that by the time of the Beijing conference NGOs had become adept at exercising influence within the process. Restrictions were imposed on NGO participation in the run up to Beijing, where one might argue important decisions were made on both the content and language of the Draft BPA.[20] Nevertheless, despite these not inconsiderable problems, women's NGOs were not entirely excluded in the process. NGOs participated in the preparatory meetings and at Beijing a caucus mechanism was established to facilitate coalition building. NGOs made more effective use of the media to publicize the cause of women's human rights and to call to account member states that they perceived to be impeding progress.

Indeed, the prominent role of NGOs at all stages of the process led Kofi Annan to declare that 'where once women fought to put gender equality on the international agenda, gender equality is now one of the primary factors shaping that agenda'.[21] At Beijing, government delegations espoused stronger political commitment to the cause of women's human rights. At the same time, the capacity of NGOs to keep the process on track appeared to bode well for future progress.[22] The forging of networks around the world to promote CEDAW has strengthened the project of advancing women's human rights.[23] Since the UN Decade for Women (1976–85), these networks have grown exponentially, aided by advances in information and global communications technologies.[24] However, if not entirely excluded women and women's groups – particularly from countries outside the affluent West – are still marginalized in the process as a whole and, as elaborated below, the marginalization of women (from the South particularly) can render UN action ineffective in a number of areas.

Contesting women's human rights

The widespread public commitment to the cause of women's human rights notwithstanding, negotiations on women's rights have often proved to be contentious. Claims of sovereignty and cultural relativism (discussed at greater length below) have been evoked to challenge sections of the BPA that deal with sexual and reproductive health, inheritance rights and unpaid work particularly. Other controversial issues include the relative weight and importance that should be attached to parental rights and the rights of the child particularly in regard to sex education. In regard to the provisions on sexuality in the BPA, conservative states, the Holy See, the Christian right and a number of Islamic fundamentalist countries formed an unlikely alliance at Beijing to resist what they represented as a 'homosexual agenda'.[25]

Following the International Conference on Population and Development in Cairo in 1994, issues of sexuality and reproduction had begun to be articulated as women's rights. At Beijing, this coalition attempted to 'roll back' the language of 'autonomy' and 'equality' in relation to sexuality and reproduction. Indeed, some 40 per cent of the entire text of the BPA was initially bracketed (contested), the so-called 'Holy Brackets'.[26] The BPA was forced to concede that the implementation of the BPA might differ in specific national, cultural and religious contexts.

After protracted negotiation, the BPA was saved from being so watered down in the area of sexuality and reproductive rights to the extent that it was meaningless, when it was agreed that the language established at earlier UN conferences would be used whenever possible. Retaining the 'Cairo language' was a crucial political achievement for women's groups since it reasserted the right of women to control their own sexuality.[27] However, many of these issues re-emerged five years later in New York at the Beijing Plus 5 Review.

Beijing initially generated optimism and expectation. The conflict surrounding sexuality, reproductive rights and sexual health notwithstanding, differences among both government delegations and NGOs from the North and the South were less prominent and divisive than they had been at previous women's conferences (notably Copenhagen, see previous chapter). There was a broad measure of agreement among both government delegations and NGOs on many of the twelve critical areas of concern identified in the BPA,[28] for example in relation to violence against women, including situations of armed conflict, or in the aftermath of armed conflict (see chapter 5). Indeed, at Beijing, the differences between women and women's groups were dwarfed by the large measure of agreement on both the principle and the content of women's human rights.[29]

And yet, even at Beijing it was clear that there was already a huge gap between the rhetoric and reality of governments' commitments to both gender mainstreaming and the promotion of women's human rights. The Commission concluded that while the principle of equality between women and men was now recognized as central to economic and social development and, therefore, a priority for the international community, the lack of progress was disappointing. By the close of proceedings at Beijing Plus 5, the atmosphere of expectation generated at the 'conference of commitments' had further dissipated. NGOs lamented the failure of states to agree on a stronger document with more concrete benchmarks, numerical goals, time-bound targets, indicators and resources aimed at implementing the Beijing Platform.[30]

Beijing Plus 5

In the four-year period following the Beijing conference, the Commission adopted a work programme to monitor the implementation of strategic objectives set forth for each of the twelve critical areas of concern.[31] Post-Beijing the Commission was fairly upbeat about the rate of progress, pointing to profound changes in the status and role of women around the world since the start of the UN Decade in 1976, but also identified the continuing obstacles in the implementation process and suggested concrete actions and initiatives to overcome them. The Beijing Plus 5 Review was designed to provide renewed momentum to the implementation of the BPA.

At Beijing Plus 5, agreement on women's health issues proved to be possible where sexuality, reproductive rights and sexual health were linked directly to measures to combat the spread of HIV/AIDS.[32] However, when not directly linked to this 'new issue area', women's rights were heavily contested. Some Islamic women's groups, conservative Catholic women's groups and delegates of NGOs affiliated to the Vatican, which enjoys permanent observer status at the UN, objected to the emphasis given to what they characterized as 'homosexual rights' and made appeals to protect the traditional family model against homosexual demands for equal rights in marriage. An Outcome Document was agreed but only after a period of difficult and protracted negotiation and after the terms 'sexual rights' and 'sexual orientation' had been removed from the document.[33]

The UN was keen to put a positive spin on the achievements of the Review. However, Amnesty International's report on the Beijing Plus 5 Review concluded that it had proved to be a disappointment with too many governments backtracking on what they had committed themselves to five years earlier. Amnesty lamented that a handful of governments had been able to hold hostage the review process.[34] Many of the measures undertaken by national governments to implement the BPA goals have subsequently been criticized on the grounds that they are fairly cosmetic.[35] Governments have displayed a persistent lack of political will to promote and protect women's human rights in all spheres of life. This lack of political will can, in turn, be explained by the under-representation of women in decision-making structures. The under-representation of women in the decision-making process also constitutes a considerable obstacle in translating commitments into concrete actions. Women's voices are still too often marginalized in the political process and the contribution of women's groups to mainstreaming projects not always fully understood or appreciated. The above-cited successes notwithstanding, male-dominated legislators and policy-making bodies are still inclined to regard gender equality as somewhat marginal to their main activities and goals. Debates on women's human rights have ensued in political forums and public spaces where elite men still frequently wield social and political power and frequently get to articulate the claims of culture and 'authentic' identities.[36]

Are human rights 'universal'?

Jack Donnelly has claimed that human rights empower citizens. Demands for human rights generate demands for social change that in turn allow for the enjoyment of the human rights that individuals have been granted.[37] Human rights have been evoked to empower individuals and specific social groups to mount a powerful moral attack on abusive institutions and practices. In many Third World countries under various authoritarian regimes, human rights have emerged as an ideology of resistance, gradually occupying the centre of the political stage.[38] Charlotte Bunch has also spoken of the 'dynamism' of human rights. She argues that their continuing relevance stems from the fact that more people are claiming them and in so doing expanding the meaning of rights to incorporate their own hopes and needs.[39] So much so that Doris Buss and Didi Herman argue that, 'just as "human rights" have become "keywords" for global political practice, "women's rights" have become a paradigmatic example of the power of international activism'.[40] The role of activism in promoting women's human rights will be revisited below. At this juncture, it is necessary to consider the debates surrounding the universality or otherwise of human rights.

Legitimate questions might be raised about whether human rights are truly universal. One objection to the concept of rights is that it is predicated on a public/private dichotomy central to liberalism and this leaves large parts of women's lives outside of the scope of legal protection or redress.[41] A second objection to rights discourse is that it is too irredeemably tainted from its association with western cultural values to be useful to women in other national and cultural settings.

The gender of rights

Rights are premised on the idea that human beings are rational beings, rationality being conceived of as the capacity to understand moral laws, or the ability to be able to determine one's own best interests (a strong argument against patrimonial or patriarchal forms of authority). One might argue that the exclusion of women from the enjoyment of rights historically is simply a consequence of bias. In so far as women have proved themselves to be capable of making moral judgements, deciding on their best interests and how to achieve them and living independent lives, women have shown themselves to be autonomous and rational subjects. However, within feminist jurisprudence, a distinctive critique of human rights has been developed that centres on the specificity of human rights with regard to class, culture and especially gender.[42] This critique focuses on both the public/private dichotomy central to liberal rights discourse, which has meant that until relatively recently the family has been considered sacrosanct in law, and the concept of universal (rational) man. Historically, rationality has been strongly associated with (white) men and 'masculine' characteristics, whereas women and the feminine have been categorized as emotional, irrational and in need of moral guidance (a strong argument for patriarchal authority). 'Rational Man' is seen to be an inherently masculinist construct (see chapter 6) that cannot in any sense represent woman.[43] Indeed, the concept of rational man can be seen to depend on the construction of the feminized 'Other'. From this perspective, the social experiences of women and the problems that women face are not easily addressed within a highly individualistic rights discourse. The championing of individual rights is not necessarily in the best interests of women, who might benefit more from the strengthening of social orderings and value systems that recognize the value of care and the role of motherhood, particularly in contributing to the good of not only families but entire communities and societies.

In the face of such criticism, Charlotte Bunch has defended rights discourse as an empowering tool for women, arguing that while the concept of rights emerged in a particular historical moment and rights were originally defined in terms of the needs of a limited section of the population, human rights have been continually transformed as a result of political struggles to claim rights for women (and, indeed, other specific groups).[44] Over time, the 'rights of man' have been extended to women, as women have demanded that they be treated equally, as in, for example, demands for equal pay. In more recent history issues of particular concern to women, such as domestic violence or reproductive rights, have come to be addressed in rights discourse and in legal instruments, the above controversies notwithstanding. The degree to which the development of women's human rights has altered the boundary between the public and private can be illustrated by the degree to which one might now speak of an international consensus that violence against women is wrong and, moreover, it is not a private matter, but constitutes a violation of women's human rights.[45] Progress in the area of violence against women in a variety of contexts also demonstrates how human rights are 'not solely a possession of middle class Western men', but an 'open text capable of appropriation and redefinition by groups in global political and legal arenas'.[46]

Gender, culture and human rights

Historically, cultural anthropologists have also tended to position themselves in critical opposition to universal values and transnational processes such as human rights. However, it is no easy task to distinguish between legitimate expressions of identity, community and culture, which should be celebrated, and the (ab)use of 'culture' and 'tradition' to legitimize the exercise of power by authoritarian governments over their people, or indeed the exercise of power over women by men. As noted in chapter 2, control over women's bodies and discourses on the 'proper' role of women in society is crucial in the reproduction of identities and in the drawing of group boundaries. Susan Okin claims that since the control of women by men is a prevalent feature of most cultures, and because there are clear disparities of power between the sexes, the more powerful, male members of cultural groups are generally in a position to determine and articulate the group's beliefs, practices and interests.[47] At such times, certain interests, needs and aspirations, arising specifically from being female, may be suppressed or subordinated by an overarching cultural paradigm favouring male dominance and privilege.[48] Moreover, cultural practices are likely to have much greater impact on the lives of women and girls than those of men and boys, since far more of women's time and energy goes into preserving and maintaining the personal, familial and reproductive side of life.

In more recent years the debate about the possible tension between women's rights and cultural difference has emerged with the publication of Okin's work '*Is Multiculturalism Bad for Women?*' Okin argues that the sphere of personal, sexual and reproductive life, including laws relating to marriage, divorce, child custody, control of family property and inheritance, forms the backbone of most cultures. In all of these domains, cultural groups engage in practices or prescribed rules that either actually or potentially limit the capacities of women and girls to live with human dignity equal to that of men and boys, and to live as freely chosen lives as they can.[49] Indeed, where religious orthodoxy or fundamentalism is a strong influence within societies, it is virtually impossible for women to choose to live independently of men, to be celibate or be lesbians, or to choose to be childless.[50]

Poststructuralists are apt to regard rights as a manifestation of the western sense of superiority. From this perspective, human rights are neither universal nor transcendent, but historically and culturally specific, arising out of particular notions of human dignity that arose in the West in response to political and social changes produced by the emergence of the modern state and early capitalist economies.[51] Thus cosmopolitan visions and the project of human rights specifically can be viewed as manifestations of cultural imperialism, a project that seeks to extend the political, economic and cultural domination of certain social groups in the West and the domination of the West over the rest of the world, undermining the autonomy of specific communities (constituted as sovereign states) in the process.

However, it is debatable whether the cultural imperialism thesis is an entirely accurate representation of the place of human rights in the world today and it is debatable whether human rights should be seen as a wholly western invention. For example, while it is often claimed that there is no equivalent to the 'Rights of Man' in Islamic doctrine, some writers argue that within Islam there are rights akin to the human rights now enshrined in international law, for example, rights to social security, limited government, protection from harm, access to justice, privacy, employment, property, political participation and freedom of expression.[52] This suggests that international human rights law is not tied to particular western values. People from various parts of the world had an input in the drafting of the Universal Declaration of Human Rights and in the formulation of subsequent treaties and conventions dealing with human rights.

Moreover, those who adopt a strong cultural relativist position tend to represent 'cultural groups' as both clearly bounded and homogeneous. This neglects the impact of transnational judicial processes. Processes of social change in domestic/national societies have been impelled through the incorporation of human rights norms into domestic systems of law.[53] During the past few decades there has been a gradual but sustained rise in the application of international human rights law, as well as the extension of a wider public discourse on human rights. Thus, rights-based discourses have been produced and translated in a variety of contexts. The growth and expansion of international human rights law in diverse societies and, more recently, international law instruments that deal with women's human rights specifically has served to challenge not only rigidly constructed boundaries between the public and the private, but also between the national and the international.[54]

A related challenge to the doctrine of cultural relativism is that it tends to emphasize the differences between groups rather than the differences within them. Cultures do not have a single set of discrete values. As is evident from the discussion of Beijing and the Beijing Plus 5 Review above, while women do not necessarily experience culture as oppressive or limiting, the 'authentic' voice of the community can be used to circumscribe political discourse and debate about women's human rights through the construction of dissent as disloyalty. Clearly, culture can be experienced as a means of providing members of the group with meaningful ways of life across the full range of human activities that encompass both public and private spheres of life[55] and also as a site of struggle and contestation over the social meanings of 'woman'.

A further problem with cultural relativism is that it can be embraced as part of the meta-narrative of governments who actively oppose the application of international human rights to their politics. The tolerance of relativism here has a directly conservative political implication in that it might result in acquiescence in state repression.[56] At a time when human rights violations have become subjected to global scrutiny, cultural relativists have often found themselves compelled to defend certain practices considered cruel and inhumane, and not just from a western perspective.

The question of what the 'balance' should be between regard for human rights and respect for cultural difference is not easy to decide. Donnelly has sought a middle ground between universalism and relativism in which cultural differences are not erased, but negotiated, in an effort to create a world in which all people are free to deliberate and develop values that will help them live more equitable lives. He argues that rather than remain wedded to a strong cultural relativist stance, one might embrace a 'cultural pluralist' position on human rights. Cultural pluralism looks for something akin to basic rights in non-western societies, which might not be identical to western rights, but which are broadly and functionally equivalent.[57] Through this means, it becomes possible to both champion the 'universality' of human rights, while allowing for some diversity and discretion in how 'universal' rights are interpreted and implemented in different cultural contexts.

At the very minimum, the women's human rights project requires a commitment to a 'thin' universalism. While in the effort to find some cross-cultural meeting ground both the cultural beliefs and practices of western and non-western societies should be open to critical interrogation, ultimately the purpose of women's human rights is to generate social changes that reinforce the equality, rather than the inequality, of women.[58] Indeed, Donnelly argues that in the final analysis, where the claims of rights to personal autonomy and choice contradict the dominant interpretation of what cultural identity requires, the emphasis must be on universality rather than relativity.[59] Women should be able to opt out of those practices that they deem to be detrimental, if they choose to do so.

Women's human rights as a political tool

Women's human rights and feminist political activism

Feminist activism has demonstrated the degree to which through political struggles the meaning of human rights has been expanded and transformed.[60] One might point here to the example of violence against women.[61] Post-Beijing, feminist activists organized transnationally to promote a gender-sensitive understanding of human rights and their violations and, intra-culturally, to change local views in such a way that women have been able to make rights claims.[62] Human rights discourse has been embraced in varied national and cultural contexts to challenge discrimination, persecution or harm, perpetuated and legitimized by ideologies of gender that naturalize inequality and that reinforce the inferiority/subordinate status of women.[63] In this process activists have exercised the political art of taking an existing discourse that has currency in the current practice of international politics and infusing it with new meanings. It is evident, therefore, that human rights should not be viewed simply as part of an imposed mission of modernity that merely reflects and legitimizes western (and male, bourgeois) interests and values since, in some contexts, human rights have served as a de-legitimising discourse, or proved to be an empowering discourse that challenges entrenched (gendered) power relations.

The women's human rights agenda has served to mobilize activists not just in the West but also across the world to monitor and, in some cases, help to implement both the CEDAW and the BPA. One might cite numerous examples here. Women's Human Rights Net (WHRnet) emerged prior to the World Conference on Human Rights, Vienna, in 1993 and expanded throughout the Fourth World Conference on Women. WHRnet has subsequently performed an important function in publicizing human rights violations across the world, as will be elaborated below.

Poststructuralist and postcolonial feminists argue that there is a need for more attention to be paid to local and specific contexts in working out strategies to empower women. However, the continuing importance of the international dimension should not be wholly discounted. Appeals to human rights have provided a powerful tool in the effort to challenge the subordinate position of women, at both local and global levels. Moreover, appeals to human rights are often useful in putting pressure on states to redress acts of violence against women, particularly when local measures and national instruments have seemingly failed them. Transnational support networks can provide support for local activists and specific individuals in their struggle to secure justice for women. One might illustrate the value of an international discourse on human rights, on human rights instruments and on transnational networks with reference to the recent case of Mukhtar Mai. Mukhtar Mai was gang-raped by a group of men after her brother had been seen with a girl from another clan, an act that was deemed to have brought shame upon the group. International human rights groups, including Amnesty International, the transnational network Women Living Under Muslim Laws and WHRnet ensured that the case received widespread publicity and put pressure on the Pakistani authorities to act.[64] In such cases, demonstrations of solidarity from both Muslim and non-Muslim organizations and the invocation of human rights was helpful in securing justice.

As activists in varied locations around the world have embraced rights discourse, the strategies that activists have adopted for pursuing and achieving their goals have undoubtedly been shaped by the need to negotiate the competing claims of culture and identity in diverse societies. Grass-roots women's organizations affirm and defend the principle of women's rights, while recognizing that differing strategies and measures are needed to realize this aspiration in concrete contexts. Brooke Ackerly has argued that in trying to bridge the gap between universal principles and local and specific measures, activists in women's groups seemingly embrace an incoherent theoretical position, in so far as human rights are held to be at once local and universal, embraced and contested.[65] She argues that women's human rights can be used to reinforce norms of international customary human rights law and to assess critically the claims of culturally legitimate deviance from these norms while respecting value plurality across and within cultures. In this way, the universality of human rights might be substantially meaningful even while the realization of human rights is not uniform.[66]

As noted above and elsewhere in this book, the reproduction of cultural or national identities often centres on the control of women's bodies and reproductive function. This is why the women's human rights agenda (in relation to reproduction, sexuality, marriage and the family particularly) continues to be contentious, with governments sometimes actively working to impede agreement on what acts should be considered violations of women's rights and dragging their feet on implementation measures. A major challenge facing women's groups at the national and local level, therefore, is how to ensure that effective means to implement relevant treaties and conventions on women's human rights are devised that serve women in different national and cultural contexts.[67] This is important because (some) national governments have succeeded in exploiting divisions among NGOs to present culture and religion as in some way trumping gender.

At Beijing, governments demanded and won the concession that respect for cultural differences would guide the way that specific measures outlined in the Platform of Action were implemented. As argued above, this is not necessarily problematic from a feminist perspective, but will be if activists are not able to provide forcible arguments for where, how and to what degree 'culture' allows legitimate deviation from internationally agreed principles and are not able to present concrete proposals for how women's human rights can be implemented in varied contexts in ways that empower women. The role of NGOs in the implementation process is, therefore, a crucial concern since the implementation of specific measures will be a future site of struggle. Activists have to ensure that the feminist interest in altering culture so as to reinforce the equality, rather than the inequality, of women is not undermined by the language of implementation that allows loopholes for governments to frustrate hard-won achievements at Beijing and elsewhere.[68]

With respect to the use of women's human rights as a political tool, it is evident that while there are some limitations, nevertheless states are clearly vulnerable to their own public rhetoric and declarations. Furthermore, human rights documentations can be successfully used, when and where political opportunities arise, to hold states to account. For example, NGOs recorded the 'list of promises' made by government delegations at Beijing and have subsequently used this to subject states to scrutiny and hold governments to account for their actions, or inaction. Transnational feminist networks, of various kinds, clearly play an important role in this process. Bunch argues that the incorporation of women's human rights by governments 'enhances womens capacity to build global alliances based on collective political goals and a common agenda' and 'because human rights is a language that has legitimacy among many individuals and governments, the appeal to human rights agreements and international norms can fortify women's networks'.[69] As she further contends, the Beijing Platform of Action is an essential tool in this process as it affirms women's rights as human rights and sets out many actions necessary to achieve women's empowerment.

CONCLUSION

There are numerous obstacles to the realization of women's human rights, but this does not refute the strategic and political necessity of speaking 'as woman' at a time when (largely) elite men continue to (largely) monopolize both global and local political space and display no timidity in asserting essentialist claims that prescribe what the role of women should be in specific societies. While the universality or otherwise of human rights and cultural difference are legitimate subjects for debate, there are perils in rejecting women's human rights given the growing influence of anti-feminist forces that contest the language of women's equality, equal worth and right to determine, as far as possible, their own destinies. Human rights is premised on some universals, but is flexible enough to accommodate potentially divisive differences, while also providing a universal idiom in which to speak about and challenge injustices at a time when this is sorely needed by activists at both the local and the global level.[70] The women's human rights agenda has also provided activists with a unifying agenda around which feminist solidarities have been forged. This is the subject of the following chapter.

TRANSNATIONAL FEMINIST SOLIDARITY

INTRODUCTION

This chapter[1] revisits one of the recurring themes of this book, the politics of transnational feminism. Historically, solidarity among women has been a core objective of the feminist movement. The need for a politics of solidarity founded on women's 'shared problems' and the necessity of speaking as 'women' remains central to contemporary feminist discourse and practice.[2] Indeed, it is difficult to imagine a feminist politics that is not predicated on the basis of solidarity among women, who understand themselves to differ in important, if not fundamental ways, from men, who display gender consciousness and who organize around issues that have the potential to unite women across boundaries of culture and nation.

And yet, it is equally evident from the history of transnational feminism[3] that forging and, particularly, sustaining solidarity has also been a 'problem' for the feminist movement. The early feminist movement organized around a platform to promote women's civil and political rights but even at this early stage in feminist organizing fissures and splits occurred on substantive issues other than suffrage.[4] In both the politics of the transnational feminist movement and debates within academic feminism in the 1980s and 1990s, it was evident that solidarity could not be assumed on the basis of a false homogeneity among women. It seemed that solidarities 'emerged along the lines of class, gender, sexuality, ethnicity and so on, and because the forms these solidarities assumed shifted and changed, movements were apt to sometimes pull apart as well as pull together'.[5] Today, the divergent political strategies of women's groups in varied locations similarly point to the potential fragility of alliances forged across boundaries of class, culture, age, ethnicity and national location.

The main aims of the chapter are to discuss the complexities of identity and difference within the transnational feminist movement and thereby challenge the notion that one can identify a homogeneous group of people called 'women' whose 'common interests' give rise to a shared identification with feminist causes. The second aim is to, nevertheless, defend the continuing importance of feminist solidarity. Differences among women do not necessarily preclude possibilities for forging solidarity, since solidarity can be secured through the negotiation of difference. However, collective identities and interests cannot simply be assumed and, similarly, solidarity does not flow from essential(ist) identities and pre-given interests. Feminist solidarity is a project that is forged through political struggle, a struggle that 'carries with it the willingness to accept responsibility for using conflict constructively'[6] and the responsibility to understand and negotiate differences between women's organizations and feminist groups.

The chapter is divided into four substantive sections. The first section is devoted to a discussion of the early feminist movement, a movement that emerged in the West in the nineteenth century and which was, initially, largely liberal in ideology and western dominated. The second section discusses the nature and basis for solidarity in human relationships. The third section documents the heterogeneity of women's groups and revisits the themes of division and fragmentation (see chapter 7). This section also reassesses the significance of diversity, and indeed conflict and division, for feminist political activity. The final part of the paper turns to contemporary feminist practice. This section includes a discussion of feminist networks that promote and defend women's human rights and also efforts to forge feminist solidarity around anti-globalization struggles.

The emergence of a transnational feminist movement

As is evident from the discussion in the previous chapter, rights discourse has been and remains fairly central to influential strands of feminist thought and to the politics of the feminist/women's movement across the world. 'Rights' are one (powerful) way in which claims on behalf of women might be articulated. Feminism[7] has never been a wholly western discourse. Fatima Mernissi, for example, has argued that there has been a debate about equality between the sexes in Muslim societies since at least the nineteenth century with the appearance of Qasim Amin's book, *Women's Liberation*, in the 1880s.[8] However, the period of Enlightenment in the West provided fertile soil to nurture a project that sought to challenge the social and political supremacy of men and 'emancipate' women.[9] In the West, the notion that 'man' was a bearer of natural or inherent rights entered into political discourse as a challenge to what were then the reigning principles of political legitimacy. Rights discourse served as a powerful challenge to forms of political authority rooted in the idea of the 'divine right' of kings (authority vested in the sovereign by God) or in notions that the aristocracy constituted a 'natural elite', a class possessed of special qualities that rendered them fit to run (or at least have great influence in) the affairs of state. Political appeals to rights made by this newly emerging class worked to challenge the vested interests of the established aristocracy and landed classes and to protect this new class of 'men of property' from the tyranny of a state whose powers were unchecked.[10]

However, while rights were held to be universal because they grew out of the universal capacity for rational thought, historically rights of citizenship were actually granted or withheld on the grounds of race, sex and/or class. To possess rights one had to be a citizen, but this effectively meant being an adult male who owned property.

Women, along with other specific social groups, were excluded from public life, denied access to political power, legal personality and citizenship.[11] As Seyla Benhabib has argued, the male bourgeois citizen fought for rights to autonomy against the absolutist state, but relations in the household continued to be built upon non-egalitarian assumptions. The family had been – and continues to be – the object of political interventions, for example, in the realm of health, education and the upbringing of children. However, the private domain was constituted in bourgeois discourse as an enclosed space or sphere of intimacy that was considered free from all social constraints and political interventions. The bourgeois family was represented as a community of care held together by solidarist bonds of love and respect. Thus, while man could not be free while ever he was subjected to arbitrary power, woman continued to be subject to her father's or her husband's arbitrary power, particularly in the private realm.[12] Rationality was, therefore, held to be a capacity that men possessed, but not an attribute of women who were constructed as 'irrational'.

In championing the principle of equality and arguing that the human person or subject was possessed of rationality, early women political activists nevertheless found liberalism useful in challenging customary prejudices about the nature and relevance of sexual difference. Written in 1792, Mary Wollstonecraft's *Vindication of the Rights of Woman* is often held up as the first attempt to make a comprehensive and coherent case for equal rights for women by invoking liberal arguments.[13] Wollstonecraft suggested that perceived sex differences were actually the consequence of discrimination, in that historically women had been confined to the home and to the domestic service of their husbands and children and so had been afforded few opportunities to exercise their intellectual faculties or develop skills other than those deemed necessary for the performance of their domestic duties. The reconstitution of the subject as a bearer of rights in liberal political discourse unsettled the prevailing gender hierarchy between the sexes, as appeals in the name of universal principles allowed women to take up their own political demands. At the same time, however, feminists were logically compelled to argue for women's equality on the grounds that women, like men, were rational beings capable of making their own decisions and determining their own best interests. In prioritizing the struggle for women's civil and political rights, liberal feminists tended to take for granted the idea that women would be 'liberated' by escaping from the family and negotiating new identities in the public sphere.[14]

When Virginia Woolf proclaimed in 1938 that 'as a woman I have no country',[15] she was espousing an internationalist sentiment that was characteristic of the early women's movement. The appeal to the idea of a 'universal sisterhood' based on shared experiences of injustice facilitated the forging of solidarity among like-minded groups across national boundaries, as women mobilized around the promotion of a political agenda that sought to expand democratic principles of participation, representation and political rights to women. Inspired by early pioneers like Wollstonecraft, women's movements emerged in many parts of North America and Europe in the nineteenth century that both contested the demands placed on women by tradition, culture and religion and started the task of mobilizing women around suffrage, property rights, representation and participation in political life.[16] While the radicalism of early liberalism was limited, these early pioneers of the women's movement went beyond calls for the right to vote, in that they also demanded that male power be circumscribed in areas of life previously regarded as 'private'. Women also became active in other social movements, for example the US abolitionist movement, often using this as a platform to disseminate ideas about the injustice of women's continuing subjugation. These nationally based organizations quickly established transnational linkages and forged solidarities across state/national boundaries, effectively establishing a network of women's groups that has since grown and expanded.

Universal claims made in the name of 'women' detracted from the elitist and heavily bourgeois nature of the movement. The vote, political participation and women's equality/rights were political demands that were particularly befitting women aspiring to economic independence.[17] Similarly, the liberal feminist conception of woman that emphasized her individuality and autonomy jarred to some degree with the championing of women as devoted mothers and dutiful wives, a discourse that was common among activists in the peace movement.[18] Women peace activists used powerful arguments for women's difference, rather than sameness/equality with men, and identified 'wartime sexual violence as a stark boundary separating women from men'.[19] However, as women mobilized politically in the service of international peace, furthering the cause of peace was in turn seen to necessitate women's participation in public life and the right to vote particularly. Thus some unity of purpose was recognized among activists, their ideological differences notwithstanding.

Verta Taylor has argued that a central problem of the early women's movement was how to reconcile the need to view the world as divided by sex, but avoid undermining the diversity of the movement.[20] This problem was, however, recognized by early pioneers like Susan B. Anthony and Elizabeth Cady Stanton who both sought to widen the social base of the women's rights movement by seeking the support of working-class women.[21] Leila Rupp has also highlighted the bourgeois and western-dominated nature of the early women's movement. However, without glossing over the tensions within the movement, she remains impressed by the 'remarkable bonds that women did forge across national boundaries and multiple languages'.[22] In foregrounding women's differences from men and creating single-sex organizations, activists were able to 'come together as women in a deeply felt solidarity based on gender'.[23]

Throughout much of the twentieth century, liberal feminism enjoyed the status of being the dominant form of feminist thought and also proved to be a powerful idea in the actual practice of world politics. However, since the 1980s differences among women have become a much more prominent theme in academic feminist discourse and have become much more salient issues in the politics of the transnational women's movement.

UNDERSTANDING SOLIDARITY

There is no single definition of solidarity, nor commonly agreed understanding of the basis upon which solidarity is or might be secured or where solidarity is grounded or located. Solidarity is often held to involve a social structure that identifies and characterizes a group; the symbolic representation of the group itself; the common emotional orientation of members towards the group; and the contribution of resources by members of the group to a collective good or to other members of the group.[24] The achievement of social solidarity has been held to depend upon the degree to which individuals are integrated into the life of a specific community, which in turn is facilitated by furnishing individuals with a common set of values and symbols around which to mobilize.[25] Solidarity might be founded on the basis of shared principles and/or generated by feelings of empathy towards other members of the group.

Social movements are often cited as examples of internationalized collective identities that serve as a locus for solidarity in world politics, uniting members around the cause of opposing the current social order and promoting an alternative set of values, beliefs and practices.[26] As Crow argues, to identify with a movement and its practices 'is to commit oneself to it in a way that normally involves endorsing its practices and seeking to promote its interests, whilst regarding one's well-being as intimately linked to its flourishing'.[27] Boundary-drawing processes are a feature of social movements. The construction of boundaries and identities encloses certain ideas and demands and excludes others.[28] Rupp and Taylor identify at least three processes involved in the formation of political identities: the creation of boundaries that mark off the group; the development of consciousness of the group's distinct and shared disadvantages; and the politicization of everyday life, embodied in symbols and actions that connect members of the group and link their everyday experiences to larger social injustices.[29]

Expressions of transnational solidarity subvert dominant discourses on identity and solidarity that privilege the nation and nationalism as a dominant discourse of political identity, source of symbolism (that generates an emotional attachment to the collective) and mainspring of political mobilization. For example, the transnational network Women Living Under Muslim Laws, which will be discussed further below, challenges the 'erroneous belief that the only possible existence for a Muslim woman that allows her to maintain her identity (however defined) is the dominant one delineated of her in her national context'.[30]

The work of WLUML bears testimony to the need to recognize how women's struggles are greatly complicated by the claims of culture, religion and national identity. Farida Shaheed argues that WLUML recognizes that the 'fear of being cut off from one's collective identity militates against women challenging "Muslim laws".'[31] However, the support provided by another collectivity that functions as an alternative reference group helps women to redefine the parameters of their current reference group. She suggests that 'the links with women from other parts of the Muslim world – whose very existence speaks to the multiplicity of women's realities within the Muslim context – provide an important source of inspiration' for women in Muslim countries. Thus, 'WLUML makes important contribution to women's struggles for justice in specific locations by opening doors to a multiplicity of possible alternatives.'[32]

Similarly, the Women in Black Women's Solidarity Network Against War links the cause of ending war with the ending of 'all forms of violence and discrimination against women'[33] and, in so doing, boldly asserts a common and collective identity shared by women, rejecting 'the imposed national identity based on the glorification of its own nation and the creation of hate towards other nations'. The rejection of national identities (thus constructed) is seen as a precondition for the development of 'the identity of woman, the other, oppressed and harassed by all war masters/mongers, without any difference as to which nation we belong'.[34] At the same time, Women in Black acknowledges diversity in experience, encouraging women to 'talk openly about their experiences in war' and 'listen with respect' to the stories of women from diverse national and religious backgrounds and different political and sexual orientations, thus acknowledging both complex identities and the varying contexts in which women experience violence.

As essentialism and essentialist claims have fallen out of favour across the social sciences and constructivist approaches to identity have gained more adherents, more attention has been paid to the means by which one's sense of identity and identification with others emerges in a social world of shared meanings and practices forged around self/other relationships. Since identity is neither fixed nor essential, it becomes necessary for social actors to establish 'a locus of attachment and secure shared meanings in order to stabilize identity', because 'in this way, political action in the name of constituted identity groups and their "interests" becomes possible'.[35]

Rather than postulating the existence of objective interests (on the basis of class, nation, gender or some other 'stable', homogeneous category) which might form the basis for solidarity, it is more fruitful to consider how both interests and identities are constructed, but nevertheless serve as a potentially unifying political force. Problematizing the primacy of collective identities and attachments to the nation-state is but a first stage in exploring 'the ways that transnational actors can design the means to facilitate the creation of a variety of international collective identities'.[36]

CONTESTING SOLIDARITY/REAFFIRMING SOLIDARITY

Yet it is evident from the earlier discussion of feminist organizing at the UN that the degree of unity in the feminist movement should not be overstated. The critique of the western, bourgeois feminist movement was covered in chapter 7 and so will not be revisited at this juncture; suffice to say that the wide-ranging critique of western feminism (both in theory and in practice) represented a fundamental challenge to the idea that women were a homogeneous group. The notion that women experienced 'common oppression' was now apt to be characterized as a 'false and corrupt platform, disguising and mystifying the true nature of women's varied and complex social realities'.[37] At the same time, the 'emotional appeal of sisterhood' was rejected on the grounds that it disguised the 'manipulative opportunism of bourgeois women'.[38] Moreover, the shift in feminist theory from championing 'woman' as a stable category of analysis to conceptualizing gender as discursively constructed served to call into question 'universal' meanings of 'woman' and, so, the politics of the transnational women's movement. The cause of empowering women necessitates a struggle to challenge multiple structures of oppression at different levels.

However, the preoccupation with difference in feminist theory and the conflicts that emerged among feminist activists did not wholly undermine the struggle to establish a basis for solidarity. As the meaning of the term 'feminist' 'shifted across time and in different contexts' and as activists sometimes disagreed on the most effective strategies to 'emancipate' or 'empower' women in varied contexts and locations, throughout these shifts and changes through 'conflict and cooperation', women's groups continued to insist on the necessity of forging a common identity that served to hold together the network of diverse groups that comprised the movement.[39] As bell hooks argued, even in the midst of conflict and contestation, it remained 'absolutely necessary for feminist activists to renew our commitment to political struggle and strengthen our solidarity'.[40] As hooks insisted, 'women do not need to eliminate difference to feel solidarity.'[41] The call by hooks, and others, to understand (and respect) differences among women generated more research on barriers that separated women and ways to overcome such barriers to solidarity, in work that explored the intersections of race, class and gender in social movement activity.[42]

The strategic necessity to speak as 'women'

Amidst debates on the importance of acknowledging specificity and differences among actual women, a tension emerged between respect for difference and the perceived political and strategic necessity to continue to speak as women. In so far as gender did determine to a large degree one's access to and control of resources and remained a significant marker of social inequality and poverty,[43] some feminist commentators warned against the prioritization of differences between women over those experiences that were shared; experiences that arose from gendered power relations, social relations of inequality and experiences of discrimination. Concerns were expressed that the deconstruction of 'woman' in academic feminism would undermine the legitimacy of the feminist movement, a movement that was engaged in concrete struggles to challenge gender inequalities and/or to promote women's rights/status in a variety of local, national and international contexts.[44] In so far as women in varied locations continued to regard gender as a 'site of contestation' and a 'mediating factor in their lives and their communities',[45] and women were able to identify collectively for some purposes, the strategic necessity of organizing as women was reaffirmed.

Solidarity as a political project

If feminist politics could no longer be based on the 'model created by bourgeois feminism', it was equally evident that feminist solidarity could not be forged on the basis of 'shared victimhood' or 'unconditional love for one another'.[46] Such assumptions encouraged women to avoid 'confronting the complexity of their own experiences' and prevented activists from reflecting upon their own social status and position and understanding and appreciating their differences. An unreflective and patently false assumption of universally constituted subjectivities, stable identities and 'objective' interests was similarly problematic. Appeals were made to the need to 'build upon women's multiple identities, experiences and locations',[47] a sentiment seemingly more in sympathy with an 'ethos of pluralism' than the cause of uniting women in the furtherance of 'universal' political projects. But if 'woman' as a theoretical construct, category and universally constituted subjectivity was deemed to be a fiction, then on what basis could chains or bonds of solidarity be forged between women in various locations around the world?

The answer to this question lay in rethinking the project of political solidarity. Conflict was recast not as divisive, but rather as constructive, while 'sisterhood' was re-visioned as an accomplishment that women must struggle to achieve. Hooks, for example, argued that conflict (between white women and women of colour) might be viewed as a 'cause of despair' since it seemingly pointed to the impossibility of women working 'together in social space that is not irrevocably tainted by the politics of domination'.[48] Confronting conflict was now presented as a necessary process in a 'sustained committed struggle' that would 'lead towards a liberatory feminist agenda'.[49] To build and sustain solidarity, it was necessary to 'respect our differences' and to 'affirm one another' by understanding and appreciating the contribution that all women made to feminist struggles.[50] Women in their diversity might then struggle in a supportive way to build the foundation for solidarity. Reflection on diversity, differences and conflict was not detrimental to the cause of building solidarity, but allowed 'individuals united by common goals' to 'consciously utilise their differences and limitations to accelerate positive advance'.[51]

This struggle was not defined only in terms of gender, but involved an appreciation of a complex web of social relations of inequality and multiple and interrelated practices of discrimination and oppression. It was imperative for activists to reflect critically upon the limitations of white, western feminism that had privileged a primarily liberal political agenda, and to address the concerns of women around the world in 'the historicised particularity of their relationship to multiple patriarchies as well as international economic hegemonies'[52] and to focus on 'multiple, overlapping and discrete oppressions rather than construct a theory of hegemonic oppression under a unified category of gender'.[53]

Negotiating differences

The project of forging solidarity necessitated not simply 'respect for difference', since respect for differences might generate separatism that 'weakens and diminishes the feminist movement'.[54] The struggle to build solidarity involves an effort to secure a basis for unity in the midst of differences. Recognizing that there are differences in how women experience discrimination and that strategies to challenge discriminatory practices necessarily differ according to specific context does not mean abandoning the aspiration to establish some common ground among activists in diverse locations, nor among individual women. Building *feminist* solidarity depends upon women being able to identify as women and perceive themselves to have some unity of purpose – to end gender oppression in the many and varied forms that it takes. Respecting differences entails the recognition that women in specific locations often share common cause with men of their own class or ethnic group, but also experience discrimination or oppression on the basis of gender and that this must also be acknowledged. Women's struggles thus reaffirm the feminist emancipatory interest in challenging gender discrimination and reinforcing 'the equality, rather than the inequality, of women'.[55]

Solidarity depends then upon the negotiation of differences and thus entails a commitment to dialogue in which women are empowered to speak as 'women' and the need for activists to reflect critically upon their own practices. Solidarity might be usefully understood as 'a relation constructed through forms of dialogue and struggle'.[56]

The potentialities and problems in achieving genuinely open and participatory dialogue, particularly in international contexts, have been extensively documented[57] and for reasons of space cannot be covered in depth here. Suffice to say that fostering dialogue is a potentially fruitful way forward in rescuing a transnational feminist project. If dialogue is to be meaningful, it must serve to empower different voices and so the project of solidarity imposes an obligation on women activists (particularly in the West) who claimed to stand in solidarity with women struggling for their rights in diverse societies to not only 'understand the oppressive relations in which women are enmeshed well enough to serve them in the struggle against those relations', but to also 'make available to them discursive and material resources to assist in that struggle'.[58] Networks of solidarity, forged among a wide array of women's groups, must function as a means of support and, possibly, resources for local groups and networks that disseminate the views of women in diverse locations. It also means that western women's groups particularly have an obligation to not only listen and to understand and appreciate differences, but to offer support to women's groups in other locations. This way, the relations that are forged between women's groups who stand in solidarity will not reproduce the worst excesses of unequal power relations. Reflexivity on one's own privileged position and voice is a central part of the struggle to build solidarity, as are efforts to dismantle 'structures of privilege' that prevent the articulation of women's interests, needs and rights, by women's groups in varied societies, from being heard.

Constructing collective identities

Most of the literature on social movements has tended to focus largely on the 'unitary aspects of collective identity and ignore significant differences of identity and interest'.[59] Reevaluating and reassessing the nature of collective identity groups (notably social movements) has been another prominent feature of recent feminist scholarship. Rupp and Taylor suggest that feminists are 'social movement actors' in so far as individual feminist activists are situated within an organizational and movement context. Feminism is more than gender ideology; it is a collective identity and so the nature of the feminist movement has to be understood in terms of 'the complex, ever-changing processes' through which boundaries are drawn that separate 'us' and 'them'. However, since diversity has, to some degree, always been a feature of the feminist movement, to understand the feminist movement it is necessary to devise an analytical framework that facilitates an understanding of how boundaries and identities are constructed, 'sometimes through conflict' and sometimes on the basis of a 'sense of togetherness'.[60]

While there have been moments when conflicts have emerged that have, or have threatened to, fragment and divide the movement in ways that seemingly defy solidarist projects, conflicts can be creative. Conflict can serve to inspire deep reflection and renewed efforts to work through differences in the interest of establishing common causes. Activists have recognized that gender relationships are constituted differently in different societies and that diverse strategies are required to challenge gender discrimination and inequality. There are possibilities for forging solidarities in varied societies and political contexts but, if these are to be realised, differences must be acknowledged, confronted and negotiated.

It is evident that there are moments in the development of the feminist movement when gender has been privileged in the narrative of feminist struggle as a significant – perhaps *the* most significant – social cleavage and category of analysis, by those struggling to critique female disadvantage and improve women's situation. However, there are other times when solidarity identities, such as race, class, and ethnicity, derived from women's specific social locations, have greatly complicated the process of constructing a collective identity. At such times, sustaining solidarity has depended to a much greater degree upon respect for the particularities of women's identities and sensitivity towards the specific contexts in which women's struggles unfold. Solidarity has then been articulated as a project that requires careful coalition building across boundaries and the construction of loose networks that allow women to share information, ideas and resources. This does not mean that the project of constructing a collective identity is wholly abandoned – networks and coalitions are established among 'women', by 'women' to support 'women', but the 'story of feminism', a narrative that underpins the entire political project, is more likely to emphasize the complexities of women's identities, the plurality of the movement and the diversity of experience as a source of strength.

Contemporary feminist discourse challenges or 'destabilizes' fixed identities in favour of 'complex and specific socially situated selves'.[61] Identity politics and claims made in the name of the collective identity group are now more likely to be viewed as problematic, if not dangerous. However, while identity categories might well be 'political fictions', they have benefits as well as costs, particularly in contexts where interest group politics are the norm and it is strategically necessary to make claims in the name of constituted identity groups. The dangers of identity politics lie in the problems of institutionalized exclusion.[62] But if identity is understood to be fluid, rather than fixed, and constructed through the dynamic interaction of groups, rather than a static precondition for political mobilization, then strategies to build alliances and support networks for groups struggling against gender injustices in specific contexts might be effectively worked out that enhance the possibilities for achieving an 'inclusive solidarity'.[63] This might well mean that 'solidarity is specific and strategic' and, moreover, might not endure over a long period of time, but is nevertheless preferable to solidarity built upon hegemonic discourses and practices that are exclusionary and ultimately divisive. It also encourages dialogue and communication to be built into feminist practice, rather than silencing particular voices in the interests of maintaining ideological 'orthodoxy'.

Taylor argues that the history of the women's movement should not so much be told as a story of waves of activism, followed by periods of fragmentation and/or the complete collapse of movement in the intervening periods, but rather as taking different forms at different periods of history, sometimes characterized by periods of 'continuity and survival', and sometimes achieving the status of a mass movement. One might speculate that the periods in which the feminist movement has been most successful in mobilizing women on a mass scale and building solid alliances have been those in which activists have been most successful in resisting or contesting discourses and political projects that privilege the claims of the nation, class or cultural group *over* the claims of gender or in privileging gender *over* the claims of nation, class or ethnicity. Certainly, one can identify 'moments of collective creation' in which members have successfully cohered around 'ideas, identities and ideals' that have 'served to provide a sense of shared purpose, or even a common bond among members'.[64] However, the diversity of women has eventually undermined solidarity built on the assumption of a singular identity and common interests that override other significant cleavages.

SOLIDARITY IN CONTEMPORARY FEMINIST PRACTICE

Forging solidarities around a women's human rights agenda

At Beijing, the NGO forum served as a site in which differences, and indeed conflicts, were openly articulated. In her 'Reflections on US Women of Colour' at the conference, Mallika Dutt recorded how all US women of colour were regarded as 'American' by women from the South and how 'Americans' were, in turn, perceived to be 'arrogant, insensitive and imperialist'.[65] Whereas women of colour generally saw themselves as 'oppositional forces' in the US, they were now compelled to confront the role of the US as 'aggressor and violator of women's human rights' in so far as the United States was held to be driving the project of economic globalization that had resulted in cutbacks in welfare, corporate downsizing, the loss of women's jobs and increasing levels of poverty among women in developing countries.[66]

The growing representation of women's organizations from the global South encouraged more open discussion of the relevance of differences among activists, but this resulted in 'creative tensions' rather than an increasing propensity towards separatism. Dutt argues that the conference had a deep impact on women's groups in the US. In their accounts of their experiences at Beijing, US women of colour described a profound shift in consciousness and a determination to struggle to implement this transformation in consciousness and perspective (on the global role of the US particularly) in their day-to-day organizing and practices.[67] While US women of colour reported experiencing 'suspicion and hostility' from Southern women, many also remarked that recognizing that women from developing countries were 'powerful voices for change' rather than 'victims' was the 'starting point in changing the dialogue between women in the US and women in many parts of the world'.[68]

Moreover, all of the women Dutt interviewed described the 'sense of the global solidarity, pride and affirmation' that they experienced in Beijing and many commented on the 'vibrancy and power of the global women's movement', a vibrancy and power that contrasted starkly with the 'lack of unity and strength in the US women's movement'.[69] Loretta Roos, of the National Black Women's Health project, implored US women to help 'build a global movement like an international human rights movement and a global labour movement' or risk becoming 'part of the global free-fall'.[70]

A recurrent theme of the work that has appeared on the Beijing conference has emphasized the way in which the NGO forum particularly functioned as a space in which activists engaged in dialogue, while also noting the further possibilities for communication opened up by global networks created to disseminate information on women's human rights.[71] Increasingly human rights have become central to the discourses and practice of many NGOs and have been embraced by diverse social movements, including feminist organizations who regard human rights as a (potentially) 'empowering tool' for activist groups and individual women.[72] Gender discrimination can be framed as a human rights issue, meaning that practices that are experienced as oppressive and/or harmful to and by women within specific societies can be addressed at both national and international levels. Governments can then be held to account when they fail to apply and implement international human rights standards that they have signed up to. Post-Beijing, the women's human rights agenda has served to mobilize women not just in the West, but women across the world.[73]

However, feminist activism around women's human rights has also demonstrated that women's rights cannot be articulated in terms of transcendental principles, but have to be worked out and negotiated. Activists can be viewed as not only lobbyists and advocates, but also participants in a dialogue involving inter-subjective negotiation on both the concept of rights and the substantive content of women's human rights and how best to advance this project in diverse societies. This dialogue has centred on what human rights for women might mean in specific locales and how relevant treaties and conventions on women's human rights might be implemented most effectively to serve women in different national and cultural contexts. In this way, the universality of human rights might be substantially meaningful even while the realization of human rights is not uniform.[74]

The women's human rights agenda provides a basis for building solidarity among activists across national boundaries without the need to embrace a 'thick' universalism as the basis for solidarity. As with many other transnational feminist organizations and networks, WLUML uses the language of human rights. Shaheed argues that WLUML's solidarity work involves initiating and responding to appeals for support from women whose human rights have been violated. The response might take the form of mobilizing international support, securing the services of lawyers, identifying support groups, providing shelter, mediating between parties or lobbying governments. Sometimes this solidarity involves ongoing campaigns to mobilize international support to reform or repeal existing laws and practices. The work of WLUML also involves campaigns for 'the repeal of discriminatory legislation to end oppressive practices and the enactment and enforcement of legislation favourable to women'.[75] However, the practice of WLUML also bears out the point that coalition building across boundaries must be, and is, sensitive to the need for 'the application of locally informed strategies of resistance'.[76] In this way, the rights and autonomy of women are at once affirmed and defended, although differing strategies and measures are utilized to realize, promote and protect women's human rights in concrete contexts.

Forging solidarities in anti-capitalist/anti-globalization struggles

As was elaborated in chapter 6, feminist commentators on globalization typically focus on the ways in which both 'the global economy affects those on the fringes of the market, the state or in households' and share a commitment to realize an 'alternative' world order characterized by higher degrees of security and justice (see also chapter

5).[77] The first task of those who seek alternatives to neoliberal globalization is to challenge the representation of globalization as a set of 'inexorable and immutable'[78] forces and to put questions of agency and politics back into the picture. While neoliberalism continues to function as a hegemonic discourse, liberalizing forces are not the only ones at work, nor are they always able to wholly trample over opposition. There is significant opposition to the neoliberal globalization project that stems from groups who promote alternative values and articulate normative visions of how the world might be differently organized. While diverse and loosely organized, reflecting a complex mix of social forces and identities, groups that collectively comprise the anti-globalization movement are increasingly appealing to the language of human rights, often conducting global campaigns to shame not only IEOs but also multinational corporations (MNCs) to grant stronger protection, including employment rights, to workers throughout the world.

In preparation for the Beijing conference, when women met in a number of regional forums to discuss the major concerns of women in those particular regions, the stress was on the need to view the problems of women in a local, national, regional and global context. The Expert Reports[79] prepared for the Fourth UN Conference on Women in Beijing recognized explicitly, and indeed placed a great deal of emphasis upon, broad disparities between North and South, rural and urban, rich and poor. In so doing, these reports demonstrated an awareness of the relationship between gender inequalities and other forms of inequality based on class or race or ethnic groups. Similarly, as NGOs worked to modify the text of the Platform of Action, they were concerned to make visible the massive economic inequalities that exist between women and that greatly add to the burden of not only women in the Third World but also working-class women and women from ethnic minorities in the West. Throughout all stages of the preparatory process, women worked to highlight the gender-specific effects of globalization and global restructuring, drew attention to the 'negative' and 'damaging' impact of structural adjustment policies forced on indebted states by the International Monetary Fund and the World Bank (see previous chapter) and generally worked hard to make explicit the linkages between gender inequalities, poverty and debt.

The 'expert report' on the ECE region, in preparation for Beijing, explicitly recognized that issues of women's rights and sustainable development could not be seriously addressed unless the consumption and production patterns in the ECE region changed. Significantly European feminists also cited the problems of racism in Europe, noting that women of colour in the region were particularly affected by global restructuring processes and made a massive contribution to unwaged and low-waged work. Women in Europe joined women in Latin America and in the Asia-Pacific region in rejecting dominant economic paradigms and arguing that the deep contradictions in economic policies of restructuring and globalization were resulting in economic and social policies that were detrimental to the rights of women. They called for gender-sensitive and socially responsible government policies. And they have also demanded that governments make multinational and transnational corporations abide by standards that promote women's equality. Consumerism as the route to personal fulfilment has been rejected because this promotes over-consumption in the West.[80]

The possibility of building solidarity among feminist organizations around anti-capitalist and anti-globalization struggles has been a theme of much contemporary feminist scholarship. Chandra Mohanty, whose seminal article *Under Western Eyes* published in the 1980s inspired a wave of postcolonial feminist scholarship, has recently called for a new feminist solidarity forged around anti-capitalist struggles (see chapter 7).[81] Mohanty argues that in *Under Western Eyes* her aim was to 'make clear that cross-cultural feminist work must be attentive to the micropolitics of context, subjectivity and struggle, as well as to the macropolitics of global economic and political systems and processes'.[82] She was at pains to point out the false universalism of western feminist claims, but it was not her intention to undermine or negate the possibility of feminist solidarity across boundaries altogether. Rather Mohanty sought to 're-emphasise the connections between the local and universal' and demonstrate 'how specifying difference allows us to theorise universal concerns more fully'.[83]

Economic globalization has impacted on the ability of countries, and particularly poor countries, to govern their own affairs. At the same time, 'the hegemony of neoliberalism, alongside the naturalization of capitalist values, influences the ability to make choices on one's own behalf in the daily lives of economically marginalized as well as economically privileged communities around the globe'.[84] Mohanty notes that feminist scholars, such as Marchand, Runyan (see chapter 6) and Hooper, have developed sophisticated feminist frameworks for understanding the gendered nature and impacts of globalization. However, she argues that we need to know more about 'the real and concrete effects of global restructuring on raced, classed, national, sexual bodies of women in the academy, in workplaces, streets, households, cyberspaces, neighbourhoods, prisons and social movements'.[85]

Globalization has produced a number of important shifts in the political and economic landscapes of nations and communities of people, such that there is now 'greater visibility of transnational women's struggles and movements, brought on in part by the UN world conferences on women held over the last two decades'.[86] However, globalization, along with the rise of religious fundamentalisms, constitutes a huge challenge for feminist struggles around the world. At a time when women's rights and feminist claims are being contested on many fronts, there is a need to build cross-cultural feminist solidarity. However, Mohanty argues that feminist solidarity can only be achieved if activists and feminist theorists are attentive to the experiences and voices of marginalized communities of women and make efforts to construct an inclusive paradigm for thinking about social justice. This 'particularised viewing allows for a more concrete and expansive vision of universal justice'.[87] Constructing a new feminist politics from the standpoint of 'poor indigenous and Third World/South women provides the most inclusive viewing of systemic power'.[88]

Conclusion

This chapter has explored how collective identities are constructed, differences negotiated and solidarities forged. The central argument has been that solidarity can, and indeed in the case of feminist groups and networks must, be forged across boundaries while recognizing and respecting differences. Conflict is apt to be viewed as the negation of solidarity. However, in the struggle to forge solidarity, conflict can serve to generate creative tensions and encourage critical reflection upon what divides women and so facilitate better understanding of where common ground might be constructed. At different times and in different locations, through the waxing and waning of the feminist movement, through periods of continuity and survival, and periods of mass mobilization, the meaning and the possibility of solidarity has been worked out in the course of feminist practice and thus affirmed the collective identity and political power of women united across boundaries.

THE GENDER(ED) POLITICS OF INTERNATIONAL RELATIONS

INTRODUCTION

As is evident from the wide range of issues and subject areas covered in this book, gender and feminist scholarship is no longer 'hidden from IR'. Indeed, Cynthia Enloe has argued that this is a time to reflect on the many successes and achievements of feminist IR.[1] Given the nature of the debates that had preoccupied the IR community (set out in chapter 2), one might have anticipated, perhaps, an initial openness to feminist questions and modes of inquiry. However, feminist scholars have contended that there is a politics at work in the construction of the 'discipline' that continues to marginalize feminist work.[2] This final chapter covers the key debates and controversies in feminist IR, concentrating on exchanges between feminists and 'mainstream' IR scholars.[3] It also assesses the place of feminist scholarship within contemporary IR theory broadly conceived.

FEMINIST ENCOUNTERS WITH THE MAINSTREAM IN IR

Academic disciplines are excellent examples of discursive communities that construct 'socially bounded' fields of knowledge. Within the academy, certain forms of knowledge are institutionalized and valorized to the degree that they assume superiority to mere 'common sense' or opinion. Academic disciplines develop theoretical and analytical frameworks, generate concepts, construct categories and develop theories about the world and how it works. As V. Spike Peterson has noted, attempts to demarcate the sphere of IR as an academic discipline and establish its core concerns are the result of the ability of socially powerful groups to impose their definitions on others.[4] Of course, any attempt to map a field of study conceptually, or delimit the scope of enquiry, inevitably involves making decisions about what should be considered 'central' or 'marginal'.[5] However, it is important to notice that such choices are never politically innocent.

Feminists have encountered a particular antagonism towards the project of 'gendering IR'. In so far as scholars located within the mainstream[6] have engaged with feminism, this engagement has been rather selective. Mainstream IR scholars have expressed frustration with feminist IR broadly conceived, but most especially in its poststructuralist guise, because of the reluctance of feminist scholars to offer up a singular, coherent perspective on IR. Ann Tickner argues that while 'feminist perspectives on international relations have proliferated, they remain marginal to the discipline as a whole, and there has been little engagement between feminists and international relations scholars'.[7] Resistance to feminist IR has come from scholars who continue to insist that production of *objective* knowledge about the world (of international relations) is both possible and desirable.

Tickner has likened engagements between feminists and the mainstream of IR to the kinds of conversations that frequently occur between men and women, fraught with the misunderstandings or the non-comprehension of people talking at cross-purposes.[8] While these misunderstandings have seemingly often been a consequence of the personal reactions that asking troubling gender questions tends to provoke, Tickner claimed that fundamentally these differences were rooted in the different ontologies and epistemologies that feminist and mainstream international relations scholars worked with.[9] Feminists also rejected the notion of a neutrality of facts in favour of subjective epistemological positions, a position 'most unsettling to proponents of scientific methodologies'.[10]

The 'good girls, bad girls and little girls' of feminist IR

At the heart of debates between feminists and the mainstream are philosophical questions concerning epistemology, ontology and method and, relatedly, the nature and purpose of IR theory or discourse.[11] It was not too long before feminist scholars were engaged by the 'mainstream' in the figure of Robert Keohane, one of the founders of neoliberal institutionalism.[12] The initial reaction to feminist scholarship in IR by mainstream IR scholars was to ask whether feminist IR implied some kind of 'reconstructive project' or perhaps the development of an overarching feminist paradigm in IR. In order to establish one's credentials within IR, feminists were charged to come up with a distinctive perspective on, for example, the conflict in Bosnia, or other conflicts that characterized the post-Cold War international landscape.[13]

Keohane afforded a cautious welcome to the project to 'gender IR'. However, for Keohane the appeal of feminist IR was primarily in its standpoint and empiricist guises, because he believed that there was potential here to mobilize feminist IR in the service of objective analyses of international relations based upon sound empirical research. In essence, standpoint was seen to be broadly consistent with the epistemological and methodological preferences of positivism and was read as an approach sympathetic to the construction of a coherent feminist paradigm or perspective in IR. In *Gender in International Relations*, Tickner was engaged in a project to construct knowledge claims from the concrete experiences of child rearing and caring shared by many women. Her claim was that 'women's experiences' could serve as a vantage point from which to construct knowledge about the world. Similarly, Tickner argued that a feminist standpoint could be used as a basis from which to rethink key concepts like power as a capacity, energy or competence, rather than as the ability to prevail or dominate.[14] The appeal of a feminist paradigm or singular feminist perspective to the mainstream in IR lay, in part, in the possibility of measuring and judging feminist empirical and theoretical claims about the world against established worldviews. Therefore, Keohane welcomed the 'contribution of a feminist standpoint' to IR theory, in so far as it could potentially contribute to the study of IR as a scientific enterprise.

Keohane's reading of feminist standpoint was, however, problematic. Certainly, standpoint made claims in the name of women as knowers, but these claims were not grounded in some notion of an essential female 'nature', but in social experiences. In postcolonial feminism, standpoint was invoked only as a useful strategic move or ploy. Crucially, standpoint theorists insisted that knowledge claims were not 'objective' but always 'situated'. Standpoint feminists resisted accommodation (or confinement) within the mainstream of IR. Indeed, Ann Tickner, a feminist IR scholar most often identified with a standpoint position, argued that the entire 'western philosophical tradition was too deeply implicated in masculinist assumptions to serve as a foundation for constructing a gender-sensitive IR'.[15]

Keohane was less enthusiastic about poststructuralist feminist IR since this strand of scholarship failed the rigorous criteria of scientific analysis. Scholars sympathetic to poststructuralism rejected the possibility of a neutral or objective stance, but also steered clear of epistemological claims made in the name of 'women'.[16] Indeed, above all else perhaps, feminist IR sought to expand the boundaries of IR and to ask troubling questions.[17] Keohane's article on the relative merits of feminist empiricism, feminist standpoint and feminist poststructuralism provoked Cynthia Weber to object that Keohane was seeking to confine feminist inquiry within the safety of the parameters of established discourse.[18]

Subsequent engagements between feminist and non-feminist IR scholars did little to assuage the feeling among feminist scholars that they were destined to engage 'from the margins'.[19] In what came to be seen as a controversial contribution to the feminist/mainstream debate, Adam Jones questioned whether gender did indeed 'make the world go around'.[20] Jones acknowledged that feminist IR had done much to rectify the invisibility of women or gender in the study of international relations, but was critical of what he saw as the shortcomings of the feminist literature. Jones criticized the feminist literature on the grounds that it limited our understanding of the role and functions of gender in IR by concentrating on women/femininity and thereby failed to recognize that men are 'victims' (in war for example). Jones argued that the central focus on women in IR served to systematically marginalize the male subject.[21] While Jones denied that he was against scholarship driven by normative concerns, he charged that feminist IR was 'one sided, selective and incomplete'.[22] What was needed to address this imbalance was a 'more balanced feminist IR' that addressed the position of men and masculinities in IR.

In so far as feminists working in IR explicitly acknowledged that 'women' and women's activities were constituted through the social relations in which they were situated and asked whether 'we should be concentrating on relocating/locating women within IR or should we concentrate instead on the functions of gender',[23] one might object that Jones's criticism of feminist IR was unfounded. Moreover, contemporary feminist theory was concerned with men and masculinities. The feminist preoccupation with issues of identity and differences among women was in part a consequence of a deep concern about whether 'women' (or indeed 'men') could be viewed as universal and stable categories. The initial question of 'where are the women in IR?' had led to rather unsettling questions about 'who are the "women", what is the difference and why does it matter?'[24]

Unlike Keohane, Jones did not focus explicitly on epistemological or methodological issues. However, it is evident that Jones's scepticism towards the contribution of feminist scholarship in IR was in part driven by what he perceived to be its 'partisan' nature and was read by Cynthia Weber as another attack on the poststructuralist 'bad girls' of feminist IR. Like Keohane, Jones also welcomed the fact that feminist empirical work providing the research agenda made both men and women visible. Similarly, just as Keohane had embraced feminist standpoint, Jones accepted that knowledge claims made in the name of women's experiences were legitimate, but only in so far as the epistemological assumptions of standpoint feminism accorded with 'the classical tradition', the standard by which feminist contributions to IR should be judged.[25] However, as with Keohane, postpositivism was rejected even though it was 'this form of feminist theorising that had arguably done most to address the tendency to collapse the categories "women" and "gender".'[26]

Gender as a 'variable' in IR

In mainstream IR, the 'engagement' with gender did not extend much beyond identifying a gender variable in IR, that is, incorporating gender as a 'variable' into explanatory theories in IR. Those who embraced positivism as a 'scientific' approach to the study of IR assumed that it was possible to identify stable and unproblematic categories (and hence have found unsettling the rather more fluid, and less ontologically secure, notions of gender and gendered subjectivities employed by poststructuralist feminists). Thus, feminist empiricism was embraced by Keohane because feminist empiricists worked with settled and essentialist conceptions of gender. This opened up the way for the introduction of a 'gender variable' in the study of IR. This move effectively reduced 'gender' to the status of one of many 'variables' that might be used to inform theories on causality or to quantify 'impacts' in international politics.[27]

Explanatory theories seek to go beyond the empirical description of an event ('what' questions) and explain why an event takes place, or why some choices are made rather than others (and so explain, for example, one policy outcome, rather than another). To speak of a 'variable', therefore, is to identify a factor that is pertinent to explaining certain events, actions or outcomes in international politics. In order to identify a gender variable, it is first necessary to appropriate gender as 'difference' and to assume that women and men can be viewed as meaningful and fairly secure ontological categories. To identify a gender variable is to identify specific contexts in which gender makes a difference in explaining (state) actions in the 'real world'.

The relevance of a 'gender variable' in explaining actions, outcomes or impacts in international politics must firstly be established by reference to an interesting empirical feature of the international realm that has not (yet) been noticed. The relevance of gender 'does not spring to one's eyes unless gender is actively used as an analytical tool'.[28] It has been the 'efforts of feminist researchers (that have) made visible the effects of gender at all levels of society. Before gender was introduced as an analytical tool, this knowledge was invisible and non-existent.'[29] However, if one accepts that a certain feminist sensibility is needed to 'notice' gender in the first place, it is then possible to expand mainstream IR to include gender as a variable.

The high politics of statecraft is an obvious domain where the predominance of men and, if not the absence of women, then at least their subordinate roles and positions is 'noticeable'. Keohane concedes as much in positing that a gender variable might be relevant in explaining the peaceful or hostile intentions of states or the likelihood of war.[30] One way in which an initial claim for the relevance of a 'gender variable' in understanding the peaceful or hostile intentions of states would be to take up the proposition that the inclusion of more women in foreign policy-making and in the high politics of statecraft would result in the pacification of states and so decrease the incidence of war. This argument was advanced by moral feminists in the peace movement, who similarly worked with a conception of gender as difference.[31]

There is certainly some prima facie evidence to support such a contention in so far as gender has been posited as a significant factor in accounting for differing levels of support for military action and increases in the level of military expenditure.[32] Thus questions can be asked about how (gender) identity 'affects views and decision making processes' and if and how (gender) identity is relevant in the constitution of interests and in explaining policy outcomes in international politics.[33] This conjecture might then be formulated 'as an hypothesis, consistent with established (scientific) theory' and the observable implications of the hypothesis could be tested to see 'whether those implications obtain in the real world'.[34] The problem is, of course, that this particular case (or hypothesis) is impossible to prove empirically since women are grossly underrepresented in policy-making bodies.[35]

In principle, the relevance of a 'gender variable' to this specific case might be established by means other than by the extent to which women participate directly in policy-making bodies. Fukuyama, for example, has pointed to the gender gap in support for defence spending in the US as evidence that seemingly supports the contention that women are more peaceful than men (hence gender difference is relevant). In this case, the connection between the pacification of states and the increasing political influence of women is less direct – it is a function of democracy – but nevertheless the increasingly political influence of women might be leading to a more 'feminized world'.[36] Changes in gender relations might explain how the prevalence of a strategic/instrumentalist rationality in foreign policy gives way to a more pacific and cooperative orientation, as women and 'feminine' identified values exert more influence over foreign policy makers. Keohane argues that this hypothesis could be tested by pointing to the degree to which 'countries with highly inegalitarian gender hierarchies behave differently from those with less gender inequality at home.' Keohane asks, as is seemingly the case with democracies, are states with more egalitarian gender relations less inclined to fight each other?

Keohane is not interested in how gender inequalities and hierarchies are structured and reproduced. Nor is he interested in what social changes or how social changes result in less gender inequality and hierarchy. The 'evidence' of less hierarchy and inequality is taken to be the increasing political influence that women enjoy in specific societies. However, introducing inequality and hierarchy into the discussion points to some of the problems in the 'gender as a variable' project. In the context of identifying 'variables', questions of power necessarily arise, specifically, power relations between those who decide who or what is 'relevant' and what is deemed to be 'not relevant'. Moreover, certain consequences flow from the appropriation of gender as difference. In taking gender as 'given', questions relating to the way in which gender is configured by social relations – by various forms of social categorization and regulation – drop out of the picture. Gender difference is afforded the status of a variable that might be helpful in 'doing some explaining' but the assumption is that gender itself does not have to be explained. It makes sense to speak of gender as difference in societies and cultures where there is a deep commitment to gender dichotomy, because in these societies gender will function as a basic category in perception and cognition and in the construction of social reality. Gender influences how we perceive, react to and evaluate ourselves and others and how we structure and assess situations. However, while gender might be 'performed' as difference, gender cannot be reduced to the dispositions or the traits people carry about inside. Gender identities do not flow from biological differences but are produced and reproduced within specific social and cultural contexts.

In western societies – indeed in many societies – gender differences are constructed around the public/private dichotomy. It might be that women are more likely to speak 'as women' on issues and in contexts where women's voices are deemed to be 'legitimate' (as in the example of the peace movement above). However, gender is not a straightforward marker of individual difference. Gender identity is fixed by 'subtle or not so subtle regulatory practices that sustain gender dichotomy and coherence'.[37] To acknowledge that gender inequality and gender hierarchy are relevant in understanding and explaining the 'real world' is also to acknowledge the exercise of social power in the production and reproduction of gender. Questions of how power/status is maintained in gender-schematic cultural contexts and how identities are constructed and socially regulated then become interesting.[38] Feminists shift the focus of interest away from gender as a 'variable' to gender as site of social regulation, because they are interested in understanding how the fixing of gender identities is central to the embedding of gender hierarchies and social relations of inequality and in how, when and where they are or might be contested in the interests of generating change. Thus, there might be some value in projects that make gender visible, but there are also inherent limitations in the same.

Furthermore, feminists recognize that it is sometimes necessary to speak about male and female and masculine and feminine to indicate differences, but insist on the importance of specifying context. It is possible to produce 'valid' knowledge within certain contexts and frames of analysis, but feminists recognize that the knowledge produced is always 'situated' within specific discourses, times and places, class relations, knowledge structures and so on. There is a politics involved in 'knowledge building'. Phillips argues that 'disciplines, the content of which is handed down, ready formed, have laboured mightily over the generations to construct the content of the field and no doubt internal politics have played some role in determining the bodies of knowledge available.'[39] The exclusion of feminism from the 'mainstream' has been represented as a consequence of feminists choosing to stay 'on the margins'.[40] However, Keohane's insistence that the *only* valid knowledge is knowledge that is proven by science says more about the politics of 'consensual knowledge building' in the discipline than it does about the status of feminist work or the proclivities of feminist scholars.[41]

Feminists have thus eschewed the project of identifying a 'gender variable' in IR that can be shown to be relevant to our understanding of, say, war and peace or conflict and cooperation.[42] Feminist IR scholars countered that Jones employed simplistic, essentialized categorizations of 'male' and 'female', 'masculine' and 'feminine'. Jones was also criticized for his lack of reflection about the rather conventional and essentialist conception of gender he worked with. Moreover, employing gender as a variable missed the point somewhat, since gender was not simply an attribute of the person – a facet of identity – but a social relationship. Gender cannot be viewed as a variable, because 'one is never outside of gender'.[43] To study gender in IR was, then, to look at 'analytically and imaginatively the who, how and why of power in the international context'.[44] In charging feminists with partiality, selectivity and bias, Jones could be said to have presented a selective, partial and rather distorted view of feminist IR. Furthermore, it was not immediately apparent how employing the 'gender variable', or focusing more on men and masculinities, would necessarily advance a feminist agenda in international politics. Jones's critics contended that the project to 'gender IR' by identifying the gender variable in war and conflict did not go far beyond a crude measure of impacts or amounted to little more than 'stacking up dead male bodies against female bodies'.[45]

Moreover, taking gender-as-difference seriously could work to engender a political backlash against feminism.[46] For example, Keohane argued that just as democracies were less inclined to fight each other, states with more egalitarian gender relations might be more peaceable. However, there were clearly dangers in such developments, since 'perhaps states with less gender hierarchy would be less aggressive, but might be more easily bullied'.[47] This was a theme of Francis Fukuyama's brief intervention in the gender/IR debate discussed in chapter 4. Both Keohane and Fukuyama continue to view the state in a rather unproblematic way as a guarantor of security in a still dangerous international environment and women are unlikely to win the argument for resources if 'national security' is compromised. Once again, one would need to move beyond the gender variable to understand the gendered nature of security/insecurity.

Constructive conversations?

Despite this seeming refusal by mainstream scholars to engage with feminist IR, in some respects today the intellectual climate in IR affords more possibility for establishing common ground between different forms of theory and different approaches in IR. There is, it seems, an increasing willingness to breach ingrained divisions between positivist and postpositivist approaches. Certainly, feminists are not averse to the idea of adopting different analytical lenses or engaging 'empathetically'.[48] As is evident from the discussion above, feminist IR is not all of one kind, and undoubtedly some scholars in the field might be interested to explore the possibilities for feminist engagements that are opened up by attempts to move beyond such dichotomies. If the 'mainstream' continued to resist feminist IR, there might well be more possibilities for an engagement between feminism and social constructivism.[49]

Non-feminist gender studies in IR

Charlie Carpenter has claimed that by not engaging with the concept of gender, IR theorists have deprived the field of an important conceptual instrument.[50] However, Carpenter argued that it was possible to gain knowledge of how gender worked in world politics without drawing upon explicitly feminist accounts. Carpenter suggested that the social constructivist concern with norms and identities was an equally good place to start to 'gender IR'. Indeed, Carpenter cited Goldstein's work on gender and war[51] as a good example of how gender might be integrated into conventional and/or constructivist literature on norms and identities in IR (see chapter 4).[52] Carpenter echoed Jones in so far as she also believed that there were shortcomings in the feminist literature, particularly in regard to the lack of attention afforded to the question of how gender constrained life chances of 'people called men'. And like Jones she pointed to men as gendered subjects and victims of war, insisting that gender violence was not only violence against women.

Carpenter also pointed to Sandra Whitworth's work as a useful place to begin talking about gender and social constructivism without necessarily advocating an explicitly normative feminist agenda. Whitworth has argued that theories of gender must be able to allow for the possibility of talking about the social construction of meaning to discuss historical variability and theorize power in ways that uncover hidden power relations. Carpenter argues that there was nothing in these contentions that required gender theories to be feminist in orientation. If constructivists had not (yet) built on feminist gender theories, this might be a reflection of gender bias (as feminists had often claimed) but it was certainly not a consequence of theoretical incompatibility (the major problem cited by Tickner in relation to rationalism). Carpenter argued that constructivism was ontologically suited to studying gender norms and identities as a specific component of the broader categories of social relations comprising world politics. This would entail a different epistemological approach from the one most favoured by feminists but would have the advantage of (potentially) doing some explaining in world politics.[53]

Generally, the project of 'gendering IR' would be better served if feminists adjusted their theoretical and analytical framework (while retaining a focus on women and a commitment to emancipation), and at the same time non-feminist scholars generated their own theories of gender in world politics without necessarily subsuming and engaging with feminist IR. In feminist IR, the normative focus was on improving the position of women, rather than understanding interactions between states. Gender constructivists could employ the analytical category of gender to understand the IR agenda as conventionally defined. In short, the analytical category of gender could be brought into scholarship not so much in the interests of generating demands for change, but in the interests of understanding the world as it is.[54]

However, this proposal to engage – or not – feminist IR was read as yet another attempt to contain or even further marginalize feminism. Carver argued that bringing men into gender studies in IR in the way that Carpenter envisaged was tricky for two reasons. First, feminism was an ongoing political project concerned with gender oppression and that this must be noticed, not marginalized on methodological grounds or hidden in 'value neutral' analysis. Second, feminist theory had not resisted the consideration of men as men, nor did feminists employ the concept of gender as a pseudonym for women in ways that erased 'men as men' (as is evident from the discussion of men and masculinities in this book). Finally, gendering IR would require acquaintance with the feminist literature – how feminist thinking has created contemporary gender studies by fostering critique and diversity in scholarship. Carver concluded that this urge to create a non-feminist IR could be read as yet another strategy in 'Othering' feminist IR.[55]

Zalewski similarly read Carpenter's project as an attempt to restrict the potentialities and possibilities in feminist IR. She concurred with Carver that advocating approaches to gender that did not engage with existing theoretical analysis risked saying nothing at all. Pondering on what she saw as a project that dismissed the achievements of feminist theories in order to clear the way for an alternative theorization of gender, Zalewski argued that this would result in, at best, 'very meagre stories about men, women and gender'. Rather than reinvent the wheels of feminism, Zalewski argued that scholars might now focus on oiling those wheels, since 'so long as opposition regularly reinvents itself as hegemony, theorists, like activists have to keep moving'.[56]

Gender in the 'middle ground' of IR

At the time of writing, IR theory is in the midst of a debate regarding the degree to which it is possible to carve out a 'middle ground' between rationalist and social constructivist approaches. The middle ground can be presented as an attempt to integrate ideas into a materialist–rationalist framework. In forging a middle ground, prominent social constructivists like Alexander Wendt have defended 'a moderate constructivism' while conceding 'important points to materialism' and endorsing 'a scientific approach to social enquiry'.[57] An accommodation between rationalist and constructivist approaches is possible if one accepts that choices do not arise from some transcendental notion of rational interest, but are made on the 'basis of normative, descriptive and causal beliefs all of which are deeply socially constructed'.[58] Choices are also constrained by structures such as demography, material scarcity and power and by institutions that affect incentives and opportunities available to actors.

There are feminist scholars who have argued that part of their project is to 'do some explaining' in IR. Enloe, for example, has been interpreted as proposing a new explanatory variable for the study of international relations: the degree to which socially constructed gender hierarchies are important.[59] Enloe claimed that in both *Bananas* and *Maneuvers*,[60] she was trying to show 'why states are so needful of ideas about masculinity and femininity' and, in so doing, 'make a theoretical argument about causality'.[61] She was also a self-proclaimed empiricist in so far as she wanted 'scholars to go out there and see which of two causal possibilities is at work in a given state at a particular time'. Enloe encouraged scholars to ask, 'under what conditions do state officials invest state resources in the manipulation of masculinity?' and 'when do state officials try to manipulate women as people?' Neglecting to ask these questions produced 'a very naive understanding of how power worked and how inter-state relations worked'.[62] However, regardless of whether one adopts an essentialist or social constructivist view of 'gender as difference', integrating a gender variable into the middle ground of IR would be open to the same criticisms as those outlined above in regard to mainstream IR.

Embracing pluralism in IR theory

In fairness to Wendt, there is rather more to his vision of the future of IR than merely integrating ideas into a mainstream framework of analysis. The middle ground debate in IR can be read as an attempt to move beyond the prioritizing of ontological, epistemological and methodological questions in debates in IR. Fearon and Wendt have argued that the priority afforded to such questions in IR theory has militated against efforts to develop problem-driven, rather than theory-driven, approaches. They have questioned 'whether progress in understanding international relations and improving human and plenary welfare is best served by the structuring of the field of IR as a battle of analytical paradigms' or whether 'important questions will be ignored if they are not amenable to the preferred paradigmatic fashion'.[63] Or that 'we know so much about international life' that we should dismiss certain arguments or positions 'a priori on purely philosophical grounds'.[64]

Fearon and Wendt see the entire positivist/postpositivist debate as one in which each side tries to marginalize or subsume the other in the name of methodological purity. The challenge, they argue, is to 'combine insights, cross boundaries and if possible synthesise specific arguments in the hope of gaining more compelling answers'.[65] IR needs to move away from debates on ontology in which 'a great deal rides on who wins' in favour of an 'ontological pluralism' which might tell us more about the conditions under which world politics would be more conflictual or cooperative.[66] Fearon and Wendt have pleaded for a more pragmatic interpretation of rationalism and social constructivism as lenses for looking at social reality or analytical tools with which to theorize about world politics.

Wendt's vision for the future of IR theory is seemingly more open than merely incorporating conventional constructivist insights into a rationalist framework, or incorporating a gender variable into a mainstream IR agenda. In affirming the legitimacy of different approaches in IR theory, Wendt does not marginalize feminist scholarship, or indeed any other kind of scholarship in IR. In feminist IR, pluralism is tolerated or even celebrated because different approaches might generate useful insights in the project of 'rethinking' IR.[67]

Keohane has similarly argued that an accommodation between rationalism and constructivism can be achieved if we recognize that knowledge is socially constructed and make efforts to widen inter-subjective agreement about important issues. He favours a sophisticated view of 'science' that overcomes any simple objectivist–subjectivist dichotomy, arguing that rather than viewing constructivist and hermeneutic approaches and positivist approaches as standing in marked opposition, we might instead view different theoretical approaches as a continuum with rationalism and poststructuralism as the 'poles'.[68] However, while theoretical or methodological innovation might be tolerated, encouraged even, in Keohane's view there are clearly limits to how far this type of project can be allowed to go before it is categorized as decidedly unscientific, unverifiable and dismissed on the grounds that it lacks explanatory power. What is needed, he argues, are 'more cogent, contingent generalisations about international relations' that are 'scientific because they are based on publicly known methods and checked by a community of scholars, working both critically and cooperatively'.[69]

An 'exhausted conversation?'

Feminists are apt to remain rather sceptical about just how far such endeavours might take feminism into what is increasingly being constructed as the 'centre ground' in IR. It seems that even projects that proceed on the basis of the inter-subjective negotiation of 'truths' would have to address the politics of knowledge claims, the politics of negotiating knowledge claims and indeed the conditions under which such engagements and conversations take place. It is surely a precondition for any meaningful dialogue that one is aware of how one is situated or positioned in a debate or conversation (whether one occupies the privileged 'middle ground' or is constructed as being 'on the margins'), is reflective and open about one's identity and the identities of others and cognisant of the complexities of our social and political relationships with others.

Feminists are certainly sceptical that some kind of inter-subjective consensus on the substance of IR or on methods and approach is possible among feminists and the mainstream on the evidence of the conversations that have taken place thus far.[70] Conversations between feminists and the mainstream are likely to be terse while ever feminists continue to be told that they will only be seriously engaged 'if feminists are willing to formulate their hypothesis in ways that are testable and falsifiable with evidence' by those who have for so long occupied the central territory in the discipline.[71] To limit or confine the discussion to the gender variable and to the scientific credentials of feminist theory is to refuse to engage in a serious discussion of either gender or feminism.

In the US in Tickner's view, positivism has yet to be displaced as the dominant approach to IR, and feminist voices continue to be marginalized, ignored or appropriated in the interests of advancing a mainstream agenda.[72] In Britain, where postpositivist approaches have been more widely embraced, the lack of attention paid to feminist perspectives by those within both rationalist and critical/constructivist schools has been disappointing.[73] Certainly there are male scholars within the discipline who had openly welcomed the contribution of feminism to IR, or had engaged with the feminist literature in a serious and reflective way, or had drawn upon feminist theories and concepts in their own work.[74] However, one continually finds examples of histories of IR that nod to feminism as a marginal voice in the postpositivist debate.[75] For this reason, feminists are likely to be both encouraged by, but perhaps also rather circumspect about, the prospects for a deeper, more productive engagement that might be opened up by recent theoretical conversations in IR that are seeking to establish a 'middle ground'.

That said, as Marianne Marchand has argued, discussions about the marginalization of gender in IR are in danger of reproducing that marginality.[76] It is important to recognize that positivism is not the only game in town, so to speak. As Marchand argues, encounters between feminism and IR have been contingent upon and embedded in different realities and attempts at making them more meaningful and substantive have to address these different contextual realities.[77] In chapter 2, feminist IR was located within the context of the fourth debate in IR. What emerged from the fourth debate was a generally 'more reflexive environment in which debate, criticism and novelty could freely circulate'.[78] Certainly, there is another story that could be told about the place of feminist scholarship within an expanding body of critical scholarship, a story that would be more celebratory about the impact of feminism in the field. There is certainly intellectual space for a debate between critical theorists (broadly conceived) and feminists, perhaps centred around shared concerns 'with the ethical dilemmas and responsibilities inherent in the practices of world politics and the theorisation of IR'.[79] However, as Marchand recognized, there has been a continual marginalization of feminism within IR to the extent that other 'critical theorists' have been more often engaged in discussion by the mainstream, whereas feminists have most often not been so engaged.[80]

CRITICAL ENCOUNTERS

In some respects contemporary feminist theorists working in International Relations, while having their own distinctive agendas, share some common ground with other critical theories. A number of Critical Theorists have drawn upon Jurgen Habermas's model of dialogue as useful in promoting 'conversation across boundaries' on the basis of a shared communicative rationality.[81] This conversation has ensued in the interest of discovering the universal conditions of communication (and so eschewed moral relativism) in an effort to discover inter-subjectively negotiated 'truths'. There have been sympathetic engagements between feminism and Critical Theory, because the commitment to universalism is seen to accord with the feminist project of emancipation, a project that depends in turn upon notions of progress and 'truth'.[82] Feminist theorizing is not a purely abstract academic activity, but an ongoing critical engagement with the world. Feminism is a point of departure, a position from which contending values and practices are assessed and evaluated. In effect, to adopt a feminist position is to adopt a normative position. Dialogue requires participants to be reflective about their own assumptions, assumptions that underlie everyday practices of communication.[83] By listening to others, participants learn about the extent to which they have had similar experiences, and this marks an important stage in establishing an 'interactive universalism' that has the capacity 'to make the claims of feminist universalism and feminist pluralism compatible'.[84]

However, as Kimberley Hutchings has argued, the commitment to rationalism in Habermasian Critical Theory necessarily generates concerns about the exclusionary character of western universal reasoning that has been a central theme in feminist theory.[85] Moreover, the nature of public space, as it is constituted in Habermas's theory, is deeply gendered. Poststructuralists have expressed scepticism about the value of Critical Theory as the 'next stage' in IR because it remains committed to 'totalizing' modes of thought and action. Poststructuralists see the project of 'emancipation' (that underpins such projects) as too closely tied to the language of old ideologies such as Marxism and socialist national liberation movements that have, in practice, produced little of consequence and have frequently engaged in repression where they have been successful in gaining power. Furthermore, emancipation implies a general prescription, a coherent plan. Poststructuralist feminists argue that difference has to be dealt with without retreating into the totalizing ideals of the Enlightenment and that sensitivity to difference enhances our ability to tolerate the incommensurable. The notion of generic 'woman' in feminist thought obscures the heterogeneity of women and prevents serious consideration of the significance of such heterogeneity for feminist theory and political activity. Poststructuralist feminists value the diversity in feminist thought and see the existence of many 'feminisms' as a reflection of the many ways of articulating the social and political experiences of concrete women. However, ultimately this view locates feminism within a politics of dissent that disrupts and erodes the theory and practice of specific power regimes.

Nevertheless, some poststructuralists are sympathetic to human-centred analysis and seek to retain or salvage something of the humanist tradition characteristic of the Enlightenment, moving beyond critique and deconstruction and finding ways in which poststructuralism can actually further our understanding of a range of human problems.[86] Indeed, some see spaces within modernist discourses of 'emancipation' that allow for critical engagement and negotiation. In the context of feminist IR, Sylvester has argued that dialogue and negotiation should be distinguished from relativism which is 'a refusal to cooperate or engage in negotiation in the name of tolerance' that effectively denies 'that the invented "other" to whom one gives space could possibly have anything in common with one's fixed sense of self'.[87] Conversations across borders must ensue on the basis of the recognition of differences and the negotiation of diverse identities. It is probably accurate to say that most (though not all) feminist scholars in IR have poststructuralist sympathies and, consequently, have more often advocated forms of empathetic negotiation and dialogue across diverse identities and boundaries, in the hope that this would facilitate a new kind of feminist politics built upon women's multiple identities, experiences and locations.[88] Hutchings has similarly championed a model of dialogue that would empower 'different voices' in a morally pluralist feminist international ethics.[89]

And yet there are more similarities between Critical Theorists, poststructuralists and feminists than have been acknowledged to date.[90] As Diez and Steans argue, all 'address ethical concerns in concrete contexts, notably in the ethical choices involved in boundary marking and processes of "Othering" in ways that confront problems of exclusion and hierarchy'.[91] Moreover, although rarely spelt out explicitly, all critical theorists recognize 'that there are different forms of Othering, and that some are preferable over others because they are less exclusionary and/or violent'.[92] Critical theorists in general have rejected the core contention of the realist/neorealist 'orthodoxy' in IR: that actions dictated by a strategic interest in the control and manipulation of others necessarily prevailed in IR because anarchy and power politics were enduring features of international relations. Feminists, poststructuralists and Critical Theorists also share common ground in their advocacy of a politics of negotiation rooted in recognition of and respect for differences, rather than a politics of force and domination over menacing 'Others'. In this regard, critical theorists generally are deeply concerned with the ethical dilemmas and responsibilities inherent in the practices of world politics and the theorization of IR.[93]

CONCLUSION

This chapter has set out some of the key debates and exchanges that have taken place between feminist IR scholars and those located in the 'mainstream' of IR and the newly constructed 'middle ground' of IR. It is evident from the above discussion that just as gender issues in international relations are highly political and often contentious, the project to 'gender IR' is also a political and politicized project. The future of feminist IR, therefore, lies very much in the outcome of ongoing struggles to carve out a space and place for feminist scholarship within what has been a highly contested field of study.

Feminist scholars have thus far contributed significantly to the field, as is evidenced from the extensive literature covered in this book. Limitations of space have meant that some promising areas of current and future research in the field have been given only scant attention in this book, for example, feminist work on cosmopolitanism and new forms of political community.[94] In what Tickner characterizes as the 'third generation' of feminist IR, postcolonial feminist scholars are producing studies that focus on specific sites of feminist activism and that map the importance of gender in understanding the politics and international relations of non-western states.

Moreover, the future of feminist scholarship within critical IR is healthy. The engagement between feminism and other strands of constructivist and critical IR theory could yet bear substantial fruit. Recent calls for IR theory to embrace a rather more pragmatic approach to theory and to put aside issues of epistemological, ontological and methodological purity in the interests of finding better answers to pressing human problems similarly bode well for the future of feminism in the field of IR.[95] It would be simply incredible to claim that gender is not relevant to 'real world' issues and problems, as the feminist literature on war, peace, security, international political economy, development and human rights graphically illustrates. Almost twenty years after the effort to gender IR was launched, feminist IR is far from being an 'exhausted' project.

NOTES

Introduction

1 Walker, R. B. J. (1992) 'Gender and Critique in the Theory of International Relations', in Peterson, V. Spike (ed.) *Gendered States: Feminist (Re)Visions of International Relations Theory*, Boulder, CO: Lynne Rienner.

2 Special Issue, Women in International Relations, *Millennium: Journal of International Studies*, 17, 3, 1988.

3 Enloe, C. (1989) *Bananas, Beaches and Bases: Making Feminist Sense of International Politics*, London: Pandora.

4 Laurien, A. (1989) 'Genderizing International Studies: Revisioning Concepts and Curriculum', *International Studies Notes*, 14, 1; Grant, R. and Newland, K. (1991) *Gender and International Relations*, Milton Keynes: Open University Press; Peterson, V. S. (1992) (ed.) *Gendered States: Feminist (Re)Visions of International Theory*, Boulder, CO: Lynne Rienner; Tickner, A. (1992) *Gender in International Relations*, New York: Columbia University Press; *Alternatives Special Edition, Feminists Write International Relations*, 18, 1, 1993; Enloe, C. (1993) *The Morning After: Sexual Politics after the Cold War*, Berkeley: University of California Press; *The Fletcher Forum of World Affairs*, Special Edition, 'Gender and International Relations', 7, 2, 1993; Hutchins, K. (1993) 'The Personal Is International: Feminist Epistemology and the Case of International Relations', in Whitford, M. and Lennon, K. (eds) *Objectivity, the Knowing Subject and Difference*, London: Routledge; Peterson, V. S. and Runyan, A. (1993) *Global Gender Issues*, Boulder, CO: Westview Press; Zalewski, M. (1993) 'Feminist Theory and International Relations', in Bowker, M. and Brown, R. (eds) *From Cold War to Collapse: Theory and World Politics in the 1980s*, Cambridge: Cambridge University Press; Williams, A. (1993) 'On the Outside Looking In; Or, Without a Look In: A Feminist Perspective on the Individual in IR', *Oxford International Review*, May; Elshtain, J. (1994) 'Reflections on War and Political Discourse: Realism, Just War and Feminism in a Nuclear Age', in Smith, M. and Little, R. *Perspectives on World Politics*, Milton Keynes: Open University Press; Sylvester, C. (1994) *Feminism and International Relations in a Postmodern Era*, Cambridge: Cambridge University Press; Whitworth, S. (1994) *Feminism and International Relations*, Basingstoke: Macmillan; Pettman, J. J. (1996) *Worlding Women: A Feminist International*

Politics, London: Routledge; True, J. (1996) 'Feminism', in Linklater, A. and Burchill, S. (eds) *Theories of International Relations*, Basingstoke: Macmillan; Steans, J. (1998) *Gender in International Relations*, Oxford: Polity.

5 Hooper, C. (1997) 'Masculinist Practices and Gender Politics: The Operation of Multiple Masculinities in International Relations', in Zalewski and Parpart *The 'Man' Question in International Relations*, Oxford: Westview.

6 Zalewski, M. and Parpart, J. (1997) (eds) *The 'Man' Question in International Relations*; Hooper, C. (2001) *Masculinities, International Relations and Gender Politics*, New York: Columbia University Press; Pease, B. and Pringle, K. (2001) *A Man's World? Changing Men's Practices in a Globalised World*, London: Zed Books.

7 More journals began to welcome pieces on gender/feminist IR themes, while publishers recognized the value (and market appeal) of feminist work. By this time, feminist IR had also gained an institutional foothold with the founding of a feminist theory and gender studies section within the International Studies Association in 1990. Panels with a focus on gender and/or feminist approaches in IR began to appear on the programme of conferences hosted in Europe, Australia, North America and Japan. By 1994, a survey of International Politics/Relations departments in the UK revealed a respectable (at the time) number of IR programmes, at both undergraduate and postgraduate level, that incorporated gender/feminist concerns, although in many cases this amounted to only one or two lectures on general IR courses. Krause, J. (1994) *Gender and International Relations: A Survey of Teaching and Research*, occasional paper, Department of International Studies, Nottingham Trent University.

8 See, for example: Sylvester, C. (1990) 'The Emperor's Theories and Transformations: Looking at the Field through Feminist Lenses', in Sylvester, C. and Pirages, D. *Transformations in Global Political Economy*, London: Macmillan; Tickner, A. (1991) 'Hans Morgenthau's Six Principles of Political Realism: A Feminist Reformulation', in Grant and Newland *Gender in International Relations*; Grant, R. (1992) 'The Quagmire of Gender and International Security', in Peterson *Gendered States*; Peterson, V. S. (1992) 'Security and Sovereign States: What Is at Stake in Taking Feminism Seriously', in Peterson *Gendered States*; Tickner (1992) *Gender in IR*; Tickner, A. (1992) 'On the Fringes of the Global Economy', in Tooze, R. and Murphy, C. *The New International Political Economy*, Boulder, CO: Lynne Rienner; Whitworth, S. (1994) 'Theory as Exclusion: Gender and International Political Economy', in Stubbs, R. and Underhill, G. *Political Economy and the Changing Global Order*, Basingstoke: Macmillan; Zalewski, M. and Enloe, C. (1995) 'Questions about Identity', in Booth, K. and Smith, S. *International Relations Theory Today*, Cambridge: Polity; Krause, J. (1995) 'The International Dimensions of Gender Inequality and Feminist Politics', in MacMillan, J. and Linklater, A. *Boundaries in Question: New Directions in International Relations*, London: Pinter; Krause, J. (1996) 'Gendered Identities in International Relations', in Krause, J. and Renwick, N. *Identities in International Relations*, Basingstoke: Macmillan; Parpart, J. and Marchand, M. (1995) (eds) *Feminism, Postmodernism, Development*, London: Routledge; Robinson, F. (1999) *Globalising Care: Ethics, Feminist Theory and International Relations*, Oxford: Westview; Peterson, S. and Parisi, L. (1998) 'Are Women Human? This is not an Academic Question', in Evan, T. (ed.) *Human Rights Fifty Years On: A Reappraisal*, Manchester: Manchester University Press; Chinkin, C. (1999) 'Gender, Inequality and International Human Rights Law', in Hurrell, A. and Woods, N. *Inequality Globalization and World Politics*, Oxford: Oxford University Press; Hutchings, K. (2000) 'Towards a Feminist International Ethics', *Review of International Studies*, 26, pp. 111–30, Special Issue.

9 'Interview with Professor Cynthia Enloe' carried out at the February 2001 Annual Convention of the ISA in Chicago in *Review of International Studies*, 27, 1, 2001, p. 649.

10 Ibid., p. 661.
11 Steans, J. (2003) 'Engaging from the Margins: Feminist Encounters with the "Mainstream" of International Relations', *British Journal of Politics and International Relations*, 5, 3, pp. 428–54.
12 Peterson, V. Spike 'Transgressing the Boundaries: Theories of Knowledge, Gender and IR', *Millennium: Journal of International Studies*, 21, 2, 1992, pp. 183–206.
13 Zalewski, M. 'Feminist Standpoint Meets International Relations Theory: A Feminist Version of David and Goliath', *The Fletcher Forum of World Affairs*, 17, 2, 1993.
14 Williams, A. (1993) 'On the Outside Looking In or Without a Look In'.
15 Since the literature that has been produced in the intervening ten years is now fairly extensive, it is not possible to discuss all feminist works in IR.
16 Grant, R. (1991) 'The Sources of Gender Bias in International Relations Theory', in Grant and Newland, *Gender and International Relations*.
17 Anderson, B. (1983) *Imagined Communities*, London: Verso Books.
18 Steans, J. (2003) 'Conflicting Loyalties: Women's Human Rights and the Politics of Identity', in Waller, M. and Linklater, A. (eds) *Loyalty and the Post-National State*, London: Routledge.
19 See, for example: Linklater, A. and Waller, M. (2003) (eds) *Loyalty and the Post-national State*, London: Routledge; Krause, J. and Renwick, N. (1996) (eds) *Identities in International Relations*, Basingstoke: Macmillan; Lapid, Y. and Kratochiwil, F. (1996) (eds) *The Return of Culture and Identity in IR*, Boulder, CO: Lynne Rienner Publications.
20 Rupp: L. J. (1997) *Worlds of Women: The Making of an International Women's Movement*, Princeton: Princeton University Press.
21 Sylvester, 'The Emperor's Theories and Transformations'; Tickner, 'On the Fringes of the Global Economy'; Whitworth, S. (1994) 'Theory as Exclusion'; Krause, J. (1995) 'The International Dimensions of Gender Inequality and Feminist Politics'.
22 Throughout the text International Relations, or IR, is used to denote the academic discipline, while international relations is used to refer to the domain of international politics, which is not necessarily limited to relations between states.
23 Grewal, I. and Kaplan, C. (1994) (eds) *Scattered Hegemonies: Postmodernity and Transnational Feminist Practices*, London: Minnesota Press; Chowdhry, G. and Nair, S. (2002) (eds) *Power, Postcolonialism and International Relations: Reading Race, Gender and Class*, London: Routledge.
24 See, for example, Halliday, F. (1988) 'Hidden from International Relations: Women and the International Arena', *Millennium: Journal of International Studies*, 17, 3, 1988, pp. 419–28; Walker, R. B. J. (1992) 'Gender and Critique in the Theory of International Relations'; Murphy, C. 'Seeing Women, Recognizing Gender, Recasting International Relations', *International Organisation*, 3, 5, 1996, pp. 513–38; Zalewski and Parpart *The 'Man' Question in International Relations*; Hoffman, J. (2001) *Gender and Sovereignty*, Palgrave: Basingstoke.
25 Carver, T., Cochran, M. and Squires, J. 'Gendering Jones', *Review of International Studies*, 24, 2, 1998, p. 298.

Chapter 1 Gender, Feminism and International Relations

1 Connell, R. (1995) *Gender and Power*, Cambridge: Polity.
2 Ibid., pp. 30–1.
3 Ibid., p. 50.
4 Lipsitz-Bem, S. (1993) *The Lenses of Gender*, New Haven: Yale University Press.

5   Tong, R. (1989) *Feminist Thought*, London: Unwin Hyman.

6   Connell *Gender and Power*, p. 80.

7   Butler, J. (1990) *Gender Trouble: Feminism and the Subversion of Identity*, London: Routledge.

8   McNay, L. (1992) *Foucault and Feminism*, Cambridge: Polity.

9   Butler *Gender Trouble*, p. 3.

10 Pease, B. and Pringle, K. (2001) (eds) 'Introduction. Studying Men's Practices and Gender Relations in Global Context', in Pease, B. and Pringle, K. *A Man's World: Changing Men's Practices in a Globalised World*, London: Zed Books, p. 2.

11 Connell *Gender and Power*, p. 85. See also Brittan, A. (1989) *Masculinity and Power*, Oxford: Blackwell; Hearn, J. (1998) *The Violence of Men*, London: Sage.

12 Connell *Gender and Power*, p. 85.

13 Ibid., p. 86.

14 Ibid., p. 83.

15 Pease and Pringle 'Introduction', p. 2.

16 Special Issue, 'Women in International Relations', *Millennium: Journal of International Studies*, 17, 3, 1988.

17 Enloe, C. (1989) *Bananas, Beaches and Bases*.

18 Harding, S. (1991) *Whose Science? Whose Knowledge?* Milton Keynes: Open University Press.

19 For a fuller discussion, see Tong, R. (1989) *Feminist Thought*.

20 Chodorow, N. (1976) *The Reproduction of Mothering*, Berkeley: University of California Press; Rich, A. (1976) *Of Woman Born: Motherhood as Experience and Institution*, London: W. W. Norton.

21 See Chodorow *The Reproduction of Mothering*; Harding *Whose Science?*; Hartsock, N. (1983) *Money, Sex and Power: Towards a Feminist Historical Materialism*, Boston: Northeastern University Press; Hirschmann, N. (1992) *Rethinking Obligation: A Feminist Method for Political Theory*, New York: Cornell University Press.

22 Tickner *Gender in International Relations*; see also Tickner 'Hans Morgenthau's Six Principles of Political Realism'.

23 See also Hutchins 'The Personal is International: Feminist Epistemology and the Case of International Relations'.

24 Alcoff, L. 'Cultural Feminism and Poststructuralism: The Identity Crisis in Feminist Theory', *Signs*, 13, 3, 1988.

25 Harding *Whose Science?*

26 There were Marxist-feminist contributions to the first wave of feminist IR literature. See Molyneux, M. (1990) 'Marxism, Feminism and the Demise of the Soviet Model', in Grant and Newland *Gender and International Relations*, pp. 51–63.

27 Delphy, C. (1984) *Close to Home: A Materialist Analysis of Women's Oppression*, London: Hutchinson.

28 Steans, J. 'The Private is Global: Global Political Economy and Feminist Politics'. *New Political Economy*, 4, 1, 1999, pp. 113–28.

29 See also Brown, S. 'Feminism, International Theory and International Relations of Gender Inequality', *Millennium: Journal of International Studies*, 17, 3, 1988, p. 471; I would locate my own work within critical feminism. See, for example, Steans, J. (1999) 'The Private is Global', *New Political Economy*, 4, 1, March 1999, 113–28.

30 See for example Whitworth 'Theory as Exclusion; Gender and International Political Economy'.

31 Whitworth *Feminism*.

32 Steans 'The Private is Global'.

33   Walker, R. B. J. (1992) 'Gender and Critique in the Theory of IR'.

34   Tong *Feminist Thought*.

35   Ibid.

36   Lorde, A. (1984) *Sister Outsider*, Boston: Crossing Press Feminist Series.

37   Tong *Feminist Thought*.

38   Goetz, A. M. (1990) 'Feminism and the Claim to Know: Contradictions in Feminist Approaches to Development', in Grant and Newland *Gender and International Relations*, pp. 133–57.

39   Peterson 'Transgressing the Boundaries'; Sylvester, *Feminist Theory and International Relations in a Postmodern Era*; Zalewski, M. 'The Women/"Women" Question in International Relations', *Millennium: Journal of International Studies*, 23, 3, 1994, pp. 407–23.

40   Butler *Gender Trouble*.

41   There is an extensive literature on postcolonial feminism. See, for example: Chowdhry and Nair; *Power, Postcolonialism and International Relations*; Alexander, M. J. and Mohanty, C. T. (1997) (eds) *Feminist Genealogies, Colonial Legacies, Democratic Futures*, London: Routledge; Ashfar, Haleh (1996) (ed.) *Women and Politics in the Third World*, London: Routledge; Davies, M. (1983) (ed.) *Third World, Second Sex*, London: Prometheus Books; Harding, S. and Uma N. (1998) (eds) *Border Crossings: Multicultural and Postcolonial Feminist Challenges to Philosophy*, Bloomington: Indiana University Press; John, M. E. (1996) *Discrepant Dislocations: Feminism, Theory and Postcolonial Histories*, Berkeley: University of California Press; Minh-ha, Trinh T. (1989) *Woman, Native, Other: Writing Postcoloniality and Feminism*, Bloomington: Indiana University Press; Mohanty, C. T., Russo, A., Lourdes, T. (1991) (eds) *Third World Women and the Politics of Feminism*, Bloomington: Indiana University Press.

42   Mohanty, C. T. 'Under Western Eyes: Feminist Scholarship and Colonial Discourse', *Feminist Review*, 30, 1988, pp. 61–88; Spivak, G. (1988) 'Can the Subaltern Speak?' in Nelson, C. and Grossberg, L. (eds) *Marxism and the Interpretation of Culture*, Illinois: University of Illinois Press; Jayawardena, K. (1986) *Feminism and Nationalism in the Third World*, London: Zed Books.

43   Grewal, I. and Kaplan, C. *Scattered Hegemonies*.

Chapter 2   Gender, Feminism and the Fourth Debate in International Relations

1   Lapid, Y. 'The Third Debate: on the Prospects of International Theory in a Postpositivist Era', *International Studies Quarterly* 33, 2, 1989, pp. 235–54.

2   Lapid 'The Third Debate', p. 237.

3   Tooze and Murphy *The New International Political Economy*.

4   The origin of IR as a distinctive discipline is often dated to the establishment of the first Chair in IR – the Woodrow Wilson Chair, at the University of Wales Aberystwyth in 1918.

5   Carr, E. H. (1939) *The Twenty Years' Crisis 1919–1939: An Introduction to the Study of International Relations*, London: Macmillan.

6   Morgenthau, H. (1948) *Politics Among Nations*, New York: Alfred Knopf.

7   In the usage employed in this text, the 'third debate' refers to the inter-paradigm debate and not the 'neo-neo debate'.

8   Vasquez, J. (1983) *The Power of Power Politics*, London: Pinter.

9   Banks, M. (1985) 'The Inter-paradigm Debate', in Groom, A. J. R. and Light, M. *International Relations: A Handbook of Current Theory*, London: Pinter.

10   Drawing on Kuhn, the generation of knowledge (in IR) came to be seen as a communal, or social, activity carried out by groups of scholars who shared common assumptions about the nature of their subject matter. Kuhn had been concerned to show how a paradigm was usually provided by a single work that was so unprecedented in its achievement that it became the 'exemplar' of scientific analysis in a particular field. This constrained scholars to the elaboration of theories that did not violate the fundamental assumptions of the paradigm. Vasquez, *The Power of Power Politics*.

11   Vasquez *The Power of Power Politics*.

12   Harding, S. (1987) 'Is There a Feminist Method?', in Harding, S. (ed.) *Feminism and Methodology*, Milton Keynes: Open University Press, p. 230.

13   Ibid., p. 230.

14   Lapid 'The Third Debate', p. 243; Tooze and Murphy, *The New International Political Economy*, p. 11; George, J. (1994) *Discourses of Global Politics: A Critical (Re)Introduction to IR*, Boulder, CO: Lynne Rienner.

15   George *Discourses of Global Politics*.

16   Lapid 'The Third Debate', p. 243.

17   Smith, S. (2001) 'Reflectivist and Constructivist Approaches', in Baylis, J. and Smith, S. (eds) *The Globalization of World Politics*, Oxford: Oxford University Press, p. 226.

18   Tooze and Murphy *The New International Political Economy*.

19   Stanley, L. and Wise, S. (1983) *Breaking Out: Feminist Consciousness and Feminist Research*, London: Routledge.

20   Ibid., p. 243.

21   Cited in McLean, J. 'Political Theory, International Theory and Problems of Ideology', *Millennium: Journal of International Studies*, 10, 2, 1981, pp. 102–25.

22   Ibid.

23   Ibid.

24   Ashley, R. K. and Walker, R. B. J. 'Speaking the Language of Exile', *International Studies Quarterly*, 34, 3, 1990, p. 259.

25   Cox, R. (1986) 'States, Social Forces and World Order', in Keohane, R. (ed.) *Neorealism and its Critics*, Princeton: Princeton University Press.

26   Ibid.

27   Whitworth, S. 'Gender in the Interparadigm Debate', *Millennium: Journal of International Studies*, 18, 2, Summer, 1989, pp. 265–72.

28   Tickner, J. A. 'You Just Don't Understand: Troubled Engagements Between Feminists and IR Theorists', *International Studies Quarterly*, 41, 4, 1997, p. 614.

29   Tickner 'Hans Morgenthau's Six Principles of Political Realism'.

30   Youngs, G. (1999) *International Relations in a Global Age*, Cambridge: Polity.

31   Morgenthau *Politics Among Nations*.

32   Grant 'The Sources of Gender Bias in International Relations Theory', p. 9.

33   Ibid., p. 9.

34   Di Stefano, C. (1990) 'Dilemmas of Difference; Feminism, Modernity and Postmodernism', in Nicholson, L. (ed.) *Feminism/Postmodernism*, London: Routledge. See also Di Stefano, C. 'Masculinity as Ideology: Hobbesian Man Considered', *Women's Studies International Forum*, 6, 1983.

35   Benhabib, S. (1992) *Situating the Self: Gender, Community and Postmodernism in Contemporary Ethics*, Cambridge: Polity.

36   Di Stefano 'Masculinity as Ideology'.

37   Peterson *Transgressing Boundaries*.

38   Hirschmann, N. *Rethinking Obligation*.

39   Ibid.

40   Ann Tickner has characterized the development of feminist IR in turns of first, second and third generations.

41   Grewal and Kaplan *Scattered Hegemonies;* Chowdhry and Nair *Postcolonialism and International Relations.*

42   Lipsitz-Bem *The Lenses of Gender.*

43   McGlen, N. and Sarkees, M. Reid (1993) *Women in Foreign Policy,* London: Routledge.

44   Enloe *Bananas, Beaches and Bases.*

45   Seagar, J. and Olson, A. (1986) *Women in the World: An International Atlas,* New York: Simon & Schuster.

46   Ibid.

47   Pettman *Worlding Women.*

48   Newland, K. (1991) 'From Transnational Relationships to International Relations: Women in Development and the International Decade for Women', in Grant and Newland (eds) *Gender and International Relations,* pp. 122–32.

49   Ashworth, G. (1991) 'An Elf Among Gnomes: A Feminist in North-South Relations', in Grant and Newland.

50   For example Marchand, M. and Runyan, A. (2000) *Gender and Global Restructuring,* London: Routledge; Peterson and Runyan *Global Gender Issues.*

51   Whitworth *Feminism and International Relations.*

52   Ibid.; Brown, S. (1988) 'Feminism, International Theory'.

53   Brown 'Feminism and International Theory', p. 471.

54   Peterson and Runyan *Global Gender Issues,* p. 18.

55   Ibid., p. 18.

56   Ibid., p. 18.

57   Zalewski, M. (1994) 'The Women/"Women" Question in International Relations', *Millennium: Journal of International Studies,* 23, 3, pp. 407–23.

58   Zalewski, M. (1994) 'Introduction: From the "Woman" Question to the "Man" Question in International Relations', in Zalewski and Parpart, *The 'Man' Question in International Relations,* p. 11.

59   Jones, A. 'Does "Gender" Make the World Go Around? Feminist Critiques of International Relations', *Review of International Studies,* 22, 4, 1996, pp. 405–29.

60   'Interview with Professor Cynthia Enloe', p. 663.

61   Ibid., p. 663.

62   Ibid., p. 663.

63   Ibid., p. 663.

64   Zalewski, 'Introduction: From the "Woman" Question to the "Man" Question in International Relations', p. 6.

65   Hooper, C. (1994) 'Masculinist Practices and Gender Politics: The Operation of Multiple Masculinities in International Relations', in Zalewski and Parpart *The 'Man' Question,* p. 33.

66   Pease and Pringle *A Man's World,* p. 10.

67   Truth, S. *Aint I a Woman.* Speech delivered at the 1851 Women's Convention, Akron, Ohio, USA.

68   See Ramazanoglu, C. (1989) *Feminism and the Contradictions of Oppression,* London: Routledge; hooks, b. and Watkin, G. (1981) *Aint I a Woman? Black Women and Feminism,* London: South End Press; hooks, b. (1990) *Yearning: Race, Gender and Cultural Politics,* London: South End Press.

69   Critical Theorists argued that positivism in IR had a pernicious impact in so far as positive work focused wholly on the problems of power and strategic interest in IR. This

militated against the development of knowledge that could be put to the service of human emancipation. Hoffman, M. 'Critical Theory and the Inter-Paradigm Debate', *Millennium: Journal of International Studies* 16, 2, 1987, pp. 231–49; see also Ashley, R. K. 'Political Realism and Human Interests', *International Studies Quarterly*, 25, 2, 1981, pp. 204–36.

Chapter 3   Gender in the Theory and Practice of 'State-Making'

1   Tickner 'You Just Don't Understand', p. 616.
2   Tickner *Gender in International Relations*, p. 39.
3   Biersteker, T. and Weber, C. (1999) *Sovereignty and Social Construct*, Cambridge: Cambridge University Press; Hoffman *Gender and Sovereignty*.
4   See Pitkin, H. (1984) *Fortune is a Woman: Gender and Politics in the Thought of Niccolò Machiavelli*, Berkeley: University of California Press.
5   Runyan, A. S. (1992) 'The 'State' of Nature: A Garden Unfit for Women and Other Living Things', in Peterson, *The Gendered State*, pp. 123–40.
6   Ibid., p. 124.
7   Pitkin *Fortune is a Woman*, pp. 80–105 and pp. 55–79.
8   Di Stefano, Dilemmas of Difference; see also Pateman, C. (1985) *The Problem of Political Obligation*, Cambridge: Polity; Lloyd, G. (1984) *The Man of Reason: Male and Female in Western Philosophy*, London: Methuen; Hartsock, N. 'The Barracks Community in Western Political Thought', *The Women's Studies International Forum*, 5, 3/4, 1982, pp. 283–6.
9   Morgenthau *Politics Among Nations*, pp. 4–5.
10   Ibid., p. 4.
11   Carr *The Twenty Year Crisis*, p. 159.
12   Ibid., p. 159.
13   Morgenthau *Politics Among Nations*, p. 103.
14   Ibid., p. 103.
15   Claude, I. (1962) *Power and International Relations*, New York: Random House, p. 55.
16   Steans 'Conflicting Loyalties'.
17   Anderson, B. (1983) *Imagined Communities*, London: Verso Books.
18   Krause and Renwick *Identities in International Relations*.
19   Ibid.
20   Chatterjee, P. 'Whose Imagined Communities?' *Millennium: Journal of International Studies*, 20, 3, 1991; Kandiyoti, D. 'Identity and its Discontents: Women and the Nation', *Millennium Journal of International Studies*, 29, 3, 1991, pp. 429–43.
21   Parker, A., Russo, M., Sommer, D. and Yaeger, P. (1992) *Nationalisms and Sexualities*, London: Routledge.
22   Anderson *Imagined Communities*.
23   Ibid.
24   Mosse, G. (1985) *Nationalism and Sexuality: Middle Class Morality and Sexual Norms in Modern Europe*, Madison: University of Wisconsin Press.
25   Yuval-Davis, N. and Anthias, F. (1989) *Woman–Nation–State*, Basingstoke: Macmillan.
26   Massey, D. and Jess, P. (eds) *A Place in the World? Places, Cultures and Globalization*, Milton Keynes: Open University Press, 1995, p. 65.
27   Ibid., p. 65.
28   Ibid., p. 65.
29   Kandiyoti 'Identity', p. 429.
30   Ibid.

31 Zalewski and Enloe 'Questions about Identity', p. 281.
32 Zalewski and Enloe 'Questions about Identity'; Krause *Gendered Identities*.
33 Callaway, H. and Ridd, R. (1986) *Caught Up in Conflict: Women's Responses to Political Strife*, Basingstoke: Macmillan; Molyneux, M. 'Mobilisation without Emancipation? Women's Interests, State and Revolution in Nicaragua', *Feminist Studies*, 11, 2, 1985, Summer.
34 Ridd and Callaway, *Caught Up in Conflict*.
35 Ibid.
36 Chatterjee, 'Whose Imagined Communities?'
37 Callaway, H. 'Survival and Support: Women's Forms of Political Action', in Callaway and Ridd *Caught up in Conflict*; Westwood, S. and Radcliffe, S. (1993) (eds) *'Viva': Women and Popular Protest in Latin America*, London: Routledge.
38 Ridd and Callaway *Caught Up in Conflict*.
39 Chatterjee 'Whose Imagined Communities?'
40 Kriger, N. J. (1992) *Zimbabwe's Guerilla War: Peasant Voices*, Cambridge: Cambridge University Press.
41 See O'Barr, J. (1984) 'African Women in Politics', in Hay, M. and Stichter, S. *African Women South of the Sahara*, London: Zed Books.
42 Harris, H. (1988) 'Women and War: The Case of Nicaragua', in Isaksson, E. (ed.) *Women and the Military System*, Brighton: Harvester Wheatsheaf.
43 Harris 'Women and War'.
44 Jayawardena, K. (1986) *Feminism and Nationalism in the Third World*, London: Zed Books.
45 Harris 'Women and War'.
46 Helie-Lucas, M. A. (1988) 'The Role of Women During the Algerian Liberation Struggle and After: Nationalism as a Concept and as a Practice towards both the Power of the Army and the Militarization of the People', in Isaksson *Women and the Military System*, p. 173.
47 Ibid., p. 176.
48 Ibid., p. 175.
49 Youngs, G. ' "Beyond Inside"/"Outside" ', in Krause and Renwick *Identities in International Relations*.
50 Kratochwil, F. (1996) 'Citizenship: On the Border of Order', in Lapid, J. and Kratochwil, F. *The Return of Culture and Identity in IR Theory*, London: Lynne Rienner, p. 182. See also Linklater, A. 'Citizenship and Sovereignty in the Post Westphalian State', *European Journal of International Relations*, 2, 1, March 1996, pp. 77–103.
51 Jayawardena *Feminism and Nationalism*.
52 Kandiyoti *Identity*, p. 431.
53 Phillips, A. (1991) *Engendering Democracy*, Cambridge: Polity.
54 Yuval-Davis and Anthias *Woman–Nation–State*.
55 Hartsock *Money, Sex and Power*.
56 Ibid.
57 Epstein, C. 'In Praise of Women Warriors', *Dissent*, 38, 1991, pp. 421–2.
58 Stiehm, J. H. 'The Protected, the Protector and the Defender', *Women's Studies International Forum*, 5, no. 3/4, 1982, pp. 367–76; see also Stiehm, J. (1984) *Women's and Men's Wars*, Oxford: Pergamon Press.
59 Linklater, A. (1998) *The Transformation of Political Community*, Cambridge: Polity.
60 Crompton, R. (1997) *Women and Work in Modern Britain*, Oxford: Oxford University Press; Dominelli, L. (1991) *Women Across Continents: Feminist Comparative Social Policy*, Hemel Hempstead: Harvester Wheatsheaf.

61 Stiehm 'The Protected, the Protector and the Defender'; Epstein 'In Praise of Women Warriors'; Chapkis, W. (1981) (ed.) *Loaded Questions: Women in the Military*, Amsterdam: Transnational Institute.

62 Stiehm 'The Protected, the Protector and the Defender'.

63 Elshtain, J. 'Reflections on War and Political Discourse', *Political Theory*, 13, 1, 1988, pp. 39–57.

64 Tickner *Gender in International Relations*; Peterson *Gendered States*.

65 Coole, D. (1988) *Women in Political Theory: From Ancient Misogyny to Contemporary Feminism*, Hemel Hempstead: Harvester Wheatsheaf.

66 Krause, J. and Renwick, N. (1996) 'Introduction', in Krause and Renwick *Identities in International Relations*.

Chapter 4 Feminist Perspectives on War and Peace

1 Von Clausewitz C. (1986) *On War* (ed. A. Rapaport), Harmondsworth: Penguin.

2 Goldstein, J. S. (2003) *War and Gender: How Gender Shapes the War System and Vice-Versa*, Cambridge: Cambridge University Press.

3 Jones, A. (ed.) (2004) *Gendercide and Genocide*, Vanderbilt University Press.

4 Dinnerstein, D. (1976) *The Rocking of the Cradle and the Ruling of the World*, New York: Harper & Row; Chodorow, N. (1978) *The Reproduction of Mothering: Psychoanalysis and the Sociology of Gender*, Berkeley: University of California Press; Gilligan, C. (1982) *In a Different Voice: Psychological Theory and Women's Development*, Cambridge, MA: Harvard University Press.

5 Elshtain, J. 'Reflections on War and Political Discourse', *Political Theory*, 13, 1, 1985, p. 57. See also Elshtain, J. Bethke (1987) *Women and War*, New York: Basic Books.

6 Roberts, Y. 'How Women's Roles are Camouflaged', *The Observer*, 23 March 2003.

7 Beevor, A. (1994) *Inside the British Army*, London: Hamish Hamilton.

8 Jones, cited in Bridget Byrne, Report No 34 Gender, conflict and development Volume I: Overview Report prepared at the request of the Netherlands. Special Programme on WID, Ministry of Foreign Affairs, Vrouwenberaad Ontwikkelingssamenwerking, July 1996.

9 Ruddick, S. (1989) 'Mothers and Men's Wars', in Harris, A. and King, Y. *Rocking the Ship of State: Towards a Feminist Peace Politics*, Boulder, CO: Westview.

10 Cetkovic, 1993, cited in Bridget Byrne Report.

11 Ibid.

12 In Afghan refugee camps in Pakistan, the influence of the religious leaders was increased, obliging all women – including urban women who had formerly been accustomed to relative freedom of movement – to go into purdah. The erosion of women's human rights can also be seen in the introduction in Iraq of a law legitimizing the murder of women suspected of offending family honour. Ibid.

13 In a bid to keep women out of combat, a House committee passed an amendment late in May that would block the US military from allowing female troops into any new jobs related to ground operations without congressional approval. The Republican-led House Armed Services Committee approved the measure to give Congress more control over which units the military opens to women and to put into law a 1994 Pentagon policy barring women from serving in 'direct ground combat' units below the brigade level. The vote along party lines followed a heated debate over the role of female troops as more women in Iraq and Afghanistan are wounded, killed and engaged in battle in insurgencies that defy the traditional military concept of a 'front line'. Tyson, A. S. 'Amendment Targets Role of Female Troops', *Washington Post*, Thursday 19 May 2005.

14   Yuval-Davis, N. and Anthias, F. (1987) *Woman–Nation–State*, Basingstoke: Macmillan.
15   Fukuyama, F. 'Women and the Evolution of World Politics', *Foreign Affairs*, 77, 5, 1998, pp. 24–40.
16   Tickner, J. A. 'Why Women Can't Run the World: International Politics According to Francis Fukuyama', *International Studies Review*, 3, 1999, pp. 3–12.
17   Ibid.
18   Hooper, C. 'Masculine Practices and Gender Politics', in Zalewski and Parpart *The 'Man' Question in International Relations*, pp. 31–2.
19   Stiehm, J. H. 'The Protected, the Protector and the Defender', *Women's Studies International Forum*, 5, 3/4, 1982, pp. 367–76.
20   Connell *Gender and Power*.
21   Ibid., p. 109.
22   Ibid., p. 109.
23   Connell argues that the key to understanding how this gendered system functions and how different masculinities are linked together lies in understanding the gendered pattern of emotional attachment that exists amongst men. Connell, *Gender and Power*, p. 108.
24   Ruddick, S. (1989) 'Mothers and Men's Wars', in Harris and King *Rocking the Ship of State*; see also Ruddick, 'Notes Towards a Feminist Peace Politics'.
25   Beevor, *Inside the British Army*, p. 59.
26   Cohn, C. (1997) 'Gays in the Military: Texts and Subtexts', in Zalewski and Parpart *The 'Man' Question in International Relations*.
27   Ibid., p. 145.
28   Ibid., p. 145.
29   Beevor records that at Sandhurst women, like men, receive lessons on dress and behaviour, but for women this includes warnings against outspoken feminism that might 'provoke' men. Women in the armed forces are frequently subjected to harassment and slander campaigns by being labelled as lesbians or whores. This is debilitating on a strategic level because it makes it harder to recruit women and to integrate them in an effective way. Beevor *Inside the British Army*; see also Yuval-Davis, N. 'Front and Rear: The Sexual Division of Labour in the Israeli Army', *Feminist Studies*, 11, 3, 1985, pp. 649–75; Stiehm, J. (1989) *Arms and the Enlisted Woman*, Philadelphia: Temple University Press.
30   Pierson, R. (1988) 'They're Still Women After All: Wartime Jitters over Femininity', in Isaksson, *Women and the Military System*.
31   Beevor has documented the profound unease that most military men feel about the participation of women in combat. Beevor *Inside the British Army*, p. 59.
32   Roberts 'How Women's Roles are Camouflaged'.
33   Enloe, C. (1988) *Does Khaki Become You? The Militarisation of Women's Lives*, London: Pandora, p. 218.
34   Kaldor, M. (1999) *New and Old Wars: Organised Violence in a Globalised Era*, Cambridge: Polity.
35   Tickner, J. A. 'Feminist Perspectives on 9/11', *International Studies Perspectives*, 3, 4, 2002.
36   Cited in Dowler, L. 'Women on the Frontlines: Re-thinking War Narratives post 9/11', *Geojournal*, 58, 2002, pp. 159–65.
37   Cited in Dowler 'Women on the Frontlines', p. 163.
38   Ibid., p. 163.
39   Cited in Dowler, 'Women on the Frontlines', pp. 159–65.
40   Dowler 'Women on the Frontlines'.
41   Tickner 'Feminist Perspectives'.

42   Stuever, 2001, cited in Shepherd, L. 'Veiled References: Constructions of Gender in the Bush Administration Discourse on the Attacks on Afghanistan Post-9/11', *International Feminist Journal of Politics*, 8, 1, 2006 (forthcoming, page references not yet available).

43   Dowler, 'Women on the Frontlines', p. 164.

44   Ibid., p. 164.

45   Cited in Shepherd 'Veiled References' (forthcoming, page references not yet available); see also Laura Bush Decries Taliban 'Brutality' at: *http://news.bbc.co.uk/1/hi/uk_politics/ 1663300*; 'Cherie Blair Attacks Taliban "Cruelty" at: *http://ww.newsmedia.com/rawa/ htm*' (accessed June 2005).

46   Shepherd 'Veiled References' (forthcoming, page references not yet available).

47   'Testimony of Tahmeena Faryal representative of RAWA before the Sub-Committee of the US House on International Operations and Human Rights', October 31 2001 at: <*http://www.rawasongs.net/testimony.htm*>. Documents last accessed November 2004.

48   Dowler 'Women on the Frontlines', p. 165.

49   Kaplan, E. A. (2003) 'Feminist Futures: Trauma, the Post-9/11 World and a Fourth Feminism', *Journal of International Women's Studies*, 4, 2, April, p. 53.

50   Contribution of Drucilla Cornell to the Roundtable on 'Gender and September 11', *Signs, Journal of Women in Culture and Society*, 28, 11, 2002, p. 435.

51   Naveh, H. Contribution to the Roundtable on 'Gender and September 11', p. 451.

52   Ibid., p. 451.

53   Radstone, S. Contribution to the Roundtable on 'Gender and September 11', p. 458.

54   Feccero, C. Contribution to Roundtable on 'Gender and September 11', p. 454.

55   MacKinnon, C. (1989) *Towards a Feminist Theory of the State*, Cambridge, MA: Harvard University Press, p. 157.

56   Ibid.

57   Ibid.

58   Roberts, M. (1956) *The Military Revolution*, Belfast. See also discussion in Hacker, B. (1988) 'From Military Revolution to Industrial Revolution: Armies, Women and Political Economy in Early Modern Europe', in Isaksson *Women and the Military System*.

59   Roberts *The Military Revolution*.

60   Ibid.

61   Connell R. (1990) 'The State, Gender and Sexual Politics: Theory and Appraisal', *Theory and Society*, 19, p. 351.

62   Ruddick 'Notes towards a Feminist Peace Politics'.

63   Ibid.

64   Enloe, C. (1987) 'Thinking about War, Militarism and Peace', in Hess, B. and Feree, M. (eds) *Analysing Gender: A Handbook of Social Science Research*, Beverly Hills: Sage.

65   Ruddick 'Notes towards a Feminist Politics'.

66   Ibid.

67   Cohn, C. (1993) 'Wars, Wimps and Women', in Cooke, M. and Woollacott, A. *Gendering War Talk*, Princeton: Princeton University Press. See also Cohn, C. 'Sex and Death in the Rational World of Defence Intellectuals', *Signs*, 12, 4, 1987, pp. 687–718.

68   Enloe 'Thinking about War, Militarism and Peace'.

69   Ibid.

70   Ibid.

71   See Connell 'The State, Gender and Sexual Politics'.

72   Harris, H. (1988) 'Women and War: The Case of Nicaragua', in Isaksson *Women and the Military System*.

73   Roberts *The Military Revolution*.

74   Enloe *Does Khaki Become You?*

75   Beevor *Inside the British Army*.
76   Ibid.
77   Goldstein, J. (2001) *Gender and War*, Cambridge: Cambridge University Press.
78   Braydon, G. and Summerfield, P. (1987) *Out of the Cage: Women's Experiences in Two World Wars*, London: Pandora.
79   Ibid.
80   Ibid.
81   Vickers, J. (1993) *Women and War*, London: Zed Books.
82   Stiehm 'The Protected, the Protector and the Defender'.
83   Pettman *Worlding Women*.
84   McGlen, N. and Sarkees, M. *Women in Foreign Policy*, pp. 1–15.
85   Steinstra, D. (1999) 'Of Roots, Leaves and Trees: Gender Social Movements, and Global Governance', in Meyer, M. and Prugl, E. (eds) *Gender Politics in Global Governance*, London: Rowman and Littlefield, p. 108.
86   Ibid.
87   Ibid., p. 108.
88   Ibid., p. 108.
89   McGlen and Sarkees, *Women in Foreign Policy*, p. 4.
90   Cited in Ahmadi, V. (2000) 'Evaluating the Impact and Effectiveness of the Transnational Feminist Movement: The UN Decade and Beyond', unpublished PhD thesis, University of Keele, UK.
91   Callaway, H. (1986) 'Survival and Support: Women's Forms of Political Action', in Callaway, H. and Ridd, R. *Caught Up in Conflict: Women's Responses to Political Strife*, Basingstoke: Macmillan, p. 76.
92   See Women in Black 'Women's Solidarity Network Against War'. *Http://lists.partners-intl/pipermail/women-east-west.* (accessed June 2005).
93   Ruddick, S. (1989) *Maternal Thinking: Towards a Politics of Peace*, Boston: Beacon Press; Ruddick, S. 'Notes towards a Feminist Peace Politics'.
94   Ruddick 'Notes towards a Feminist Peace Politics'.
95   McGlen and Sarkees *Women in Foreign Policy*.
96   Dinnerstein, D. (1989) 'What Does Feminism Mean?' in Harris and King *Rocking the Ship of State*.
97   Ibid.
98   Enloe 'Feminist Thinking about War, Militarism and Peace'.
99   Chapkis, W. (1981) *Loaded Questions: Women in the Military*, Amsterdam: Transnational Institute.
100 Di Leonardo, M. 'Morals, Mothers and Militarism; Anti-Militarism and Feminist Theory', *Feminist Studies*, 11, 3, 1985; Richards, Radcliffe J. (1990) 'Why the Pursuit of Peace is No Part of Feminism', in Elshtain, J. and Tobias, S. (eds) *Women, Militarism and War: Essays in History, Politics and Social Theory*, Savage: Rowman & Littlefield. See also Epstein, C. Fuchs 'In Praise of Women Warriors', *Dissent*, 38, 1991, pp. 421–2.
101 Hartsock 'The Barracks Community in Western Political Thought'.
102 Stiehm 'The Protected, the Protector and the Defender'.
103 Enloe 'Feminist Thinking about War, Militarism and Peace'.

Chapter 5   Re-Visioning Security

1   Scruton, R. (1983) *A Dictionary of Political Thought*, London: Pan.
2   Turpin, J. and Lorentzen, L. A. (1996) *The Gendered New World Order*, London: Routledge; Seagar, J. and Olson, A. (1986) *Women in the World: An International Atlas*, New York: Simon & Schuster.

3   Peterson, V. S. (1992) 'Security and Sovereign States: What is at Stake in Taking Feminism Seriously', in Peterson *Gendered States*; Grant, R. (1991) 'The Quagmire of Gender and International Security', in Peterson *Gendered States*; Tickner *Gender in International Relations*.

4   Oniang'o, R. and Mukudi, E. (2005) 'Nutrition and Gender.' At: www.unsystem.orgscn/publications/foundation4dev/07Gender.pdf.

5   Buzan, B. (1991) *People, States and Fear: An Agenda for International Security in a Post Cold War Era*, Hemel Hempstead: Harvester Wheatsheaf.

6   Scruton *A Dictionary of Political Thought*.

7   Ibid.

8   Tickner, J. A. (1995) 'Revisioning Security', in Booth, K. and Smith, S. *International Relations Theory Today*, Cambridge: Polity.

9   Buzan *People, States and Fear*.

10   Ibid., p. 39.

11   Ibid., p. 38.

12   Ibid., p. 177.

13   Ibid., p. 188.

14   Jervis, R. (1981) 'The Spiral of International Insecurity', in Smith, M., Shackleton, M. and Little, R. *Perspectives on World Politics*, Milton Keynes: Open University Press.

15   Youngs, G. (1996) 'Beyond the Inside/Outside Divide', in Krause, J. and Renwick, N. *Identities in International Relations*, Basingstoke: Macmillan.

16   Krause, K. and Williams, M. C. (eds) (1997) *Critical Security Studies*, Minneapolis, MN: University of Minnesota Press; see also Baylis, John (1997) 'International Security in the Post-Cold War Era', in Baylis, J. and Smith, S. (eds) (1997) *The Globalization of World Politics: An Introduction to International Relations*, Oxford: Oxford University Press, pp. 193–211; Teriff, T. et al. (1999) *Security Studies Today*, Cambridge: Polity; Tickner, J. A. 1996 'Revisioning Security', in Booth, K. and Smith, S. *International Relations Theory Today*; Katzenstein, Peter J. (ed.) (1996) *The Culture of National Security: Norms and Identity in World Politics*, New York: Columbia University Press; Shultz, Richard H. et al. (eds) (1997) *Security Studies for the 21st Century*, Washington, DC: Brassey's.

17   Lapid, J. and Kratochwil, F. (eds) (1996) *The Return of Culture and Identity in IR Theory*, London: Lynne Rienner.

18   Krause and Williams *Critical Security Studies*.

19   Campbell, D. (1992) *Writing Security: United States Foreign Policy and the Politics of Identity*, Manchester: Manchester University Press. See also discussion in Tickner, 'Revisioning Security'.

20   Elshtain, J. (1985) 'Reflections on War and Political Discourse: Realism, Just War and Feminism in a Nuclear Age', *Political Theory*, 13, 1, pp. 39–57.

21   Campbell, D. *Writing Security*.

22   Elshtain 'Reflections on War and Political Discourse'.

23   Diez, T. (2005) 'Social Constructivism', in Steans, J. and Pettiford, L. *International Relations: Perspectives and Themes*, London: Pearson.

24   Ibid., pp. 181–202.

25   Ibid., pp. 181–202.

26   Elshtain, J. 'Reflections on War and Political Discourse'.

27   Ibid.

28   Ibid.

29   Enloe 'Feminist Thinking about War, Militarism and Peace'.

30   Ibid.

31   Hartsock 'The Barracks Community in Western Political Thought'.

32   Gilligan *In a Different Voice*.

33   Tickner *Gender in International Relations*.

34   Ibid.

35   Beneria, L. and Blank, R. (1989) 'Women and the Economics of Military Spending', in Harris, A. and King, Y. *Rocking the Ship of State*.

36   Ibid.

37   Enloe 'Feminist Thinking about War, Militarism and Peace'.

38   Beneria and Blank 'Women and the Economics of Military Spending'.

39   Ibid.

40   Report commissioned by the Netherlands Special Programme on WID, Ministry of Foreign Affairs (DGIS) of the Netherlands, as a background paper for a conference on gender, conflict and development organized by Vrouwenberaad Ontwikkelingssamenwerking held in Amsterdam in January 1996.

41   'Guns or Growth?' Control Arms Campaign, June 2004 1 Guns or Growth? Assessing the impact of arms sales on sustainable development. At: <www.controlarms.org/the_issue/guns_or_growth.htm> (accessed June 2005).

42   United Nations Charter, Articles 1, 26, 55 and 56.

43   Galbraith, J. K. (1987) 'Weapons and World Welfare', *Development Forum*, XV, 3; George, S. (1992) *The Debt Boomerang*, London: Pluto.

44   Cited in 'Guns or Growth?'

45   Ibid.

46   Ibid.

47   See United Nations General Assembly Special Session (UNGASS) 'Women 2000: Gender Equality, Development and Peace for the Twenty-first Century', New York, 5–9 June 2000, (UN Department of Public Information DPI/2035/N. 1.

48   Copelon, R. R. (1995) 'Gendered War Crimes: Reconceptualizing Rape in Time of War', in Peters, J and Wolper, A. (eds) *Women's Rights, Human Rights: International Feminist Perspectives*, London: Routledge.

49   See <www.peacewomen.org/un/sc/1325.htm>.

50   C. Corrin (2003) 'International Interventions–Gendered Impacts and Consequences in Kosovo and Afghanistan', paper presented at the 28th Annual Conference of the British International Studies Association, University of Birmingham, 15–17 December.

51   Ibid.

52   Ibid.

53   Diez, 'Social Constructivism'.

54   Sen, A. (1981) *Poverty and Famine*, Oxford: Clarendon.

55   United Nations, Human Development Report Office 1999: *A Human Face for Globalization*, <http://www.undp.org/hdro/E1.html>.

56   See, for example, (1991) *World Women's Conference for a Healthy Planet*, Official Report, Miami, published by WEDO, New York. See also Commission on Environment and Development (1987) *Our Common Future*, Oxford: Oxford University Press.

57   Poku, N. K. (2001) AIDS in Africa: An Overview, *International Relations*, xv, pp. 5–14.

58   Sen, A. *Poverty and Famine*.

59   See: <www.un.org/womenwatch/un/unagency/htm>.

60   Vickers *Women and War*.

61   Vickers *Women and War*.

62   Peterson and Runyan *Global Gender Issues*.

63   Booth, K. (2004) (ed.) *Critical Security Studies and World Politics*, Boulder, Co: Lynne Rienner.

64   Brock-Utne, B. (1985) *Educating for Peace*, Oxford: Pergamon.

Chapter 6   The Gender Dimension of International Political Economy

1   Steans 'The Private is Global'.
2   Frieden, J. A. and Lake, D. A. (1995) *International Political Economy: Perspectives on Global Power and Wealth*, London: Routledge, p. 1.
3   Sylvester 'The Emperor's Theories and Transformations'.
4   Tickner, A. (1992) 'On the Fringes of the Global Economy', in Tooze, R. and Murphy, C. *The New International Political Economy*, Boulder, CO: Lynne Rienner.
5   Mies, M. (1986) *Patriarchy and Accumulation on a World Scale*, London: Zed Books.
6   Tickner 'On the Fringes of the Global Economy', p. 191.
7   Runyan, A. S. (1997) 'Of Markets and Men: The (Re)Making(s) of IPE', in Burch, K. and Denemark, R. A. (eds) *Constituting International Political Economy*, London: Lynne Rienner, p. 79.
8   See: *http://www.allwomencount.net.* (accessed June 2005).
9   Waring, M. (1988) *If Women Counted: A New Feminist Economics*, San Francisco: Harper and Row.
10   Tooze and Murphy *The New International Political Economy*.
11   Tickner 'On the Fringes of the Global Economy'.
12   Sylvester 'The Emperor's Theories and Transformations'.
13   Nelson, J. (1998) 'Abstraction, Reality and the Gender of Economic Man', in Carrier, J. and Miller, D. (eds) *Virtualism: A New Political Economy*, Oxford: Berg, p. 75.
14   Tickner 'On the Fringes of the Global Economy'.
15   De Goode, M. 'Mastering Lady Credit', *International Feminist Journal of Politics*, 2, 1, 2000, pp. 58–81.
16   Tickner 'On the Fringes of the Global Economy'.
17   Youngs *International Relations in a Global Age*.
18   Tickner 'On the Fringes of the Global Economy'; Sylvester 'The Emperor's Theories and Transformations'; Whitworth, S. (1994) *Feminism and International Relations*; Waylen, G. 'Gender, Feminism and Political Economy', *New Political Economy* 2, 2, 1997, pp. 205–20.
19   Tickner 'On the Fringes of the Global Economy', p. 202.
20   Ibid., p. 206.
21   Ibid., p. 206.
22   Vickers, J. (1991) *Women in the World Economic Crisis*, London: Zed Books.
23   See, for example: Mies, M. (1986) *Patriarchy and Accumulation on a World Scale*, London: Zed Books; Mitter, S. (1986) *Common Fate, Common Bond: Women in the Global Economy*, London: Pluto Press; Young, K., Wolkowitz, C. and McCullagh, R. (1991) *Of Marriage and the Market: The Subordination of Women Internationally and its Lessons*, London: Routledge.
24   Whitworth, S. (1999) 'Theory and Exclusion', in Stubbs, R. and Underhill, G. (eds) (2nd edition). *Political Economy and the Changing Global Order*, London: Palgrave, p. 91.
25   See, for example, Spike-Peterson, V. 'Rewriting (Global) Political Economy as Reproductive, Productive and Virtual (Foucauldian) Economies', *International Feminist Journal of Politics*, 4, 1, April, 2002, pp. 1–30.
26   True, J. 'Expanding Markets and Marketing Gender: the Integration of the post-Socialist Czech Republic', *Review of International Political Economy*, 6, 3, 1999, pp. 360–89.
27   De Goode, 'Mastering Lady Credit'.
28   McGrew, A. and Lewis, P. (1992) *Global Politics*, Cambridge: Polity.
29   Cerny, P. (1996) 'What Next for the State?' in Kofman, E. and Youngs, G. (eds) *Globalization: Theory and Practice*, London: Pinter, pp. 123–37; Stopford, J. and Strange, S.

(1991) *Rival States, Rival Firms: Competition for World Market Shares*, Cambridge: Cambridge University Press.

30 Hay, C. and Marsh, D. (2000) *Demystifying Globalisation*, London: Palgrave.

31 Held, D. et al. (1999) *Global Transformation: Politics, Economics, Culture*, Cambridge: Polity, p. 191.

32 Jameson, F. and Miyoshi, M. (eds) (1998) *The Cultures of Globalization*, London: Duke University Press.

33 Ohmae, K. (1995) *The End of the Nation-State: the Rise of Regional Economies*, New York: Free Press; Kofman, E. and Youngs, G. (eds) (1996) 'Introduction: Globalization – the Second Wave' in Youngs, G. and Kofman, E. *Globalization: Theory and Practice*, London, pp. 1–10.

34 Hay and Marsh *Demystifying Globalisation*, p. 3.

35 Kofman and Youngs *Globalisation: Theory and Practice*; Hay and Marsh *Demystifying Globalisation*.

36 Peterson 'Rewriting (Global) Political Economy', p. 2.

37 Marchand, M. and Runyan, A. (2000) *Gender and Global Restructuring*, London: Routledge.

38 Meyer, W. H. (1998) *Human Rights and International Political Economy in the Third World*, Westport, CT: Praeger.

39 Ibid.

40 Ibid.

41 Birdsall, N. and Graham, C. (2000) (eds) *New Markets, New Opportunities? Economic and Social Mobility in a Changing World*, New York: Brookings Institute.

42 Meyer *Human Rights and International Political Economy*.

43 Marchand and Runyan *Gender and Global Restructuring*.

44 Waylen, G. 'Putting Governance into the Gendered Political Economy of Globalisation', *International Feminist Journal of Politics*, 6, 4, 2004, p. 561.

45 Mitter *Common Fate, Common Bond*.

46 Ibid.

47 Mitter, S. and Luijken, A. (1989) *The Unseen Phenomenon: The Rise of Homeworking*, London: Change Publications.

48 Ashworth, G. and May, N. (1990) *Of Conjuring and Caring*, London, Change Publications.

49 Elson, D. and Pearson, R. (1991) 'The Situation of Women and the Internationalisation of Factory Production', in Young, Wolkowitz and McCullagh, *Of Marriage and the Market*.

50 Mitter and Luijken *The Unseen Phenomenon*.

51 See Mitter *Common Fate*; Elson and Pearson 'The Situation of Women and the Internationalisation of Factory Production'.

52 Meyer *International Political Economy and Human Rights*.

53 Marchand and Runyan *Gender and Global Restructuring*.

54 Elson and Pearson 'The Situation of Women and the Internationalisation of Factory Production'.

55 Rai, S. (2002) *Gender and the Political Economy of Development*, Cambridge: Polity.

56 Mackintosh, M. (1984) 'Gender and Economy: The Sexual Division of Labour and the Subordination of Women', in Young, K., Wolkowitz, C. and McCollagh, R. *Of Marriage and the Market*, London: Routledge.

57 Mitter *Common Fate, Common Bond*.

58 Elson, D. (1991) *Male Bias in the Development Process*, Manchester: Manchester University Press.

59 Enloe *Bananas, Beaches and Bases*.

60   Terrell, K. (2000) 'Worker Mobility and the Transition to a Market Economy', in Birdsall and Graham *New Markets, New Opportunities?*

61   True 'Expanding Markets and Marketing Gender'.

62   Umfreville, M. (1990) *$£XONOMIC$: An Introduction to the Political Economy of Sex, Time and Gender*, London: Change Publications; Pettman, J. (1996) 'An International Political Economy of Sex', in Kofman and Youngs *Globalization: Theory and Practice*.

63   Hooper, E. (1994a) *Report on the UN LAC Regional Preparatory Meeting for the Fourth World Conference on Women*, La Plata; Hooper, E (1994b) *Report on the UN ESCAP Regional Preparatory Meeting for the Fourth World Conference on Women*, Jakarta.

64   Truong, Thanhn Dan (1985) 'The Dynamics of Sex Tourism: The Case of South East Asia', *Development and Change*, 14, pp. 533–53.

65   Ibid.

66   Enloe *Bananas, Beaches and Bases*.

67   De Groot, J. (1991) 'Conceptions and Misconceptions: The Historical and Cultural Context of Discussions of Women in Development', in Ashfar, H. *Women, Development and Survival in the Third World*, London: Longman.

68   George, S. (1992) *A Fate Worse Than Debt*, Harmondsworth: Penguin; George, S. (1989) *The Debt Boomerang*, London: Pluto.

69   See for example: Development Alternatives with Women for a New Era, *Alternatives*, vol. 1, and vol. 2, Rio de Janeiro: Editora Rosa dos Tempos, 1991; Elson *Male Bias in the Development Process*; Kardam, N. (1990) *Bringing Women In: Women's Issues in International Development Programs*, Boulder, CO: Lynne Rienner; Marchand, M. and Parpart, J. (eds) (1995) *Feminism, Postmodernism, Development*, London: Routledge; Momsen, J. H. (1996) *Women and Development in the Third World*, London: Routledge; Tinker, I. (1990) *Persistent Inequalities: Women and World Development*, Oxford: Oxford University Press.

70   Beneria, L. (1981) 'Conceptualizing the Labour Force: The underestimation of Women's Economic Activities', in Nelson, N. (ed.) *African Women in Development*, London: Frank Cass.

71   Whitworth *Feminism in International Relations*.

72   Hoogvelt, A. (1997) *Globalisation and the Postcolonial World*, London: Macmillan, p. 167.

73   Elson *Gender Bias in the Development Process*.

74   Ibid.

75   Moser, C. (1993) 'Adjustment from Below: Low Income Women, Time and the Triple Role in Guayaygil', in Westwood, S. and Radcliffe, S. (eds) *'Viva': Women and Popular Protest in Latin America*, London: Routledge.

76   See: *http://www.un.org/millenniumgoals/*

77   Mayoux, L. 'Questioning Virtuous Spirals: Micro-Finance and Women's Empowerment in Africa, *Journal of International Development*, 11, 1999, p. 957 Available at: *http://www3.interscience.wiley.com/cgibin/fulltext?ID=68501662&PLACEBO=IE.pdf&CRETRY=1&SRETRY=0*

78   Ibid., p. 974.

79   Cornia, G., Jolly, R. and Stewart, F. (1987) *Adjustment with a Human Face: Protecting the Vulnerable and Promoting Growth*, A Study by UNICEF, Oxford: Oxford University Press.

80   O'Brien, R., Goetz, A. M., Scholte, J. A. and Williams, M. (2000) *Contesting Global Governance*, Cambridge: Cambridge University Press; Special Issue 'Gender, Governance and Globalisation', *International Feminist Journal of Politics*, 6, 4, pp. 553–55.

81   See: *www.dawn.org.fj*.

Chapter 7   Promoting Women's Status at the UN: Gender in Development

1   Reanda, L. (1995) 'The Commission on the Status of Women', in Alston, P. (ed.) *The United Nations and Human Rights: A Critical Appraisal*, London: Clarendon Press.
2   Ibid.
3   United Nations Department of Public Information (1995) 'The United Nations and the Advancement of Women', New York: UNDPI.
4   Boserup, E. (1989) *Women's Role in Economic Development*, London: Earthscan.
5   Reanda, 'The Commission on the Status of Women'.
6   Pietila, H. and Vickers, J. (1994) *Making Women Matter: The Role of the UN*, London: Zed Books.
7   Of the mandates concerning women adopted by UN system between 1975 and 1988 75 per cent related to development. Reanda, 'The Commission on the Status of Women'.
8   Joachim, J. 'Framing Issues and Seizing Opportunities: The UN, NGOs and Women's Rights', *International Studies Quarterly*, 47, 2, June, 2003, pp. 247–74; see also 'Report of the World Conference of the UN Decade for Women, 1980, Copenhagen', New York: United Nations, 1980.
9   Available at: http://*www.un.org/womenwatch/confer/nf/s* (accessed June 2005).
10   Available at: http://*www.unesco.org/education/information/ufsunesco/pdf/BEIJIN_E.PDF* (accessed June 2006).
11   In the 1980s a survey conducted by INSTRAW found that out of 96 countries, only six included women's issues as central issues in their development plans.
12   Molyneux, M. 'Mobilisation without Emancipation? Women's Interests, State and Revolution in Nicaragua', *Feminist Studies*, 11, 2, Summer, 1985; Moser, C. (1995) 'Gender Planning in the TW: Meeting Practical and Strategic Gender Needs', in Wallace, T. and March, C. *Changing Perceptions: Writings on Gender and Development*, Oxford: Oxfam Publications.
13   Ashworth, G and Bonnerjea, L. (1985) *The Invisible Decade; UK Women and the UN Decade for Women*, London: Gower.
14   Muntemba, S. (1986) (ed.) *Rural Development and Women: Lessons from the Field*, vols. I and II, Geneva: ILO.
15   Penny, A. (1991) The Forward Looking Strategies', in Wallace and March, *Changing Perceptions*.
16   Ashworth, G. 'An Elf Among Gnomes: A Feminist in North–South Relations', *Millennium: Journal of International Studies*, 17, 3, 1988, pp. 497–537; Ashworth and Bonnerjea *The Invisible Decade*; Tinker, I. and Jaquette, J. 'UN Decade for Women; Its Impact and Legacy', *World Development*, 15, 3, 1987, pp. 419–27.
17   Allison, H., Ashworth, G. and Redcliffe, N. (1980) *Hardcash: Man Made Development and its Consequences; A Feminist Perspective on Aid*, London: Change Publications.
18   Tinker *Persistent Inequalities*.
19   Kardam, N. (1994) 'Women and Development', in Beckman, P. and D'Amico, F. *Women, Gender and World Politics: Perspectives, Policies and Prospects*, London: Bergin and Garvey.
20   Waylen, G. (1996) *Gender and Development in the Third World*, Milton Keynes: Open University Press.
21   Goetz, A. M. (1995) 'The Politics of Integrating Gender to State Development Processes: Trends, Opportunities and Constraints in Bangladesh, Chile, Jamaica, Mali, Morocco and Uganda', United Nations Research Institute for Social Development, Geneva, p. 8.
22   Ibid., p. 3.

23   *The Ecologist*, Special Edition, Women in Development, 22, 1, Jan/Feb 1992; Dankelman, I. and Davidson, J. (1994) *Women and the Environment in the Third World: Alliance for the Future*, London: Earthscan Publications.

24   Dankelman and Davidson *Women and the Environment in the Third World*.

25   UNIFEM World Survey of the Role of Women in Development, New York, United Nations Publications, 1989, and UNIFEM Newsletter, 2, 1, New York, United Nations Publications, February 1994.

26   See *http://www.dawn.org*; see also Antrobus, P. (2005) *The Global Women's Movement*, London: Palgrave.

27   Jayawardena *Feminism and Nationalism in the Third World*.

28   Jaquette, J. 'Women and Modernization Theory: A Decade of Feminist Criticism', *World Politics*, 34, 2, 1982.

29   Mohanty, C., Rosso, A. and Torress, L. (1991) *Third World Women and the Politics of Feminism*, Indiana: Indiana University Press; Amos, V. and Parmar, P. 'Challenging Imperial Feminism', *Feminist Review*, 17, 1984, pp. 13–19.

30   Spivak, G. ' "Woman" as Theatre; United Nations Conference on Women, Beijing, 1995', *Radical Philosophy*, 75, January/February, 1996, p. 2.

31   Spivak, ' "Women" as Theatre', p. 3.

32   Spivak, ' "Woman" as Theatre'.

33   Mohanty, C. 'Under Western Eyes: Feminist Scholarship and Colonial Discourse', *Feminist Review*, 30, 1988, pp. 61–88.

34   Grewal and Kaplan *Scattered Hegemonies*.

35   Mohanty 'Under Western Eyes'.

36   Mohanty argued that there was urgent political necessity of forming strategic alliances across class, race and national boundaries, but argued that the analytical principles of western feminist discourse limit the possibilities of coalitions amongst white western feminists, working-class women and women of colour around the world. See Mohanty, 'Under Western Eyes'.

37   Tohidi, N. (1994) 'Modernity, Islamisation and Women in Iran', in Moghadam, V. *Gender and National Identity; Women and Politics in Muslim Societies*, London: Zed Books.

38   See, for example, Autobus, P. *The Global Women's Movement*; DAWN; Mohanty, C. 'Under Western Eyes Revisited', *Signs*, 28, 2, 2003, pp. 499–535.

39   Bulbeck, C. (1998) 'Women's Movements in the Asia Pacific', in Maidman, R. (ed.) *Culture and Society in the Asia Pacific*, London: Routledge.

40   Ferree, M. and Martin, P. Y. (1995) *Feminist Organisations: Harvest of the New Woman's Movement*, Philadelphia: Temple University Press.

41   Ibid.

42   Bryson, V. 'Adjusting the Lenses: Feminist Analysis and Marxism at the End of the Twentieth Century', *Contemporary Politics*, 1, 1, Spring, 1995, p. 5.

43   Kourany, J., Sterba, J. P. and Tong, R. (eds) (1993) *Feminist Philosophies*, Hemel Hempstead: Harvester Wheatsheaf.

44   Amos, V. and Palmer, P. 'Challenging Imperial Feminism', *Feminist Review*, 17 (Autumn), 1984, pp. 3–19.

45   See MacNay, L. (1994) *Foucault and Feminism*, Cambridge: Polity.

Chapter 8   Women's Human Rights

1   C. Bunch (1995) 'Transforming Human Rights from a Feminist Perspective', in Peters and Wolper *Women's Rights, Human Rights*; A. Afsharipour, 'Empowering Ourselves: The

Role of Women's NGOs in the Enforcement of the Women's Conventions', *Columbia Law Review*, 99, 1, 1999, pp. 129–72.

2   United Nations General Assembly Special Session (UNGASS) 'Gender Equality, Development and Peace for the Twenty-first Century', New York, 5–9 June 2000. (UN Department of Public Information. DPI/2035/N), p. 1 (accessed November 2004).

3   Amnesty International 'Women's Rights Are Human Rights. Commitments Made by Governments in the Beijing Declaration and the Platform for Action' at: *http://www2.ammesty. se/wom.nsf/f64b3a7cOpenDocument*, p. 1 and pp. 19–22; *www.amnestyusa.org/news/ 2000/A7701100.htm* (accessed November 2004).

4   Jill Steans and Vafa Ahmadi 'Negotiating the Politics of Gender and Rights: Some Reflections on the Status of Women's Human Rights at "Beijing plus Ten"', *Global Society*, Vol. 19, No. 3, (July 2005), pp. 227–45.

5   *http://www.un.org/overview/rights.htm* (accessed June 2005).

6   Ibid.

7   Joachim 'Shaping the Human Rights Agenda'.

8   Reanda 'The Commission on the Status of Women'.

9   The process was kept on track largely by European countries. See Reanda 'The Commission on the Status of Women'. The EU continues to promote CEDAW and sponsors the ratification of CEDAW and the lifting of all reservations. Commission of the European Communities 'A New Partnership Between Women and Men', COM (95) 221, Luxembourg: Official Publications of the European Communities, 1995.

10 Reanda 'The Commission on the Status of Women'.

11 CEDAW provides few specific rights based upon life experiences of women and states retain considerable discretion as to what constitutes 'appropriate measures' to eliminate discrimination. See Chinkin 'Gender, Inequality and International Human Rights Law.'

12 Reanda 'The Commission on the Status of Women'.

13 Cited in Ahmadi *Evaluating the Impact and Effectiveness of the Transnational Feminist Movement.*

14 Reanda 'The Commission on the Status of Women'.

15 Ngan-ling Chow, E. (1996) 'Making Waves, Moving Mountains: Reflections on Beijing '95 and Beyond', *Signs* 22, 1, p. 187.

16 The Beijing Platform for Action, Global Framework, point 9. At: *http://www.un.org/ womenwatch/daw/beijing/platform* (accessed November 2004).

17 Ibid.

18 DAW (1999) 'An Optional Protocol to CEDAW'. At: *http://www.un.org/womenwatch/ daw/CEDAW/protocol/index.html.*

19 NGO Forum on Women: Final Report United Nations Publications, 1996.

20 Clark, A. M. 'Non-Governmental Organizations and their Influence on International Society', *Journal of International Affairs* 48, 2, 1995, pp. 507–25.

21 United Nations General Assembly Special Session (UNGASS) 'Gender Equality, Development and Peace'.

22 DAW (2001) 'State Parties to the CEDAW'. At: *http://www.un.org/daw/CEDAW* (accessed November 2004).

23 The International Women's Right Watch started life at the Third United Nations Conference on Women in Nairobi, while the Institute for Women, Law and Development; the Latin American Committee for the Defence of Women's Rights; the Asia-Pacific Forum of Women, Law and Development; Women in Law and Development in Africa; GABRIELA in the Philippines; Women Living Under Muslim Law in France and the Global Fund for Women in the USA are all examples of transnational non-governmental groups which

have become established since 1985. Chinkin 'Gender, Inequality and International Human Rights Law'.

24 Harcourt, W. (1999) *Women@Internet: Creating New Cultures in Cyberspace*, London: Zed Books.

25 Buss, D. and Herman, D. (2003) *Globalising Family Values: the Christian Right in International Politics*, Minneapolis: University of Minneapolis Press.

26 Poole, T. (1995) 'UN Women's Conference Watered Down, but Still a Cause for Hope and Pride', *The Independent*, 16 September.

27 Mufson, S. (1995) 'UN Women's Meeting Settles Key Disputes', *Washington Post* (14 September), 1995, both cited in Ahmadi *Evaluating the UN Women's Conferences*.

28 The Beijing Platform of Action identified twelve critical areas of concern: women and poverty; education and training of women; women and health; violence against women; women and armed conflict; women and the economy; women in power and decision-making; institutional mechanisms for the advancement of women; human rights of women; women and the media; women and the environment; and the girl-child.

29 Dutt, M. 'Some Reflections on U.S. Women of Color and the United Nations Fourth World Conference on Women and NGO Forum in Beijing, China', *Feminist Studies*, 22, 3, 1996, 528.

30 Steans and Ahmadi 'Negotiating the Politics of Gender and Rights'.

31 DAW (2000) 'Preliminary Analysis of the Beijing +5 Outcome Document'. *http://www.un.org/womenwatch/daw/follow up/analysis.html* (accessed June 2005).

32 UNGASS (2000) *Fact Sheet no. 12*; Report A/54/264: P 7; Report A/54/26, 8. (accessed November 2004).

33 G. Urquhart 'Homophobia: winning and losing', *The Guardian* (16 February 2000); Steans and Ahmadi 'Negotiating the Politics of Gender and Rights'.

34 Amnesty International (28/03/96) Women's Rights Are Human Rights. Commitments Made by Governments in the Beijing Declaration and the Platform for Action (Index number: IOR 41/005/1996) found at Amnesty Website: *http://www2.ammesty.se/wom.nsf/f64b3a7cOpenDocument*; 1 and 19–22; *www.amnestyusa.org/news/2000/A7701100.htm* (accessed November 2004); Ahmadi *Evaluating the Women's Conferences*.

35 Beijing Plus 10 passed off relatively quietly in New York in March 2005, hardly noticed by the world's media, but reaffirming most of the political commitments espoused at Beijing and with renewed commitment to move forward on specific areas such as gender inclusion in governance and UN peacekeeping.

36 Corrin, C. 'International Interventions – Gendered Impacts and Consequences in Kosovo and Afghanistan'.

37 Donnelly, J. (1993) *International Human Rights*, Boulder, CO: Westview Press.

38 Gaete, R. (1993) *Human Rights and the Limits of Critical Reason*, Aldershot: Dartmouth.

39 Ibid., p. 565.

40 Buss and Herman *Globalising Family Values*, p. 138.

41 Bottomley, A. (1996) (ed.) *Feminist Perspectives on the Foundational Subjects of Law*, London: Cavendish Publishing Limited.

42 Ibid.

43 Peterson and Parisi 'Are Women Human?'

44 Bunch 'Transforming Human Rights from a Feminist Perspective'.

45 Joachim J. 'Shaping the Human Rights Agenda' in Meyer, M. and Prugl, E. *Gender Politics in Global Governance*, Oxford: Rowman and Littlefield.

46 Bunch 'Transforming Human Rights from a Feminist Perspective'.

47 Okin, S. (1999) 'Is Multiculturalism Bad for Women?' in Cohen, J. and Howard, M. (eds) *Is Multiculturalism Bad for Women?*, Princeton: Princeton University Press.

48   Lawson, S. (1998) 'The Culture of Politics', in Maidment, R. (ed.) *Culture and Society in Asia-Pacific*, London: Routledge.

49   Okin 'Is Multiculturalism Bad for Women?'

50   Ibid.

51   Taylor, C. (1989) *The Sources of the Self: The Making of the Modern Identity*, Cambridge: Cambridge University Press.

52   Cited in Piscatori, J. P. (1980) 'Human Rights in Islamic Political Culture', in Thompson, K. W. *The Moral Imperatives of Human Rights*, Washington, DC.: University of America Press, p. 153.

53   Risse, T., Ropp, S. C. and Sikkink, K. (1999) (eds) *The Power of Human Rights: International Norms and Domestic Change*, Cambridge: Cambridge University Press.

54   Erikson, T. H. (1997) 'Multiculturalism, Individualism and Human Rights', in Wilson, R. *Human Rights: Culture and Context: Anthropological Perspectives*, London: Pluto Press.

55   See Kymlicka, W. (1989) *Liberalism, Community, and Culture*, Oxford: Clarendon Press; Kymlicka, W. (1995) *Multicultural Citizenship: A Liberal Theory of Minority Rights*, Oxford: Oxford University Press.

56   Lawson 'The Culture of Politics'.

57   Donnelly *International Human Rights*.

58   Ahmed, L. (1992) *Women and Gender in Islam: Historical Roots of a Modern Debate*, New Haven: Yale University Press.

59   Donnelly *International Human Rights*.

60   The section of the chapter, human rights as a political tool, has been reproduced from: Steans, J. (2005) 'Debating Women's Human Rights as a "Universal" Feminist Project: Defending Women's Human Rights as a Political Tool'. Submitted to the *Review of International Studies* (under review at the time of writing).

61   Joachim 'Framing Issues and Seizing Opportunities'.

62   Ackerly, B. (2001) 'Women's Rights Activists as Cross-Cultural Theorists', *International Feminist Journal of Politics*, 3, 3, pp. 311–46.

63   Afsharipour 'Empowering Ourselves'.

64   BBC News, 28 June 2005. At: *http://news.bbc.co.uk/2/hi/south_asia/4620065.stm* (accessed June 2005).

65   Ackerly 'Women's Rights Activists', p. 312.

66   Ibid., p. 312.

67   Bunch argues that in international UN meetings, controversies over language are debates about the direction of government policy and so attention has to be paid to the detail of compromises as well as the subtext of the disputes they represent. Nevertheless getting reluctant governments to agree to even a weak text can represent an advance on their prior position and, therefore, be important. Bunch, C. 'Beijing '95: Moving Women's Human Rights from Margin to Centre', *Signs*, 22, 1 (Autumn), 1996, pp. 200–4.

68   This was not just an issue at Beijing, but at the 1993 Vienna conference on Human Rights too. The West mounted a strong endorsement of universality in wake of a challenge from Asia-Pacific countries (The Bangkok Declaration) who acknowledged that human rights were universal but argued that they must be considered in the context of the dynamic and evolving process of international norm-setting, bearing in mind the significance of national and regional peculiarities and various historical, cultural and religious backgrounds. But there is little guidance on what this means in operational terms. This is an issue for feminists, precisely because it is in the 'private sphere' where agreement is hardest to reach and so in the absence of such guidance much of the substance of women's human rights – issues such as marriage, divorce, reproductive rights – is up for grabs. Cerna, C. M.

'Universality of Human Rights and Cultural Diversity: Implementation of Human Rights in Different Socio-Cultural Contexts', *Human Rights Quarterly*, 16, 4 (November), 1994, pp. 740–52.

69   Charlotte Bunch 'Beijing '95'.

70   Steans, J. 'Debating Women's Human Rights as a "Universal" Feminist Project'.

Chapter 9   Transnational Feminist Solidarity

1   This chapter is based on a paper produced for the British International Studies Association's Solidarity in International Relations Working Group, University of Aberdeen, May 2004. It was submitted to the *Review of International Studies* in January 2006 and is under review at the time of writing. I am grateful to Martin Weber for his comments on the earlier draft.

2   Bryson 'Adjusting the Lenses', p. 10.

3   In the usage employed in this paper, the 'transnational feminist movement' refers to a broad and heterogeneous network of NGOs and women's groups who nevertheless are a 'movement' to the extent that they share a common aim of achieving social and political changes at the international and national/local level that will lead to a better position for women in specific societies. See Ferree and Martin *Feminist Organisations*.

4   LeGates, M. 'Feminists before Feminism: Origins and Varieties of Women's Protests in Europe and North America Before the Twentieth Century', in Freeman, J. (1995) *Women: A Feminist Perspective*, London: Mayfield, pp. 494–508.

5   Crow, G. (2002) *Social Solidarities: Theories, Identities and Social Change*, Buckingham: Open University Press, p. 23.

6   hooks, b. 'Sisterhood: Political Solidarity between Women', *Feminist Review*, 23 (Summer), 1986, p. 125.

7   Ibid.

8   Mernissi, F. (1987) *The Veil and the Male Elite: A Feminist Interpretation of Women's Rights in Islam*, New York: Addison Wesley.

9   There is evidence of reflection on and criticism of women's assumed nature and purpose in pre-modern Europe. In 1404 Christine de Pisan attacked misogyny and male culture that perpetuated negative views of women. LeGates has identified a 'querelle des femmes', or debate about women, from the fifteenth century onwards, although the ability of actual women to mobilize to challenge patriarchal beliefs and transform social institutions and structures that embedded male privilege was severely circumscribed by prevalent traditions and religious beliefs. LeGates, M. (1995) 'Feminists before Feminism', pp. 500–2.

10   Gaete, R. (1993) *Human Rights and the Limits of Critical Reason*, Aldershot: Dartmouth.

11   This is an extensive literature. See, for example, Coole, D. (1993) *Women in Political Theory: From Ancient Misogyny to Contemporary Feminism*, London: Harvester Wheatsheaf; Di Stefano, C. (1983) 'Masculinity as Ideology: Hobbesian Man Considered', *Women's Studies International Forum*, 6; Elshtain, J. (1981) *Public Man/Private Woman*, Princeton: Princeton University Press; Evans, J. (ed.) (1986) *Feminism as Political Theory*, Beverly Hills, CA: Sage Publications; Okin, S. (1979) *Women in Western Political Thought*, Princeton: Princeton University Press; Pateman, C. (1985) *The Problem of Political Obligation*, Cambridge: Polity; Sunstein, C. (1990) *Feminism and Political Theory*, Chicago: University of Chicago Press.

12   Benhabib, S. (1992) *Situating the Self: Gender, Community and Postmodernism in Contemporary Ethics*, Cambridge: Polity.

13   Wollstonecraft, M. (1985) *A Vindication of the Rights of Woman*, London: Penguin.

14   Although, even as women rallied to the cause of sexual equality and the desire to be treated like men, their sense of difference was never fully erased. Liberal feminism did not entirely displace the idea that women and men had different social functions. The idealization of motherhood and women's roles within the family might have been a way for women to compensate for their economic marginalization at a time when 'home' and 'work' were increasingly being viewed as distinctive and separate spheres. In nineteenth-century Europe, the education of women was limited to ensuring that they could carry out their primary roles as wives and mothers. In some parts of Europe, a more conservative political culture also meant that arguments based on women's familial and communal roles were more likely to be sympathetically received than arguments based on an individualistic ethic. See LeGates, 'Feminists Before Feminism', p. 503.

15   Woolf, V. (1963) *Three Guineas*, London: Harvest.

16   Caine, B. 'Feminism, Suffrage and the Nineteenth Century Women's Movement', Women's Studies International Forum, 5, 6, 1982, pp. 306–30.

17   Caine, 'Feminism, Suffrage and the Nineteenth Century Women's Movement'.

18   McGlen and Sarkees *Women in Foreign Policy*; Meyer, M. (1999) 'The Women's International League for Peace and Freedom: Organising for Peace in the War System', in Meyer and Prugl *Gender Politics in Global Governance*.

19   Rupp, L. J. and Taylor, V. 'Forging Feminist Identity in an International Movement: A Collective Identity Approach to Twentieth Century Feminism', *Signs*, 24, 2, Winter, 1999, p. 365.

20   Taylor, V. 'Sisterhood, Solidarity and Modern Feminism', *Gender and Society*, 3, 2 (June), 1989, p. 278.

21   The Working Women's Association created alliances between feminists and labour unions and encouraged both groups to understand the relationship between gender issues and economic issues. Ibid., p. 278.

22   Ibid., p. 278.

23   Wares, S. 'Review of Leila Rupp's "World of Women: The Making of the International Women's Movement"', *Journal of American History*, 85, 3 (December), 1998, p. 1123.

24   Noah, M. 'Review of The Problems of Solidarity: Theories and Models', *Theory and Epistemology*, 2001, p. 91.

25   Useem, B. 'Solidarity Model, Breakdown Model and the Boston Anti-Bussing Movement', *American Sociological Review*, 45, 3 (June), 1980, pp. 357–69.

26   Crossly, N. (2002) *Making Sense of Social Movements*, Buckingham: Open University Press.

27   Crow *Social Solidarities*, p. 23.

28   Rupp and Taylor, 'Forging Feminist Identity', p. 379.

29   Ibid., p. 365.

30   See *http://www.wlulm.org.*, Mission Statement, p. 1 (accessed June 2004).

31   Shaheed, F. 'Controlled or Autonomous: Identity and the Experience of the Network Women Living Under Muslim Laws', *Signs*, 19, 4 (Summer), 1994, p. 1005.

32   Ibid., p. 1007.

33   See Women in Black 'Women's Solidarity Network Against War'. *Http://lists.partners-intl/pipermail/women-east-west*, p. 2 (accessed June 2005).

34   Crow *Social Solidarities*, p. 23.

35   Ibid., p. 25.

36   Ibid., p. 27.

37   hooks 'Sisterhood: Political Solidarity between Women', p. 127.

38   Ibid., p. 127.

39   Rupp and Taylor 'Forging Feminist Identity'.

40   hooks 'Political Solidarity between Women', p. 125.

41   Ibid., 1986, p. 138.

42   See, for example, Caplan, P. and Buirjra, J. (1979) (eds) *Women United, Women Divided: Comparative Studies of Ten Contemporary Cultures*, Indiana: Indiana University Press.

43   *http://www.un.org/womenwatch* (accessed June 2005).

44   Udayagiri, M. (1995) 'Challenging Modernization: Gender and Development, Postmodern Feminism and Activism', in Marchand, M. and Parpart, J. (eds) *Feminism, Postmodernism, Development*, London: Routledge, p. 167.

45   Lea Wood 'Gendered Imagination: Women's Resistance to Islamist Discourse' at: *http://www.ilstu.edu/-mtavokol/lwood/htm.*, p. 9 (accessed June 2005).

46   hooks 'Political Solidarity between Women', p. 128.

47   Grewal and Kaplan *Scattered Hegemonies*, p. 18.

48   hooks 'Political Solidarity between Women', p. 125.

49   Ibid., p. 125.

50   Ibid., p. 129.

51   Ibid., p. 129.

52   Grewal and Kaplan *Scattered Hegemonies*, p. 18.

53   Ibid., p. 18.

54   hooks 'Political Solidarity between Women'.

55   Wood *Gendered Imaginations*, p. 9.

56   Pfeli, F. (1994) 'No Basta Teorizar: In-Difference to Solidarity in Contemporary Fiction, Theory and Practice', in Grewal and Kaplan, p. 225.

57   The notion of dialogue across boundaries is not uncontroversial, particularly in its Habermasian guise, but might be reformulated to accommodate feminist concerns. Kimberly Hutchings 'Speaking and Hearing: Habermasian Discourse Ethics, Feminism and IR', *Review of International Studies*, 31, 1, January, 2005, p. 162.

58   Pfeli, 1994, p. 225–6.

59   Rupp and Taylor 'Forging Feminist Identity', p. 364.

60   Ferree, M. M. and Roth, S. 'Gender, Class and Interaction between Social Movements: A Strike of West Berlin Day Care Workers', *Gender and Society*, 13, 6 (December), 1998, p. 628.

61   Ibid., p. 627.

62   Ibid., p. 628.

63   Ibid., p. 629.

64   Eyerman, R. and Jamison, A. (1991) *Social Movements: A Cognitive Approach*, Cambridge: Polity, p. 4.

65   Dutt, M. 'Some Reflections on US Women of Colour', *Feminist Studies*, 2, 3 (Autumn), 1996, p. 523.

66   Ibid., pp. 521–2.

67   Ibid., p. 520.

68   Ibid., p. 520.

69   Ibid., p. 519.

70   Ibid., p. 522.

71   C. Bunch and S. Fried 'Beijing '95: Moving Women's Human Rights from Margin to Center', *Signs*, 22, 3, 1996, pp. 200–4.

72   Afsharipour, A. 'Empowering Ourselves: The Role of Women's NGOs in the Enforcement of the Women's Conventions', *Columbia Law Review*, 99, 1 (1999), pp. 129–72; C. Bunch, (1995) 'Transforming Human Rights from a Feminist Perspective', in Peters, J. and Wolper, A. (eds) *Women's Rights, Human Rights: International Feminist Perspectives*, London: Routledge; Chinkin, C. (1999) 'Gender Inequality and International Human

Rights Law', in Hurrell, A. and Woods, N. (eds) *Inequality, Globalization and World Politics*, Oxford: Oxford University Press.

73   For example, advocacy in the interests of promoting women's reproductive and health rights are now a central plank of the work of DAWN (although human rights are by no means the exclusive focus of their work). In addition, there are a large number of NGOs and networks that have grown up in the wake of the Convention on the Elimination of Discrimination Against Women, including transnational organizations like Women's Human Rights Net (WHRnet).

74   Ibid., p. 311.

75   Ibid., p. 1013.

76   Ibid., p. 315.

77   Tickner, A. (1992) 'On the Fringes of the Global Economy'.

78   Hay, C. and Marsh, D., *Demystifying Globalisation*; Kofman, E. and Youngs, G. (1996) 'Introduction: Globalisation – the Second Wave', in Youngs and Kofman *Globalisation: Theory and Practice*.

79   Hooper, E. *Report on the UN ECE Regional Preparatory Meeting for the Fourth World Conference on Women*, Geneva, 1994; Hooper, E. *Report on the UN ESCAP Regional Preparatory Meeting for the Fourth World Conference on Women*, Jakarta, 1994c.

80   Ibid.

81   Mohanty, C. 'Under Western Eyes Revisited: Feminist Solidarity through Anticapitalist Struggles', *Signs: Journal of Women in Culture and Society*, 28, 2, 2002, pp. 499–535.

82   Ibid., p. 501.

83   Ibid., p. 505.

84   Ibid., p. 508.

85   Ibid., p. 516.

86   Ibid., p. 508.

87   Ibid., p. 510.

88   Ibid., p. 511.

Chapter 10   The Gender(ed) Politics of International Relations

1   'Interview with Professor Cynthia Enloe', carried out at the February 2001 Annual Convention of the ISA in Chicago, in *Review of International Studies* (2001), 27, pp. 649–66.

2   Tickner, J. A. 'You Just Don't Understand: Troubled Engagements Between Feminists and IR Theorists', *International Studies Quarterly*, 41, 4, 1997, p. 661.

3   Part of this chapter was originally published as Steans, J. 'Engaging from the Margins: Feminist Encounters with the "Mainstream" of International Relations', *British Journal of Politics and International Relations*, 5, 3, 2003, pp. 428–54.

4   Peterson, V. Spike 'Transgressing Boundaries: Theories of Knowledge, Gender and IR', *Millennium: Journal of International Studies*, 21, 2, 1992, pp. 183–206.

5   Banks, M. (1985) 'The Inter-paradigm Debate', in Groom A. J. R. and Light M. *International Relations: A Handbook of Current Theory*, London: Pinter, pp. 7–26.

6   The term 'mainstream' in this context, embraces both neorealism and neoliberal institutionalism since both are rationalist approaches to the study of IR.

7   Tickner 'You Just Don't Understand', p. 623.

8   Ibid., p. 623.

9   Ibid., p. 663.

10   Ibid., p. 621.

11 Weber, C. 'Good Girls, Bad Girls and Little Girls: Male Paranoia in Robert Keohane's Critique of Feminist International Relations', *Millennium: Journal of International Studies*, 23, 2, 1994, pp. 337–49.

12 Keohane, R. 'International Relations Theory: Contributions of a Feminist Standpoint', *Millennium: Journal of International Studies*, 18, 2, Summer, 1989. See also Keohane, R. 'Beyond Dichotomy: Conversations Between International Relations and Feminist Theory', *International Studies Quarterly*, 42, 1, 1998, pp. 193–8.

13 Zalewski, M. 'Well, What is the Feminist Perspective on Bosnia?' *International Affairs*, 71, 2, 1995, pp. 339–56.

14 Tickner *Gender in International Relations*.

15 Tickner 'You Just Don't Understand', p. 617.

16 Sylvester *Feminist Theory and International Relations*; Sylvester, C. 'Empathetic Cooperation: A Feminist Method for IR', *Millennium: Journal of International Studies*, 23, 3, 1994, pp. 315–34.

17 Weber, C. (2001) 'Gender', in *International Relations Theory: A Critical Introduction*, London: Routledge, p. 82.

18 Weber 'Good Girls, Bad Girls and Little Girls'.

19 Peterson 'Transgressing Boundaries'; Tickner, J. A. 'Continuing the Conversation', *International Studies Quarterly*, 42, 1, 1998, pp. 205–10.

20 Jones, A. 'Does "Gender" Make the World Go Around? Feminist Critiques of International Relations', *Review of International Studies*, 22, 4, 1996, pp. 405–29.

21 Ibid., p. 303.

22 Ibid., p. 301.

23 Zalewski, M. 'The Women/"Women" Question in International Relations', *Millennium: Journal of International Studies*, 23, 3, 1994, p. 428.

24 Ibid.

25 Carver, Cochran and Squires 'Gendering Jones', p. 298; Jones, A. 'Engendering Debate', *Review of International Studies*, 24, 2, 1998, pp. 299–303.

26 Carver, Cochran and Squires 'Gendering Jones', p. 294.

27 Jones 'Does "Gender" Make the World Go Around?'

28 Berg, A. and Lie, M. 'Feminism and Constructivism: Do Artefacts Have a Gender?' *Science, Technology and Human Values*, 20, 3, *Special Issue: Feminist and Constructivist Perspectives on New Technology*, Summer, 1995 p. 344.

29 Ibid., p. 345.

30 Keohane, R. (1998) 'Beyond Dichotomies: Conversations between International Relations and Feminist Theory', *International Studies Quarterly*, 4, 3, 193–8.

31 McGlen and Sarkees *Women in Foreign Policy*.

32 Goldstein, J. (2005) 'Feminism', in *International Relations*, London: Pearson; Fukuyama, F. 'Women and the Evolution of World Politics', *Foreign Affairs*, 77, 5, 1998, pp. 24–40.

33 Goldstein 'Feminism', p. 113.

34 Keohane 'Beyond Dichotomies', p. 196.

35 Goldstein 'Feminism', p. 113.

36 Fukuyama, F. (1998) 'Women and the Evolution of World Politics', *Foreign Affairs*, 77, 5, pp. 24–40.

37 Rooney, P. 'Methodological Issues in the Construction of Gender as a Meaningful Variable in Scientific Studies of Cognition, *Proceedings of the Bi-ennial Meeting of the Philosophy of Science Association*, 1, 1994, pp. 109–19.

38 Zalewski, M. and Eloe, C. (1997) 'Questions of Identity', in Booth, K. and Smith, S. *Theories of International Relations*, Cambridge: Polity.

39   Phillips, D. 'The Good, the Bad and the Ugly: the Many Faces of Constructivism', *Educational Researcher*, 24, 7, October, 1995, pp. 5–12.

40   Carpenter, C. R. 'Gender Theory in World Politics: Contributions of a Non-Feminist Standpoint?' *International Studies Review*, 4, 3, 2003, pp. 153–66.

41   Weber *Good Girls, Bad Girls and Little Girls*; Tickner You Just Don't Understand; Tickner *Continuing the Conversation*; Weber, C. (2001) 'Gender', in Weber, C. *International Relations Theory: A Critical Introduction*, London: Routledge; Smith, S. 'The United States and the Discipline of International Relations: Hegemonic Country, Hegemonic Discipline', 4, 2 (Summer), 2002, pp. 67–86; Carver, T. 'Gender/Feminism/IR' *International Studies Review*, 5, 2 (June), 2003, pp. 288–90; Zalewski, M. ' "Women's Troubles" Again in IR', *International Studies Review*, 5, 2 (June), 2003, pp. 291–4; Kinsella, H. 'For a Careful Reading: The Constructivism of Gender Constructivism', *International Studies Review*, 5, 2 (June), 2003, pp. 294–7; Steans 'Engaging from the Margins'.

42   Jones 'Does "Gender" Make the World Go Around?'; Carver, Cochran and Squires, 'Gendering Jones.'; Weber 'Gender'.

43   Weber 'Gender', p. 83.

44   Carver, Cochran and Squires 'Gendering Jones', p. 297.

45   Ibid., p. 296.

46   Carver, Cochran and Squires 'Gendering Jones'.

47   Keohane 'Beyond Dichotomies', p. 197.

48   Peterson and Runyan 'Global Gender Issues'; Sylvester 'Empathetic Cooperation'.

49   Steans, J. (2006) 'Feminism and Social Constructivism: Revisiting and Recasting the Debate'. (work in progress).

50   Carpenter, C. R. 'Gender Theory in World Politics: Contributions of a Non-Feminist Standpoint?' *International Studies Review*, 4, 3, 2003, pp. 153–66.

51   Goldstein *Gender and War*.

52   Carpenter 'Gender Theory in World Politics.'

53   Ibid.

54   Ibid.

55   Carver 'Gender/Feminism/IR'.

56   Zalewski ' "Women's Troubles" Again in IR'.

57   Wendt, A. (1999) *Social Theory of International Politics*, Cambridge: Cambridge University Press, p. 5.

58   Ibid., p. 195.

59   Ibid.

60   Enloe, C. (2000) *Maneuvers: The Militarisation of Women's Lives*, California: University of California Press.

61   'An Interview with Professor Cynthia Enloe', p. 656.

62   Ibid., p. 657.

63   Fearon, J. and Wendt, A. (2002) 'Rationalism v. Constructivism: A Skeptical View', in Carlsnaes, W., Risse, T., and Simmonds, B. *Handbook of International Relations*, Sage, London, p. 52.

64   Ibid., p. 52.

65   Ibid., p. 68.

66   Ibid., p. 68.

67   Steans, J. (1998) *Gender and International Relations*, Cambridge: Polity.

68   Keohane 'Beyond Dichotomies', p. 194.

69   Ibid., p. 196.

70   Zalewski ' "Women's" Troubles Again'.

71   Keohane 'Beyond Dichotomies', p. 197.

72   Tickner 'You Just Don't Understand'.

73   Marchand, M. 'Different Communities/Different Realities/Different Encounters: A Reply to J. Ann Tickner, *International Studies Quarterly*, 42, 1 (March), 1998, pp. 199–204.

74   See for example, Carver, T. (with M. Cochran and J. Squires) 'Gendering Jones', *Review of International Studies*, 24, 2, 1998, pp. 283–98; Halliday 'Hidden from International Relations', pp. 419–28; Hoffman *Gender and Sovereignty*; Murphy 'Seeing Women, Recognizing Gender, Recasting International Relations'; Walker 'Gender and Critique in the Theory of International Relations'; Zalewski and Parpart *The 'Man' Question in International Relations.*

75   Schmidt, B. (2002) 'On the History and Histography of International Relations', in Carlsnaes, Risse and Simmonds *Handbook of International Relations.*

76   Marchand 'Different Communities, Different Realities'.

77   Ibid.

78   Lapid 'The Third Debate'.

79   Diez, T. and Steans, J. 'A Useful Dialogue? Habermas and International Relations', *Review of International Studies*, 31, 1 (January), 2005.

80   Marchand 'Different Communities, Different Realities'.

81   Dallmayr, F. 'Conversation across Boundaries: Political Theory and Global Diversity', *Millennium: Journal of International Studies* 30, 2001, pp. 331–47.

82   Seyla Benhabib, for example, has reformulated discourse ethics as 'interactive universalism'. Cited in Hutchings 'Speaking and Hearing'. See also Fraser, N. 'What's Critical about Critical Theory? The Case of Habermas and Gender', *New German Critique* 35, 1985, pp. 97–131; Ackerly 'Women's Rights Activists'.

83   Hutchings 'Speaking and Hearing'.

84   Ibid., p. 158.

85   Ibid., p. 158.

86   Rosenau, P. (1994) *Postmodernism and the Social Sciences*, Princeton: Princeton University Press.

87   Sylvester 'Empathetic Cooperation'.

88   See Sylvester 'Empathetic Cooperation'; Grewal and Kaplan *Scattered Hegemonies.*

89   Hutchings 'Speaking and Hearing'.

90   Diez, T. and Steans, J. (2005) 'A Useful Dialogue?'

91   Ibid., p. 134.

92   Ibid., p. 138.

93   See, for example, Robinson *Globalising Care*; Campbell, D. (1993) *Politics without Principle: Sovereignty, Ethics, and the Narratives of the Gulf War*, Lynne Rienner, Boulder, CO; Frost, M. 'A Turn not Taken; Ethics in IR at the Millennium', *Review of International Studies*, 24, special issue, 1998, pp. 119–32.

94   Eschele, C. 'Engendering Global Democracy', *International Feminist Journal of Politics*, 4, 3, 2002, pp. 315–41.

95   See, for example, M. Cochran, 'Deweyan Pragmatism and Post-Positivist Social Science in IR', *Millennium: Journal of International Studies*, 31, 3, 2002, pp. 525–48; Owen, D. 'Re-Orienting International Relations: On Pragmatism, Pluralism and Practical Reasoning', *Millennium: Journal of International Studies*, 31, 3, 2002, pp. 653–73.

INDEX